Modern Teaching of History

Modern Teaching of History

Theories & Practices

Edited by

G.D. Gururani

AKANSHA PUBLISHING HOUSE
NEW DELHI - 110 002 (INDIA)

AKANSHA PUBLISHING HOUSE
4649/21-B, Ansari Road,
Daryaganj, New Delhi - 110 002
Phones: 23263193, 9811582579
E-mail: ektabooks@yahoo.com

Modern Teaching of History: Theories & Practices

First Published, 2006
Reprint- **2015**
ISBN 81-8370-034-9

PRINTED IN INDIA

Published by M.P. Misra for Akansha Publishing House, New Delhi - 110 002 and Printed at Tarun Offset Press, Delhi

Contents

	Preface	*vii*
1.	An Introduction to History	1
2.	Classification of History	13
3.	History and Other Subjects	23
4.	Teaching History: Aims, Objectives and Values	32
5.	Main Methods	47
6.	Golden Tips for Effective History Teaching	78
7.	Principles of Teaching History	84
8.	Curriculum Development	89
9.	Teaching History for Citizenship in the Elementary School	112
10.	Techniques of History Teaching	117
11.	Lesson Planning & Time Sense in History	127
12.	History Library & Role of Text Books	145
13.	The History Teacher and The History Room	158
14.	Evaluation in History	173
15.	Teaching Aids	188
16.	Salient Features of Ancient Indian History	206
	Select Bibliography	285
	Index	287

Preface

History is the story of the progress of mankind since times immemorial. If history is taken from this point of view we can easily conclude that there is one history of the whole world and such a history could only be world history. However, for the convenience of study historians have divided history into various parts or branches. Every such part is complete in itself. No one can be called a true historian if he has read only a part of this long and varied journey of the progress of mankind.

"History is the record of man's steps and slips. It shows us that the steps haver been slow and slight: the slips, quick, and abounding. It provides us with the opportunity to profit by the stumbles and tumbles of our fore-runners. Viewed a right History is the broadest studies, embracing every aspect of human life. It lays the foundation of education by showing how mankind repeats it errors and what those errors are. Bismarck used to remark, "fools say that they learn by experience. I prefer to learn by other people's experiences." These study of history offers us that opportunity. It is universal experience—infinitely longer, wider and more varied than any individual's experience."

The main topics, elaborately dealt in this book are: An Introduction to History; Classification of History; History and Other Subjects; Teaching History: Aims, Objectives and Values; Main Methods; Golden Tips for Effective History Teaching; Principles of Teaching History; Curriculum Development; Teaching History for Citizenship in the

Elementary School; Techniques of History Teaching; Lesson Planning & Time Sense in History; History Library & Role of Text Books; The History Teacher and The History Room; Evaluation in History; Teaching Aids; Salient Features of Ancient Indian History; etc.

Amidst the plenty of literature available, this book is has some unique features. Besides the fundamental issues pertaining to teaching of history some tips are also added to enhance the applicability. A chapter on salient features of Indian History is also given highlighting all significant point of that phase of our great history, which every present-day history teacher should know.

Substantially based on the authoritative information derived from the works of great historians, this book presents a blend of unique synthesis. I am grateful to all those scholars whose works are liberally cited to and drawn from. The entire credit for this venture ought go to them. Friends and colleagues deserve my praise for their inspiration and assistance. Last but not the least, Mr. M.P. Misra deserves all appreciation for bringing out this book superbly within very short period of time.

Hopefully this book will prove a dependable handbook to teachers, teacher-trainers, teacher-trainees, students and all others interested in the study of history, historiography and history teaching.

—Editor

1

An Introduction to History

"Not to know what has been transacted in former times is to continue always a child."

—*Seneca*

The word "History" is derived from the greek word "Historia" which means "what has actually happened in the past". Thus history is just "man — his story."

History deals with our social, political and economical aspects of life. Though History is an independent subject in many an Indian states but in some states it is taught as a past of social studies. No doubt, History dominates the entire course of social, studies, and forms its major and important part.

History is an important subject because it tells us about the human civilization of the yore days. To quote the words of a famous historian, history is, "what men have done and said and above all what they have thought" According to Johnson, "History has always been what human beings thought about the past and in this sense it has always been of creation of the past." From the mass of details available about man's recorded past it can easily been seen that history is the story of man's effort to satisfy his craving for an orderly social life, to satisfy his love for freedom and to satisfy his thirst for beauty, knowledge, and learning.

Henry Johnson says "history is a detailed account of

the events that have taken place". From this definition it became quite clear that history mainly deals with the events of the past. In history there is description of the events only.

"History is the record of man's steps and slips. It shows us that the steps haver been slow and slight: the slips, quick, and abounding. It provides us with the opportunity to profit by the stumbles and tumbles of our fore-runners. Viewed a right History is the broadest studies, embracing every aspect of human life. It lays the foundation of education by showing how mankind repeats it errors and what those errors are. Bismarck used to remark, "fools say that they learn by experience. I prefer to learn by other people's experiences." These study of history offers us that opportunity. It is universal experience—infinitely longer, wider and more varied than any individual's experience."

In view of some historians it is a "new date calendar" while others consider it a "collection of events of war."

The definition given by Rapson is quite scientific. According to him, "History is a Connected account of the course of events and the progress of ideas".

In the words of Prof. Ghose, "history is a scientific study and record of our complete past".

Dr. S. Radhakrishnan has defined history as, "The memory of a nation or a race."

Rabindranath Tagore says, "There is only one history—The History of Man." In the words of Pt. Jawahar Lal Nehru. "History is the story of Man's struggle through the ages against Nature and the elements; against wild beasts and the jungle and some of his own kind who have tried to keep him down and to exploit him for thieir own benefit".

Jones states, "History is a veritable mine of life

experiences and the youth of today studies History that he may profit by the experiences of the race".

In Carr's words, "History is a continuous process of interaction between, the historian and his facts. It is an unending dialogue between the present and the past".

"History is the record of what one age finds worthy to note in another, "remarks Burckhardt.

Keeping in view all these interpretations regarding the nature and concept of History we may say that History is not a mere chronicle of events as generally understood by common man. It is actually, "a wraths with the events strung on the thread of the ideas". "History is not simple information regarding the affairs of kings, also have passed away but is a science which expands the intellect and furnishes the wise with examples."

DEVELOPMENT OF HISTORY

To show how immensely in depth and notion a brief account of development of history is given here.

Wrong Notion About History

In view of some thinkers, "God manifested himself in history".

In view of the remarks made by Napoleon that, "history is a fable agreed upon", people started thinking that they cannot consider history to the quite dependable thing and actually it is not quite dependable. Spencer has remarked, "Read them (the facts of history) if you like, for amusement, but do not flatter yourself. They are instructions".

In the opinion of Sigmund Freud; "Historical records area law of right or wrong".

According to Jones, "History is precious store-house of the experiences of human race. History is recorded so that people may take advantage of the experience of people of the past generation".

Henry Johnson opines, "History is itself a phase of development and, therefore, never entirely new. History began as enquiry and is still enquiry. History began as a record and is still a record. History became what actually happened and is what actually happened."

The above notions cannot be considered the perfect notion of history.

Old Concept

In the beginning history was nothing more than a local saga a collection of legendary stories, heroic ballads and folk-tales, sung in praise of great heroes on ceremonial occasions. Its aim was partly to provide entertainment and partly to breathe heroism into the hearts of young warriors on the eve of some battle. In these histories facts and fictions were quite freely mixed up together. The credit of giving history the status of an independent field of study goes to the Greek historian Herodotus, who lived in 5th century B.C. He collected a lot of information about present and past of places and then gave an interesting narration of these.

Thucydides, a contemporary of Herodotus gave a true picture of political conditions and events of his own time and not of past. His writings can be called "didactic history" and in his field he still remains a model and master. For the next two thousand years history remained either story-telling history or didactic history.

With the advancement of physical sciences in the 19th century, attitudes of the students of history completely changed. Germany became the house of scientific history The history was raised to the level of a science, during this period by two great German historians (i.e. Leopold Von Ranke and Nietruhr). They used scientific principles and methods. Because of such a vast change in attitude the 19th century in called "the century of history". However, it may be clearly noted that this age being the age of empires, monarchies and political alignements, history emphasised mainly mainly the military and political aspects of human life. It was not at a later date, under the influence of Karl Marx that emphasis was shifted from political to economic and social aspects of man and cultural history came to be recognised as an invaluable aspect of the achievements of mankind.

Indian History

History in India has had an oral tradition. The achievements of ancient Indian heroes were preserved in the form of sagas or *gathas*. The 'bards' and other people used to learn by heart various events and deeds of the people, because the arts of writing and printing books were unknowns. The historical events were used to literary, artistic, political and religious purposes. In "Puranas" and other historical writings of India, events have not been arranged in a systematic and chronological order. There is more of praise of kings and warriors.

It was only under the English system of education that history was introduced as a school subject in India. Thus in the beginning most of the text-books on Indian History were written by European scholars, who have no clear understanding of Indian society, its ethos and its problems. The result was that history in Indian schools had little educational value, either individual or social.

Modern Views

We can state the modern concept of history as under:

1. *History is a study of the present in the light of the past:* The present social life of man has been a result of evolution through centuries of human efforts in various directions. Modern history helps us in understanding the process of evolution and how society has come to its

present form. It also helps us to discover and explain how this adjustment has taken place in the past and how it is taking place today. It is likely to give us not only a sense of national patriotism and an appreciation of national heritage but also a clear sense of world unity

2. *History is a scientific study and a faithful account of past:* According to its modern concept, history is not confined to one period or country or nation. It begins from the appearance of man on this earth and deals with all places whose man has gone and lived. It also deals with various aspects, such as political, social, economic, religious, literary, aesthetic etc., of human life. It has now actually become a study of man's evolution on earth.

3. *History is growth and development of human civilisation through the ages :* Since it is dynamic so it implies growth, development and evolution. "It traces the fascinating story of how man has developed through the ages, how man has studied to use and control his environment and how the present institutions have grown out of the past. Man's struggle with his. environment man's use and abuse of his powers and resources, his development and essential unity of human civilisation are the main themes of history."

History as a Science

Some scholars consider that history is a science. As a science it aims at discovering facts of the past as they really were and then interpreting them correctly. It also makes use of various methods of enquiry like observation, classification, formulation of the hypothesis and analysis of evidence before interpreting and reconstructing the past. Science has been defined in various ways.

According to Galbraith, "By science we mean a body of knowledge that seeks to tell the truth, the whole truth and nothing but the truth." Science has also been defined as a

"Systematic study of knowledge" concerning the relationship between cause and effect of a particular phenomenon.

History too, "is an inquiry, designed to find the truth" so it is a science.

But in a strict sense, history cannot be termed as science. It is not a science in the sense physics and chemistry are sciences. It is so because history is not based on certain theories and the facts of history are too complicated and unique. They seldom repeat in the real sense of the word Historical data ate not available for observation and experimentation. It may be called a concrete science because it is concerned with the experiences of human beings.

Sciences are of two kinds, physical science and social science. History is not a physical science but it is certainly a social science. It may not use the methods of physical sciences bat it do use the methods of social science in the following form.

(i) in it, we have a collection of data. Such data may be secured from any quarter. The whole of the data that forms history has been collected at a place,

(ii) the collected data can be analysed quite carefully, it can be classified and sorted out The laboratory of history is the universe, and

(iii) we can lay down certain theories after proper observation, analysis and comparative inspection of the available data.

History as an Art

Art is nothing but the practical application of knowledge acquired by science. Art is also a part of literature and Fine Art. Here we have a display of emotions and fine feelings. This element is also available in history. Many scholars consider that history is an art.

Spencer says, "History deals with unroganised facts from which no conclusions can be drawn."

In addition to this they give the following arguments to show that history is not a science no conclusions can be drawn. Besides this statement, Spencer and his followers have based their arguments on the following facts:

1. *Historical methods of arriving at facts differ radically from the methods of natural sciences:* Natural sciences generally deal with facts which can be observed directly and which can be tested by experiment Historical facts on the other band, cannot be observed directly. They can be arrived at only indirectly through inference and through various sources. This indirect method of history is plainly a different method and the general status of facts, established by this method, is also quite different

2. *Non-scientific historical data for scientific observation and experiment:* History deals with thoughts and actions of human beings, who possess a tree will. Collingwood says that every historical event has two aspects, the internal and the external; Its outside describes the external factors and inside, the thoughts and feelings of the people, involved in the event. The historian is concerned with both these aspects because he investigates the actions which depict both the outside and the inside of an event. "Events of history are the things which the historian looks, not at, but through, to discern the thought within. And free human activities cannot provide material for scientific experimentation and formulation of scientific laws. Moreover, experiment in history is not possible because it deals with events that have already happened and cannot be repeated. Secondly, the intentions which a human action expresses, cannot be directly observed. These can only be reached by a process of inference and apprehended through the imaginative powers of the mind.

3. *Historical synthesis:* The fundamental quest in history is for what is important. As such, historical synthesis, is completely different from that of natural sciences. In history, past must be seen through the eyes of the past and not through the eyes of the present. If history is determined by what matters most in the present, it would inevitably miss what mattered most in the past and would, therefore, "neither correctly represent nor correctly explain the past." As Walsh says, "The historian is taking not as a scientist would, about all men, past present and future, who have certain characteristics, but about all the man who lived at a certain time and in a certain area.

4. *Neither generations can be formulated nor future can be predicted with certainty:* Science consists of a body of general truths. A scientist looks at knowledge from a universal angle and arrives at certain generalisations. This helps him control the present and predict the future. But for a historian, it is not possible to arrive at general principles or laws which may enable him to predict with certainty the recurrence of like events, under given conditions.

From the foregoing discussion we may infer that history is an art as well as science. As an enquiry to elicit truth it is science and as a narrative account of that truth it is an art or a piece of literature. Science supplies only day lifeless facts and it is only historian with great literary genius, high imagination and sympathetic bent of mind, who puts life and soul into lifeless historical events and thus makes history live for us. Hence history may be considered as a science and historiography, an art. However, for a historian both these facts (i.e., history and historiography) are important. In history knowledge and action both go together. In the words of Lord Action. "Study of history is critical, objective and view." In this statement he has put in the elements of both science and art.

In modern times the historian is expected not only to keep himself abreast of recent trends in historical research and interpretations but he has also to reconstruct the life of the past, re-interpret the process of history and also to represent the historical truths in the light of the latest researches and discoveries, without any bias or falsehood.

SCOPE OF HISTORY

By history we understand the breadth, comprehensiveness, variety and extent of learning experiences, provided by the study of a particular subject The growth of history has accompanied with the growth of human race. Thus history and man are inter-related or that history is a story of human race from beginning upto the present day. History at present is no more confined to the study of political activities of man but it also includes astudy of his achievements in the physical, social, economic, religious, philosophical, literary, artistic, cultural, industrial, technological and scientific fields, starting from ancient times upto, the modem age. In this way its scope is very wide and varied—infact as wide as the world and as long as the existence of man on earths. History links the present of mankind with his past. We cannot say that future is outside the scope of history. Experiences of history will form the history of tomorrow and in this way history is connected with future as well.

The most interesting fact about the extent and comprehensiveness of history is that today we hear of "History of Art," "History of Culture," History of Civilisation," "History of Religion." "History of Music," "History of Geography." "History of Physics." "History of Philosophy," "History of Education," "History of Biology." "History of the Atom," "History of Literature," "History of Mathematics." and History of what not. A learned speaker on a political, religious, literary or any other platform connected with any field of human activity, will place before his audience pure and simple history, connected with the life and achievements of some past of great human beings and nothing else. This makes the scope of history almost limitless, which knows no ends and also speaks of the importance of history as a teaching subject in schools and universities.

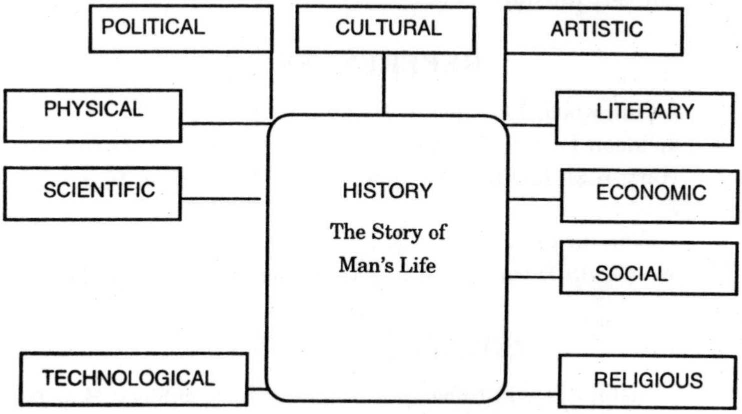

Diagramatical Presentation of Scope of History

Thus, history has expanded both vertically and horizontally. Its close connection with the allied fields of human sciences, has given new effects to historical studies. In the words of Lord Acton, "If the past has been an obstacle and a burden, a knowledge of past is the safest and surest emancipation". In the words of E. Lewis Hasluck, "A knowledge of history illumines the whole of human life. It adds to our knowledge of the existing state of world, a knowledge in which the human society and institution has grown up, a knowledge for future."

At becomes clear from the above discussion that the subject of history has no frontiers and that it is limitless and fathomless ocean, with no ends in view. However for instructional purposes in schools and colleges, we have to limit its scope and frontiers.

For deriving fullest benefit of historical studies, we should place before our students the broad outlines of development down the ages on one hand and the detailed study of a short period of history, on the other. The former will provide the whole sweep of the story of the past while the latter will give the varied aspects of the life of a people for a chosen period.

REFERENCES

1. Collingwood, *The Idea of History,* p. 214.
2. Johnson Henry, *Teaching of History.*
3. Hart, B.M. Laddell, *Why does not We Learn from History,* p. 2.
4. *Tarikh-e-Daudi.*
5. Walsh, *An Introduction to Philosophy of History,* p. 40.

REVIEW QUESTIONS

1. History is said to be a multi-disciplinary subject. How far do you agree with this statement and why?
2. What is History? Interpret it in modern context.
3. Is history a science or an art?
4. What is the modem concept of history?
5. "The scope of history is wide, the theme is the whole life of man, the world over." In the light of the above statement, discuss briefly the scope of history.
6. "History is scientific study and a record of our complete past." Comment and discuss the nature of History as a science.
7. "In spite of the fact that history is an all-encompassing subject it has its frontiers." Elucidate this statement by discussing the nature and scope of history.

2

Classification of History

> **Don't keep forever on the public road, going only where others have gone. Leave the beaten path occasionally and dive into the woods. You will be certain to find something you have never seen before. It will be a little thing but do not ignore it. Follow it up, explore around it, one discovery will lead to another and before you know it, you will have something really worth thinking about.**
>
> *—Alexander Graham Bell*

For systematic study of any subject, it is most necessary that teacher should classify it in proper way. All aspects of the subject have their own significance as such we must have a clear notion of a particular aspect or all aspects in mind. Thus, arise the need of classification.

History is the story of the progress of mankind since times immemorial. If history is taken from this point of view we can easily conclude that there is one history of the whole world and such a history could only be world history. However, for the convenience of study historians have divided history into various parts or branches. Every such part is complete in itself. No one can be called a true historian if he has read only a part of this long and varied journey of the progress of mankind.

History can be classified in different branches on the following main considerations.

1. Classification of History on the Basis of Geographical Boundaries

On this basis history is classified as:

(a) World history,
(b) National history,
(c) Provincial or regional history, and
(d) Local history.

2. Classification of History on the Basis of Time or Period

On this basis history is classified as:

(a) History of early ages,
(b) Ancient history,
(c) Medieval history, and
(d) Modern history.

3. Classification of History on the Basis of Circumstances

On this basis history is classified as:

(a) Political history.
(b) Economic history, and
(c) Social history.

In the light of above classification history is taught at different levels. A brief description of these is as follows.

1. World History

When should we teach the world history to our students? Various educationists have given their opinion and there are two prominent schools of thought on this question: One is of the opinion that it should not be taught to the children at the lower stages of education. This is meant only for the students of higher classes. The Second School of Thought is of the opinion that the student must be given a glimpse of the world history. This is not likely to be difficult for them. On the other hand, they shall evidence curiosity in it. They shall also acquire acquaintances with the ways of living of the people of the other countries. This view is based on the Child psychology. These thinkers also believe that while presenting a picture of the history of the world to the children, an attempt should be made to start this at the earliest possible ages to awaken greater curiosity in the students.

Now educationists have come to realise that at the secondary level of education history should be taught in the background of world history, however, such a background should be sketchy only and should not go into details of world history. Since it will not be possible to take up world history at the elementary school stage because of the fact that at this stage the students are too young to understand things or even events beyond their immediate social and physical environment.

At this stage we can teach them the biographies of some prominent "world figures" or great men of the world. At the middle stage we can introduce the study of certain important social and religious movements. Finally a comprehensive course of world history in a sketchy form be taught at the higher secondary stage.

2. National History

Nation is a geographical, social and political entity of the world the similar units in a country are known as regions for the purpose of historical studies. However, such a view may not be quite useful in the present age of internationalism. It is this desirable to introduce the study of national history or regional history in such a way that it does not develop regionalism or provincialism in them.

A famous British historian V.A. Smith has described India as "an ethnological museum in which numberless races of mankind may be studied". However, through all these diversities, these runs a strong invisible under-current of unity that nourishes and sustains the tremendous variety. This is India's cultural unity. While ancient cultures of other countries such as Egypt, Mesopotamia, Rome and Greece etc., are now mere memories and have no direct link with the life of the present generation in these countries, our ancient culture and civilisation have survived through the ages and still have direct bear - on our present day life. This is the most notable feature of our history. As Dr. A.C. Majumdar says, "Indian history and institutions form an unbroken chain by which the past is indissolubly linked with the present". Though we have varieties of traditions which differ from state to state and each state has a history of its own. It is the duty of the history teacher to present a comparative picture of these various histories but always keeping in mind to not let the unity or spirit of oneness slip of his hands.

3. Regional History

Regions are the smaller units in a country. In spite of the fact that such a study of history may be desirable and useful it is more likely to prove harmful in spirit.

The usefulness of such a study lies in the feet that each region (e.g. In case of India, Maharashtra, Punjab, Rajasthan, Andhra Pradesh, J&K etc.) have got their fascinating history. Different sages and seers, political leaders, social reformers from across the country have kept alive the great traditions of India culture and civilisation in their respective areas, however, their teachings never remained confined to any particular area or region but effected Indian life as a whole.

4. Local History

Though the term in self-explanatory but in history it does not necessarily mean only the history of a town or village in which the child lives. It definitely includes the history of the suburbs and the neighbourhood with which the child is familiar. The materials in and around his neighbourhood will stimulate more interest in the child and it could be a profitable starting point in the teaching or history. Though there exist innumerable monuments and other sources of historical importance throughout the length and breadth of our country but only resourceful teachers can make a full use of these in teaching effectively many of the important topics and events of national or provincial history. It is the duty of the history teacher to familiarise this students with their immediate surroundings and make the fullest possible use of such information in further enrichmemt of their knowledge of history.

(a) Importance of Local History

The various advantages of teaching local history can be summarised as under:

(i) The children became acquainted with the local customs and traditions which broaders their out look.

(ii) It is quite interesting to the students because it is related to their ancestors.

(iii) It develops in students emotional feelings towards their religion and they become interested to work for its development.

(iv) It develops in students a scientific out look.

(v) Local surveys give valuable training in history. These are as useful as laboratory work in the teaching of science.

(vi) It helps in the development of skills and right attitudes.

Writing about the importance of local history, E.S. Hasluck, "The study of Local history is of real importance and should most certainly find some space, however, small, in the school history syllabus. It helps and brings home to the pupil, by everyday contact with historical scenes, names and buildings, the sense of the development which his country has undergone, and removes his thoughts from time to time away from the present to the contemplation of the ages that are passed".

(b) Teaching of Local History at Different Levels

It is true that the Local history is of great importance, but the teacher should not wholly depend upon the Local history. It should serve just to illustrate and illuminate National or International history. It should be taken as supplementary study. Local history is of great importance to the students of primary classes as well as to the student's of junior classes. It teachers the boys to respect the customs and traditions of that place because they are germs of the life of the citizens. Due emphasis should be given to the Local history at the primary and higher secondary stages. However, in the higher classes.

Local history is not so much important. It must be taught but it shall not be of great use for the students of these classes. At the higher secondary stage, the students should be asked to take excursion to the neighbouring places. They should be encouraged to collect materials from the different parts of the locality which are of historical importance. The students must know about the historical buildings of their locality and their impact upon the social life. They should be encouraged to collect models, specis, coins etc., and take pictures of the different material of historical importance.

(c) Method of the Study of Local History

While teaching Local history, the following methods may be employed;

1. Excursions and tours should be arranged for the places that have importance in the Local history.

2. An attempt should be made to present a history of the local community and social groups.
3. An attempt should also be made to present before the students, a history of the various changes that have taken place in the locality, in political, social and economic life.
4. Students should be encouraged to have a look at various places of historical importance in the locality.
5. They should be encouraged to have knowledge of the history of the names of the roads of the locality.
6. During the teaching of history of higher classes, the teacher should often refer to Local history for illustrating the influence of the past on the present and to make clear how present is the product of past.

We may come to conclusion from the above discussion that local history can become a valuable aid both to the teacher and the student of history.

(d) Mediaeval Ages

During this period human civilisation progressed a good deal. From the Indian point of view, this is called the period of Rajputs and Muslims. So far as the religious conditions are concerned, it was the age of multifarious religions. It will not be wrong to call it a period of religious and political activities.

(e) Ancient History

It includes the history of stone age. In those days the life was difficult and it was quite difficult to get food, clothing, dwelling units etc. He lived in open space, resorted to hunting for his food and used barks of trees or skin of animals to cover his body. This story of man's life in different parts of the world is quite interesting to the children and enables them to understand how civilisation has developed through the ages. After the stone age started the ancient age when man began to settle in social groups. He started performing certain religious and social acts and it led to the classification of society into various categories. During this period some ard ant literature also developed. The scene was dominated by heroes and warriors.

(f) Modern Period

Modern period is the period of the highest development of culture and civilisation. Various political, social, economic and religious changes have taken place during this period. Science, literature, art, etc., have worked wonders. It shall not be wrong to call it an Age of science. It is an Age of Space Conquest. Man has established his supremacy not only over the nature but over the space as well. Every day the train of progress is going ahead. Modern history deals with all these things.

(g) Political History

Freeman, a great historian, opines history, is essentially a record of political events because political events greatly influence the life of a community. But history must not remain only a record of political events. It must throw light on all aspects of community life the study of all aspects of political history not only satisfies the human curiosity but it also enable the students to have a knowledge of political events of the past. However, it should not be studied in a narrow manner, i.e., the deads of the rulers and the political changes should not be the only concern of the political history.

(h) Social History

Social history deals with the development of family and the related problems such as social organisations, traditions, education, agriculture etc. Thus, it is very wide subject and actually it indirectly deals with political history. It should be taught very cautiously and never in isolation.

(i) Religious History

There is a class of educationists that lays great stress on the study of Religious history. It says that religion has influenced our civilisation and culture since the early ages. All the political and social events have taken place only on account of religion. Form this point of view, the study of Religious History is very important

While studying Religious history, we should keep in mind that we do not look at religion from a universal and human point of view. It should be treated as a collection of virtues and good qualities that are helpful for the preservation of human race.

Great caution must be taken while teaching Religious History A teacher has to present things in a very objective manner. He should not criticise any religion because this is likely to hurt the susceptibilities of the followers of that faith.

(j) Economic History

While emphasising the importance of economic needs as the spring of all social conduct. Karl Marx has clearly laid down that *it is the economic condition that determines and influence the progress of society and human beings.* State, society, culture, art and literature etc., all depends upon economic circumstances. Since it all gives a central place to economic history so the study of economic history is very important Economic history should not be studied in isolation and an attempt be made to assess other types of events as well. We will come across many an instances in different period of history. When a powerful and strong willed ruler or conqueror appeared on the scene and brought about tremendous changes that greatly affected the social and economic life of the community.

REVIEW QUESTIONS

1. What are the main bases of classification of history?
2. What do you understand by micro and macro study of history?
3. In which period of Indian history, would your local history prove most useful to you as a history teacher in that locality?
4. What precautions a teacher must take while teaching local history?
5. Is religious history teaching is good for the health of a multi-religious society?
6. What is the value of the local material in the teaching of history? What are its various varieties and how would you use them at the higher secondary stage?

3

History and Other Subjects

> The difference between a river and a swamp is that a river is confined within banks, while a swamp is not . . . Because a river is confined, and channeled, it has life. It is a mighty, moving, living thing. Because a swamp has no restrictions, it becomes thin and stagnant. . . . In our modern life we boast of freedom. We want life without restrictions and without confinement. Only we forget that such living becomes stagnant.
>
> —*Leonard Cochran*

Fundamentally, education aims at the unification of knowledge existing in different branches of learning. To achieve such a unification a conscious effort has to be made by teachers teaching various subjects. It is only by such a joint venture that we will be able to achieve the goal of unification of knowledge as a whole.

No subject can be taught in isolation especially History. To take the learning process to its devised and we have to take full advantage of various correlations and applications of history. Just for our convenience we have divided history in different branches of study. However, a conscious effort is made now-a-days to integrate various branches of history and to treat the subject as a synthetic whole. Teaching of history is done keeping in view its correlation with other subjects. It helps the students in understanding of subject matter by the students. It is possible to correlate different experiences and at the same time, allow different aptitudes and incluciation to work with co-ordination and correlation.

The unit of the students works in such a manner that he can understand a subject that is being taught, keeping in view its correlation with other subjects. Such a teaching brings about a healthy development of personality.

CORRELATION OF HISTORY WITH OTHER SUBJECT

Basically, all tte social education is nothing but a short course of history, depicting social, economic, industrial, scientific and cultural aspects of man's life. It throws light on the inter-dependence of man and man, nation and nation and country and country.

Dr. Terevelyan is of the opinion, "History is not a subject at all but a house in which all subjects dwell." In Ziller's opinion, " History is the central subject round which all other subjects can revolve". Prof. Johnson opines, "History with or without the name, certainly has been and is a background for other social sciences. History may indeed be regarded as the only field in which all other social sciences meet".

Koerner says in this connection, "Occupying as it does an intermediate position between the humanities and social sciences and employing both the qualitative approach of the humanist and the quantitative data of the behaviourist, it serves as a medium through which student can learn some thing of literature and arts on the one hand, and politics, economics and social behaviour on the other".

1. History and Geography

History in intimately correlated to Geography and till 1950's the two subjects were taught together. In fact they are twins, one stresses time and the other space. History studies people of different times and geography deals with the people of different places. The two subjects are now studied separately for convenience of study but we cannot completely separate the two subjects. In the words of Prof. Immanuel Kant, "Geography and history fill up the entire circumference of our perceptions, geography, that of space and history that of time." No history can be complete without some reference to space. Similarly no geographical account can be intelligible without reference to development in time. So both history and geography are concerned with the inter-play of human and physical factors.

Geography is the stage on which drama of history is enacted and it is the geography which determines the historical events and offer an explanation for historical actions of mankind. Similarly historical facts can serve as a good basis for arousing interest in geographical studies. In explanation of historical fact geographical factors are taken into consideration. Various factors taken into consideration are physical conditions of the life of man, climate, means of communication etc. All these factors determine the direction of human life and history increased by human life and his activities. History of each and every country is governed by there factors. Truly speaking historical studies desired of geographical background would be inaccurate and unscientific. The story of man's evolution since primitive stage, cannot be told without the varied geographical settings of the world. Man's mode of living, dieting and dressing etc., are all determined by his physical environment.

If United States of America grew into a powerful nation and acquired a rich history, it was very much due to its geographical conditions. Geographical factors were the sole cause of the downfall of many empires. The growth of Delhi, Dhaka or Beijing can be better understood by considering various geographical factors. The history of hostility between France and Germany can be explained on the basis of existence of river Rhine and Lorrain coal-fields. The correlation between history and geography becomes quite evident if we look at the equipments/apparatus used for teaching of these subjects. For teaching these subjects we make use of maps, pictures and atlases and other visual aids.

2. History and Civics

Till recently, civics was thought to be a part of history. It is now treated as a separate subject but there is a direct correlation between the two. Civics describes the pattern of administration of present day while history gives an account of the pattern of administration that existed in the past. The knowledge of civics cannot be obtained without reference to history. Even constitution is an outcome of the long history behind it. It is history that guides the actions and foundations of the government. In the words of Prof. Johnson, "The study of history in schools has, from beginning in large past, been a study of the forms of the government, of changes in government and of actions by the government, civil government can best be studied as a part of history". Again it is history that describes the progress of human ideas and institutions through the ages. It is history from that we get an up-to-date knowledge about the origin, development and progress or decline of some of the social institutions. Thus, there is close relationship between the two subjects.

3. History and Literature

History of development of literature is a part of history at large. Imagination which is an essential part of literature, imparts human touch to the teaching of history. It is only by "interpreting his sentiments and feelings as they are expressed in literature that the study of either literature or history can be made vital". History provides material, inspiration and background of contemporary events and conditions to literary persons. In its turn literature throws a light on popular taste, moral and intellectual standards, prejudices, ideals and inspirations of a nation. So both history and literature are closely correlated subjects.

4. History and Language

A thorough knowledge of language is quite essential to have a thorough knowledge of any subject. While teaching languages various stories are taken out from different pages of history. Students are quite frequently required to write essays on topics of historical importance.

Oral (words of mouth) and written expression is also very essential. In teaching history we provide opportunities to the students for discussing, speaking, debating, paper reading as also of narrating their experiences in black and white. Thus, we find a lot of correlation existing between history and language.

5. History and Art

Art activities are quite intimately related to history. In history students are required to draw pictures, battle-plans, graphs, maps' time lines and time charts etc. They are also required to prepare models of buildings, costumes and stage scenery for dramatic performance. This type of teaching aids area must for the teaching of history. All these aids are the products of Art and crafts. Thus, art provides a base to teaching of history. It also makes the subject interesting and delightful. Art is the practical application of the scientific knowledge. This practical application can be of two types: (i) Utilitarian, and (ii) Fine.

Whether the art is utilitarian or fine, it presents a picture of the things. Various events of history are presented before our eyes in the form of pieces of art. The paintings of Ajanta and Ellora are presented through art. Taj Mahal represents the whole reign of Shahjahan. It very clearly indicates the history of the economic conditions of that period. Coins, arms and other pieces of art are helpful in ascertaining the history of that period.

The history of development of art forms the subject-matter of history. What was the condition of the art during Gupta period or Buddha period or Mughal period can be known to us only through history. Had there been no history, we would not have learnt about the various styles of art. In short, both these subjects are inter-linked.

6. History and Economics

Economics is the study of wealth which deals primarily with production, distribution, consumption and exchange. But this study is in relation to man and his daily life activities. Thus a correlation between history and economics is quite natural. Economic conditions play a vital role in the course of history. If a country could attain a height of civilisation in a period, it must have been because of good economic conditions of a country or various countries in various periods. To know the economic conditions of India during reign of Akbar or Shahjahan we shall have to go through the pages of history. In history we are also told that certain empires faced liquidation only because of economic reasons.

Similarly, the course of economic events have been influenced by historical circumstances, e.g. Mohd. Tughlak had certain plans, but the historical conditions of his time did not favour them and so he could not succeed, however, afterwards these plans were considered to be good and scientific.

7. History and Physical Sciences

Apparently, though no direct relationship is there between history and physical sciences but indirectly there is a definite correlation between the two. All the principles and theories of science are based on facts and these are found out after a good deal of scientific study. But the knowledge as to how these principles evolved, developed and came into actual practice, can be acquired through the study of history. Thus, it is history that gives us a picture of the development and progress of science. The development of science takes a long period and it may take generations and centuries to evolve and reach perfection. It is only through the knowledge of history that the work done by one generation is known to other generation. It is history that tells us how much has actually been done and what still remains to be done. This history teacher is working very closely with the science teacher when he is tracing the history of a scientific invention, narrating the biography of an eminent scientist or describing the impact of scientific development on human society. In fact, advances in science and technology, as applied to human life, have revolutionised our social relationships to a great extent, in the present-day world.

8. History and Mathematics

The relationship between history and Mathematics is reciprocal. History helps mathematics to know about various mathematicians who were pioneers in their field and enriched mathematics by their contributions. History also provides the information about the origin and development of mathematics. Mathematics helps history in regards to calculation of dates and days etc. of various historical events. Acquisition of time sense in history is based on the knowledge of mathematics. These two subjects are complementary to each other. Really, speaking, there is a vast difference between the two subjects. Mathematics is generally called a dry subject, while history is supposed to bean interesting subject. But the knowledge of history can make teaching of mathematics quite interesting.

9. History and Handicrafts

There is a definite relation between history and handicraft. While teaching history, we make use of models, charts, pictures, toys etc. Teaching aids are an essential part of the teaching of history. These aids are the product of craft or hand-work. Thus, hand-work provides a lease of the teaching of history.

The most important educational slogan of the day in *'learning by doing'* and doing involves hand-work. The involvement of hand-work in teaching of history helps to co-ordinate the activities of hand and mind, thus correlation of hand-work and history is not only good for the general development of child's mind but it is also quite effective in teaching of history. Thus, we find a close correlation between history and hand-work.

11. History and Theology

History and theology are intimately related. Religion has influenced the course of history to a very great extent. In older times, it was the religion that guided people to make conquests and fight certain battles that have now become a part of the history. Many of the wars and political upheavals were caused by religious feelings. Therefore, the knowledge of theology is very helpful for a historian. Without the knowledge of theology, it is difficult to have a thorough knowledge of history.

In like way the knowledge of history is also helpful for the knowledge of theology. The birth and growth or the establishment and foundation of various religions and sects, are studied under history. The causes of failure and success of various religions form the subject matter of history. It is the history that gives us the knowledge about the spread and importance of religion in a certain period or certain periods.

In short, it may be said that both the subjects are intimately related.

10. History and Sociology

No doubt, sociology is the mother of all social sciences. Sociology has a wide scope of study. It studies the development of the human society at large. Really speaking, the subject-matter of history, geography, civics, political science etc., could very safely be included within the broad scope of the study of sociology. In fact, sociology gives us knowledge of the development of the society. It aims at developing man into an ideal social being History is very helpful in acquiring the knowledge of the development of society under various periods and under various conditions. The teaching of history should invariably be guided by the knowledge of sociology. Similarly, study and teaching of sociology can draw a lot from the knowledge of history.

The above description, make clear that history a multidisciplinary subject having direct correlation with all social sciences, even with mathematics, and other physical sciences with applied notion. A history teacher must have good acquaintance of this correlation.

REVIEW QUESTIONS

1. Do you agree with the saying that "History is a subject which is closely correlated with other social sciences."
2. Can Physical Sciences and Mathematics be helpful to the teaching of history? State your views with examples.
3. Discuss the relationship of history with Geography and Sociology and state how far these subjects can be helpful in making History teaching more effective and functional.
4. What is the importance of correlating the teaching of history with other school subjects ? Discuss with illustrations.
5. How can history be taught effectively, correlating it with other subjects?
6. Give a categorical account of correlation between history and other social sciences. Elucidate its importance in present day context.

4

Teaching History: Aims, Objectives and Values

> Every man is to be respected as an absolute end in himself; and it is a crime against the dignity that belongs to him as a human being, to use him as a mere means for some external purpose.
>
> —*Immanuel Kant*

As is the basic prerequisite of teaching, which a teacher-trainee is taught, first explain and chalkout the aims, objectives and value of a particular lesson or subject. Thus he can proceed successfully to his goal step-by-step.

Before starting to teach a subject it is essential to have a knowledge of aims and objectives of teaching that subject. It is also true for the teaching of history. In the absence of clear aims and objectives, the teacher will lead his pupils in a position of dilemma without destination.

Unless we determine the aims, it is not possible for us to work out a plan for attaining those aims. Once the aims and objectives are determined, then various methods of teaching are evolved according to these aims and objectives. Formulation of aims also helps in keeping the teacher and taught on the right track. Aims and objectives indicate the way and point to the ideas. No doubt aims are idealistic, but they are indispensable.

Writing in this context Henderson says, "we teachers, need to know where we want to go. Otherwise we may walk a long way, get very tired and accomplish practically nothing".

For determining the aims of teaching any subject we have to take into consideration the utility and usefulness of that subject. We have material as well as spiritual aspects in our life. For a successful spiritual life it is essential that we have a well-founded material life.

The aims and objectives of teaching various subjects are normally very similar and they are generally guided by economic and social consideration. The aims and objectives of teaching history include all the aims and objectives of education. These aims and objectives of teaching history have undergone changes with the change in the philosophical thinking of the time and changes in social and political practices.

In the nineteenth century the effects of Karl, August, Muller and Von Ranke bore signs of present day aims of teaching history. Towards the close of the century, if one surveyed the different aims of teaching history, ope would find the aims frequently mentioned to be accruing from historical instruction were: discipline of the memory, the imagination, the judgement; the setting up of ideas of patriotism, of conduct, of social service; the illumination of other studies especially geography and literature; and the establishment of intimate relations with current events. Apart from these, training in historical evidence; training, to develop habits of accuracy in dealing with facts; skill in putting facts together, and insight into causal relations; training in the use of books and the cultivation of a discriminating taste for historical reading were also considered important.

AIMS AND OBJECTIVES IN INDIAN PERSPECTIVE

In India we had very few historical texts and writings

before the advent of Muslims. "History," as Basham remarks, "in fact, in so far as it existed (in India) was a branch of religion......" Its aim was to instruct the pupils in Dharma (morals), Artha (wealth), Kama (desire) and Moksha (salvation). The Ramayana and the Mahabharata throw a flood of light on the lives of people and the "ideals they were expected up to".

Kalhana Pandita of Kashmir was to first to scientifically analyse past events and present them in an artistic way.

Various periods of history such as the Muslim history, European history, history of England and history of India were taught in such a way as to fulfil the requirements of examination and syllabus for these school subjects.

When the Secondary Education Commission formulated the objectives of secondary education as. "the training of character to fit the students to participate creatively as citizens in the emerging social order, the improvement of their practical and vocational efficiency so that they may play their part in building up the economic prosperity of their country; and the development of their literary, artistic and cultural interests which are necessary for self-expression and for the full development of human personality without which a living national culture cannot come into being." In the light of these aims the social studies movement was given a trial for about a decade. However, now we have again switched over to the old pattern of instructions.

The aim of history, as given in its report by Kothari Commission, is "to increase productivity, achieve social and national integration, accelerate the process of modernisation and cultivate social, moral and spiritual values." The role of history in strengthening "social and national integration" and cultivation of social, moral and spiritual values cannot be minimised.

Aims of Teaching History

In the foregoing discussion we have already given a broad hint to the aims of teaching history. In this sub-section these are listed in a more systematic and easily understandable form.

Though history teaching may not be able to achieve all the aims of education, such as:

(i) development of qualities of ideal citizenship,
(ii) development of qualities of leadership,
(iii) all round development of personality, and
(iv) development of character building and economic efficiency, yet it is helpful in the achievement of some of these aims, e.g. development of qualities of citizenship, qualities of leadership, character building etc.

As already pointed out the aims of teaching history have changed many a times in the past. They can be classified as:

(i) aims of teaching history in ancient times,
(ii) aims of teaching history in the 19th century, and
(iii) aims of teaching history in modern times.

(i) Aims of Teaching of History in Ancient Times: In ancient times history was only a chronology of events. It was intended to preserve the memorable events of life. In those days; history was a part of literature. Then the main aim of teaching of history was in preserving and keeping in memory those events that had some importance for the people at large. By and by the aims changed.

(ii) Aims of Teaching History in the 19th Century. Nineteenth century saw the development of scientific outlook in the various aspects of life. Teaching of history was now based on scientific outlook. It aimed at reviving the past

events of the society with a view to help the present day set-up.

With the development of the democracy and nationalism, teaching of history assumed a different outlook. It is now thought to be an integral part of education. Karl Auguste and Muller made a good deal of efforts in this direction. These educationists thought that history should help the understanding of other subjects of studies. They have laid down the following, as the aims of teaching of history:

(a) Understanding the present in a better manner, with the help of the study of the past;
(b) Bringing about the intellectual development of the children, and
(c) Helping the study and understanding of other subjects.

(iii) Aims of Teaching History in *Modern Times.* Today, we see that there are definite aims laid down for the teaching of history. These aims are based on scientific outlook. Various thinkers and scholars have tried to assess and study aims of teaching of history. These aims are briefly as under:

Miss Drummond in her book *History in Schools* has tried to make a thorough study of the aims and objectives of the study of history. She has laid down the following aims for the study of history:

(a) Interest for the Study of History. The first aim of the teaching of history is to create interest in the future. The history, in fact, is a treasure of knowledge so its study can be quite useful for young children.

To stabilise interest of students in the study of history we need very capable and devoted teachers who are able to link the past with the day-to-day life of the present

(b) Formation of Scientific Attitude: One of the aims of teaching history is the development of scientific attitude in the student. To develop such an attitude the vast historical data should be used in a scientific way.

(c) Development of International Outlook and Understanding: Since at present we live in an era of international understanding and outlook so to be able to live we must be prepared to understand the outlook of the people of other countries. This should, therefore, be one of the aims of teaching of history.

Many other scholars have also laid down the aims of the teaching of history. There may be summarised as under:

(i) Utilitarian Aim. Like any of the subject the study of history helps us in earning bread and butter and so it is one of the main aims and we study history to earn our livelihood. History helps us to grow out of narrow outlook and enables us to take a proper place in life.

(ii) Intellectual Aim: The basic aim of education is to bring about an all round development of the personality of the child. It includes the intellectual development as well. In this respect we reproduce the remarks of F.C. Hoppold, "Study of history results in clear and vivid form, freedom from bias and irrational prejudices, ability to think and argue logically, and to form aim independent judgment supported by the evidence which is available and at the same tune, the realisation that every conclusion must be recorded as a working hypothesis to be modified or rejected in the light of fresh evidences".

The correct picture in this respect is presented in the following extract,

"It (history) trains memory and power of concentration. It improves the reasoning and judgment of pupils by presenting facts in logical sequence and by providing opportunities for weighing evidence and for shifting the right from the wrong."

(iii) *Social and National Aim:* Through the study of history, it is accepted that the students will develop the spirit of sociality and sociability and the knowledge acquired by history will, help them to know what their forefathers have done. They will also know how their forefathers tried to raise the social status and help their fellowmen. That was an age of social interaction and social get-together.

It is a broad and human patriotism that develops rational humanity rather than overbearing audiciousness and it is desired to perpetuate the principles of justice and humanity that control the life of a nation.

(iv) *Moral Aim:* Study of history also aims to develop the qualities of morality in the educants. it is the duty of the teacher to acquaint the students with the lives and deeds of great men of the past. Sacrifices and noble deeds of great men shall inspire the young souls to acquire those moral qualities that are helpful in raising the society and its values.

It has rightly been remarked: "But the teacher must not regard history as a series of object lessons in morality, and must realise the danger that children may also see how wicked have flourished in past and are still flourishing. The moral aim, therefore, cannot be overemphasised."

According to Prof. Linwood Chase, the aims of teaching history are as follows:

(1) To collect the data pertaining to history.
(2) To evaluate the contributions of the past.
(3) To develop the consciousness in the pupils about society and social values.

(4) To help the students in having a correct idea about the importance and meaning of liberty and freedom.

(5) To help the students to understand the influence of historical facts and situations upon life.

(6) To develop the spirit of patriotism.

(7) To help the students to understand the series of social changes and their importance in social progress.

(8) To inculcate the interest of the pupils in the study of history and to encourage them to have a proper idea of time, place and their relationship.

(9) To understand the sequence of historical events since ancient times.

(10) To have a clear idea of historical facts and to give them a shape in order to have their practical utility.

(11) To study the development of human race.

Objectives of Teaching History

The objectives are the specific and precise behavioural outcome of teaching a particular topic in history. Any topic in history helps in realising some general aim of teaching history. The two important characteristics of a good objective are:

(i) It should be specific and precise and

(ii) It should be attainable.

Bloom's Taxonomy

Bloom's taxonomy of objectives is a classification of instructional objectives in a hierarchy. According to it the specific objectives have been classified into the following three categories:

(a) cognitive domains objectives,

(b) affective domains objectives, and

(c) psychomotor domains objectives.

The cognitive domain objectives include knowledge, understandings, applications, analysis, synthesis and evaluation.

The affective domain objectives include the appreciations, values, altitudes, interests and feelings.

The Psychomotor domain objectives include skills.

Now an attempt will be made to briefly discuss these objectives.

1. Knowledge of Objectives

To impart knowledge in the basic aims of education and so it naturally is the basic aim of teaching of any subject including history. By imparting knowledge of history to the student it is expected that he acquires a knowledge of the following;

(i) The student acquires knowledge of terms, concepts, events, facts, ideas, trends, movements, related to historical phenomenon, e.g., Recalls terms, recognises, reads maps, locates maps, charts etc.

(ii) Acquires, comprehension of terms, concepts etc., e.g., translates mutually different forms of communication, differentiates compares and contrasts, classifies and classifications, expands and summarises, illustrates, detects and rectifies errors, interpolates and extrapolates the required information.

(iii) Applies knowledge to unfamiliar situations e.g., selects facts, concepts etc., establishes relationships, employs known procedures in new situations, restructures given materials, predicts outcomes restates problems in new perspectives.

(iv) Develops critical and creative thinking, e.g., discovers difficulties involved, detects the logical fallacies, hypotheses, verifies, infers, generalises, evaluates, writes historical fiction.

(v) Developes practical skills in the field study of history e.g., improvises tools and apparatuses, prepares models, draws maps and charts, reserves specimens and exhibits, manipulates things, organises display of exhibition etc.

2. *Affective*

(i) Developes desirable attitudes, e.g. develops a sense of patriotism, becomes open minded and receptive, developes social virtues accepts civic responsibilities developes feelings of national integration and international understanding, realises the importance of international co-operation and piece and justice, values human rights and privileges, evaluates social changes critically.

(ii) Developes interests and appreciations, eg. reads voluntarily and appreciates literature and fiction of historical type. e.g. collects relevant materials, produces display material, discusses in historical perspective the social, political, economic and educational problems, visits places of historical interests, writes articles and fiction on subjects of historical importance.

The psychomotor domain objectives include skills.

Teaching History at the Primary Stage

At this stage of education the main objectives of teaching history to pupils are:

(i) *To Develop in the Students the Interest far History:* For achieving this aim it is desirable that the pupil is not burdened with a lot of information. He should not have a fear of examination.

(ii) *Development of the Power of Imagination:* The power of imagination which is an essential characteristic of childhood can be developed through teaching of history. This can be achieved by using story-telling method. Since pupil are quite fond of stories so it is quite natural for them to get interested in history if they are taught by story-telling method.

(iii) *To Make Students Conscious of the Influence of Past on Their Present Life.* It is desirable to develop in students the sense of time and this can be achieved with the help of time charts, time curves, time graphs and their frequent use in the teaching of history.

(iv) *To Develop Spirit of Patriotism and World-Brotherhood:* While teaching history an attempt be made to inculcate in the pupils a sense of patriotism and world-brotherhood.

Teaching History at the Junior High School Level

Teaching of history to the students of the Junior High School level should be done with the following objectives in mind:

1. The real interest in the history should be developed in the students.
2. Various mental facalties of the children should be developed. They should be encouraged to take up independent thinking. Critical faculty should be developed in them. They should be encouraged to look at various historical facts from a critical point of view.
3. The students should be encouraged to look at the present in the light of the past, and also to dream future.
4. The sense of time, as developed at the primary stager should be further developed. More abstract

means should be employed to develop this sense of time.

5. Patriotism and world-brotherhood should be developed in greater respect.

Teaching History at the Higher Secondary Level

At the Higher Secondary level, teaching of history should be carried on with the following objective in view:

1. Interest in the study of history, as developed at the primary and junior stages, should be strengthened and consolidated.
2. Mental faculties of the students should be so developed that they may acquire the power of reasoning and arriving at the decisions. The students should be encouraged to examine wings critically and accept them only when their power of reasoning accepts them.
3. The students should be given idea of the exchange of the various cultures of the world. They should be made to realise that every country of the world has to depend upon the other with regard to its culture in one way or the other.
4. The students should be encouraged to judge the present in the light of the past. They should also be made capable of looking forward.
5. They should be acquainted with the 'Law of Cause and Effect.'
6. Their sense of time, as developed at the primary and junior stages of education, should be strengthened and consolidated. A scientific outlook should be developed in them.
7. An attempt be made to acquaint the students with the social, political and religious problems of society and their possible solutions.

8. An attempt be also made to teach them about the development of the civilisation of the world.

Values of Teaching History

We have already seen a relationship between *aims* and *objectives*. Aims are nothing but set objectives according to which the teacher acts. The values are the gains of those aims. Actually speaking, the values are achieved when the aims are acquired. So we can say that aims are, in itself, where as the values are the product.

An analysis of aims and objectives of teaching of history reveals that its study will not lead to any materialistic gains. Its value is cultural, humanising and disciplinary. The study of history leads to development of the understanding of the cultural heritage, provides the pupil some intellectual training and inculcates in them moral virtues. It also arouses in pupils a patriotic fervour.

The important values of teaching history can be categorised as follows:

1. History leads to the intellectual development of the child. The child tries to employ his intellect in the solution of various problems. Children, when they study the deeds of great heroes like Rana Pratap, Shivaji or Razia Begum, feel to be like them. If this thinking, could be given a practical shape, it shall be very useful for the students and the society at large.
2. Though history, an attempt is made to enrich the knowledge of the students on the basis of the past experiences. An attempt is also made to develop the spirit of sympathy and self-confidence.
3. It develops in the students the qualities that may help them to adjust themselves with society.

4. Through the teaching of history, an attempt is made to inspire the students to achieve great deeds.
5. Teaching of history also strengthens the relationship between the teacher and the taught.
6. Through the study of history it is possible to develop effectiveness in our life.
7. Teaching of history can generate, in the students, the interest of studying the deeds of great men. This interest helps them to employ their leisure in the study of the lives of great men and women. With this study, their feelings are directed towards the high ideals and values.
8. It also developes, in the pupils, the quality of objectivity and impartiality. It encourages them to undertake the service of mankind without any self-interest
9. Serious students of history can develop the qualities of partiotism, ideal citizenship and service for the motherland. It is possible for the students to develop all these qualities when the teacher has given a real turn to their interest and talents.
10. It develops the power of reasoning and thinking in the pupils.

REFERENCES

1. Basham. A.L., *The Indian Sub-continent in Historical Perspective,* p. 23.
2. Government of India (1952-53), *Report of Secondary Education Commission,* p. 23.
3. Government of India (1966), *Report of the Education Commission,* p. 613.
4. Henderson, S.V.P. (1947), *Introduction of Philosophy of Education,* p. 15.
5. Johnson, Henry (1940), *Teaching of History.* New York Macmillan Company, p. 25.

REVIEW QUESTIONS

1. Comment with illustration on 'Teaching of History in our high school can be used for developing civic and moral sense in the students."
2. What aims of teaching History in Indian Schools be specially emphasised by the teacher in the present socio-political conditions of our country? Give sound arguments to justify your answer.
3. What are the aims of teaching history at the secondary school stage ? What changes will you suggest in the context of present political and socio-economic changes ?
4. Write a short essay on the "Aims of Teaching History to class VIII".
5. Discuss briefly the values of teaching History in Indian schools.

5

Main Methods

> The difference between man and the animals is that man is, or should be, aware that there is more to life than begin, beget and be gone.
>
> —*Imogene Fey*

> A mature person is one who does not think only in absolutes, who is able to be objective even when deeply stirred emotionally, who has learned that there is both good and bad in all people and in all things, and who walks humbly and deals charitably with the circumstances of life, knowing that in this world no one is all-knowing and therefore all of us need both love and charity.
>
> —*Eleanor Roosevelt*

For achieving the aims and objectives of teaching of a particular subject certain maxims are laid down. The teaching of the subject is then planned and carried out keeping these maximum as the guiding principles. No doubt teaching is an art but the success of a teacher lies in making his subject so simple as to make it intelligible for his students even to slow learner.

Method is a procedure which teacher follows to make learning easy and effective. It is made up of various important steps. Many of these steps used in one method may also be used in other method. Generally speaking, method is the, "process of planning, guiding, sharing and evaluating learning with a group of students." It is, therefore, that the method is one of the most fundamental aspect of education and central problem of teaching.

Generally it is found that every teacher develops his or her own method of teaching. A method may be successful for one teacher but the same may not be successful with other teacher. A method should always be in accordance with the requirements of the age of students, their stages of education and their physical environments. A method should never be stereo typed. It should be workable and flexible. To be a successful teacher one should be familiar with all the methods of teaching but should be able to select one that suits him best at a particular time and place for directing and learning process.

In the words of C. P Hill, "Method must be appropriate to the teacher's own personality, his gifts and his feelings; the teacher who has learned from the jawns of his students that they cannot tell a tale vividly must resist the temptation to plunge into narrative description, where as the teacher who has flair for swift blackboard sketches, should make full use of them". Method of teaching history in the means by which knowledge of history is imparted to the students.

DIFFERENT METHODS OF TEACHING OF HISTORY

Following are the important methods of teaching of history which are widely used by the teachers:

(i) Biographical method,
(ii) Story-telling method,
(iii) Source method,
(iv) Text-book method,
(v) Laboratory method,
(vi) Problem method,
(vii) Project method,
(viii) Lecture method,
(ix) Self-study method,

(x) Discussion method, and
(xi) Unit method.

For better comprehension, these methods can be elaborately described.

1. Biographical Method

As per dictionary meaning, Biography is the story of life of a great-man or woman living or dead. By using this method the great events of history can be taught as the events turning round the lives of great individuals. Teacher can make use of his method for inculcating in his students the values and ideals of life. Carivle says, "The history of what man has accomplished in this world is at the bottom, the history of great man who have worked here."

This method is useful in primary classes and to some extent in secondary classes. Making use of this method teacher is in a position to put various historical facts in an interesting and lively manner. It is also helpful in motivation and can lead to the development of the qualities of patriotism and nationalism in the students.

Merits of Biographical Method

Some of the advantages of this method are:

(i) It provides natural interest to students.
(ii) It is a simple method.
(iii) It is helpful to inculcate social and moral virtues.
(iv) It provides motivation to the students.
(v) It leads to the study of social life.

Limitation

The major arguments against the use of this method are:

(i) It is undemocratic, because instead of laying stress as society it lays stress on a few great personalities.

(ii) It does not provide continuity of subject matter.

(iii) It tends to develop hero-worship.

(iv) It is not possible to teach complete history by this method.

(v) This method can not be used to teach world movements.

(vi) Many a times great ruler do not represent their times.

(vii) By adopting this approach it become difficult to follow the chronological order.

2. Story-telling Method

It is considered as the best method of teaching history at all stages, however, it is more useful at early stages of education i.e., elementary and primary stage of education. Since the students in elementary and primary classes are fond of listening to stories, so, if the teacher tell them about the lives of great men of various ages it definitely arouses their interest and provides a scope for imagination development. Plato laid much stress on story-telling method.

The following points be kept in mind while using story-telling method of teaching:

(i) Teacher should ensure that he has full control over the subject matter that he is likely to present in the form of a story.

(ii) His style should be natural and interesting.

(iii) He must know the art of acting and he should be able to lay stress on emotions as and when required.

(iv) While telling a story, there should not be too much of personal element in it.

(v) Teacher must always keep an eye on chronological order, and the sense of time and space.

Various Types of Stories

The stories being related to young children can mainly be classified as:

(a) True Stories. Such stories occupy a unique position in the teaching of history and are quite valuable in the teaching of history.

(b) Myths. This refers to those stories that are mainly about fairies and other super-natural objects. Such stories are false and are of little or no historical value. As such they do not have much importance in the teaching of history.

(c) Legends are those stories which do have certain elements of truth in them but their details are generally incorrect. The use of such stories can be made in junior and middle classes where we are not much concerned about the accuracy of details. In this regard we reproduce the words of Prof. Jarvis, "Truthfulnes should be the major criterion to guide as in taking the help of stories, while teaching history. Historical stories whether facts or legends, must be formulated by a truthfulness which is higher than mere accuracy of incidents".

Merits of Story-telling Method

Some of the advantages of this method of teaching are as under:

(i) It enthuses interest in the subject.

(ii) It helps firing and development of imagination.

(iii) It inculcates good virtues which are likely to be inculcated in the students if they are told the life-stories of great men and women. Good virtues are truthfulness, charity, value, etc.

(iv) It inspiration for creative exercise.

3. Source Method

It is a common knowledge that doing a certain thing is a better of learning it Personally visiting a factory, a building, a mountain or a dam, is much better method of learning about them than merely reading or hearing about them. Similarly the study and use of original material and original sources, will give a much better understanding of subject, like history, as compared to any other method. This is known as source method of teaching and learning history.

Source method is considered to be a very important method of teaching history. It helps the students of higher classes to construct a superstructure of historical facts with the helps of the source materials such as, written cards, old chronicles, diaries, fermans, letters, contemporary documents, old inscriptions, statues, rains, battlefields, pottery, tools, clothes, arms, armours, roads and bridges, monuments, building etc.

Classification of Sources

Historical sources are classified as under:

(i) *Archaeological sources:* e.g., monument finds, epigraphics, numismatics.

(ii) *Literary sources:* e.g., sacred or religious literature, secular, literature, foreign accounts.

(iii) *Oral traditions,* e.g., Local history etc.

These are further classified as: (i) Primary sources, and (ii) Secondary sources.

Important Sources

Some important sources of history can be appraised as follows:

1. *Old Written Records:* These are the important sources of history. Written records comprise of old biographies,

autobiographies, diaries, official despatches, letters, legal decrees, business documents, charters, accounts of journeys, religious books, accounts of kings and their courts written by old historians.

2. *Old Coins:* Old coins are very useful source of history. By these, we know about the dynasties and chronology. They also throw some light on the social conditions and development of art.

3. *Metal and Stone Inscriptions:* Indian kings issued grants of lands or cash *inams* to saints and other important persons. The orders to the effect were inscribed on the copper plates and stones. So, they are also the source of ancient history.

4. *Ancient Tools, Implements and Pieces of Pottery:* So many tools, implements and pieces of pottery are buried in the olden ruins. They throw light on the civilisation of the ancient times. The study of these tools, implements and pieces of pottery also tell us the continuous story of the development of human race.

5. *Inscription or Buildings, Rocks and Pillars.* Inscriptions on old buildings, rocks and pillars also throw much light on the dim past Ashoka's history is known to us from his inscriptions.

6. *Ancient Buildings, Ruins and Monuments:* These are the very important source of history. The ruins of Taxila and Mohanjodaro, the art works of Ellora and Ajanta and the old buildings of Delhi and Agra speak the glory of the ancient India.

7. *Traditions Recorded in Literature:* Old traditions recorded in literature and folk songs also throw light on what and how men thought and felt in the past.

Utilization of Sources

The suitable way of utilisation of sources, which are

available in such large numbers, is not an easy task. To make proper use of available sources the need of a "source book", is felt, which may be useful in the acquisition of knowledge of history. The following extract is this context in worth-noting. "The original documents are too difficult, too technical and laborious to be properly interpreted and grasped. The paucity of such source books, however, cannot be over-looked."

Since students are not familiar with the purpose and utility of source material so it becomes the duty of the teacher to describe and explain such materials to students. For this purpose teacher can use same or more of the following ways:

1. *Demonstration.* The teacher should give an actual demonstration, to his students of the way in which a particular source can be utilised.
2. *Assigned Reading.* This can be achieved by the teacher if he asks some selected students to read certain selected passages that may be assigned to them.?
3. *Problem Solving.* Problems can be easily solved by making use of source materials. Source materials help the student to reach the truth.

The use of source material can be made in the beginning of the lesson, during the lesson, at the end of lesson or even after finishing the lesson.

Importance of Sources

In the teaching of history various sources are quite important because of the following reasons:

(i) Sources are quite useful to make the history real and alive for the students.
(ii) Sources make history concrete and meaningful.
(iii) Sources help in stimulating the imagination of children.

(iv) Sources make the children research minded. They do not accept the facts without proper reasoning and analysis. In this way they become critical-minded.

(v) Sources supplement the text-book knowledge and make the lesson vivid. In this respect they act as visual aid in the teaching of history.

(vi) They reveal the nature of reliable evidence and give a sense of reality.

(vii) This provide functional knowledge.

Difficulties in Utilising Original Sources

Though there are various advantages in utilising original sources but there are a few limitations in the use of such original sources. Some of the difficulties are given below:

(i) Sources of real value are not available.

(ii) In case of Indian students there in the *problem of language.* Most of the original sources of historical or cultural value, are in languages, foreign to Indian students, (e.g., in Persian, English, Arabic, etc.)

(iii) Conflicting views of different contemporary writers.

Importance

This method is used by history teacher in a scientific background and on the basis of certain facts.

This method is more suitable for the students of secondary classes. It is quite useful for developing the power of thinking, reasoning and drawing inferences, in such students. A few important advantages can be listed as under:

(i) Sources reveal the nature or reliable evidence.

(ii) They give a sense of reality

(iii) They provide training in reasoning and judgment.

(iv) They provide functional knowledge.

Because of the above advantages source method in quite useful for a history teacher.

Limitations

Some of the limitations of source method are as under:

(i) It cannot be used at the lower levels of education.

(ii) Even expert historian cannot interpret all the sources, so the teacher feels difficulty in making use of this method.

(iii) A great-skill on the part of teacher is needed for proper use of this method.

(iv) It is not a complete method.

(v) This method can not be used to teach all the topics in history.

(vi) It is a time consuming and expensive method.

4. Text-book Method

The text-book method is used for teaching of history event in great progressive countries. This method of teaching we revolve round the textbooks.

In this method, the students are asked to learn certain facts given in a lesson of history book. They are asked to memorise and learn by heart some facts. The students may some times be asked to go through history textbooks and grasp the material given therein.

As with any method of teaching, this method also has its advantages and shortcomings. Some of these are given here.

Merits of Text-book Method

(i) It helps develop in the students, the efficiency to acquire knowledge by reading the books.

(ii) It encourages students to remain active and learn things by themselves.

(iii) It helps the students know the length of answer to a particular question set in the examination.

(iv) It helps developing the memory of the students.

(v) It gives an accurate account of the subject.

(vi) It suggests various application of the material.

(vii) It reflects and establishes standards.

(viii) It gives the teacher to expand or limit the size of a topic according to needs.

(ix) It can serve as basis of all other methods of teaching history.

(x) It presents to the student, different and opposing points of view as historical and current events.

Limitation

(i) This method narrows the out-look of students and they become inactive and lethargic. They do not take an active part in the acquisition of knowledge.

(ii) This method does not develop the scientific out look in the pupils.

(iii) This method does not employ or use the maximum and principles of education.

(iv) In this method the scope of revision is very much limited and the knowledge acquired by the students is not permanent.

(v) It retards the originality in the students.

(vi) There past experience remain dormant.

(vii) This method leads to the development of cramming tendency in the students.

(viii) In case only are text-book is used by the teacher, then this method becomes even more rigid and unscientific.

(ix) Text-books contain only minimum essentials.

(x) Since the whole matter is condensed in a text-book there is a possibility of error of details or of interpretation.

5. Laboratory Method

This is scientific method of teaching history where history is taught like a science subject. It is quite a new method for a country like India. However, this method is quite useful in imparting the knowledge of history to the students in a scientific manner. We came across the demand raised by history teachers of some countries that a laboratory be established for the study of history in a scientific manner. Such a laboratory should be equipped with the following apparatus:

(i) Table for practical and experimented work.
(ii) Black-board.
(iii) Radio.
(iv) Show Case
(v) Magic Lantern
(vi) Projector, screen etc.
(vii) Historical maps
(viii) Time curves and time-graphs etc.
(ix) Pictures of great rulers and persons etc.

In this method the teacher provides an outline of the work before the students and the students are required to fill the details from the knowledge they acquire through presentation.

Merits of Laboratory Method

(i) It develops in the students the qualities of self-study and experimentation.
(ii) In this method the students acquire the knowledge as an active partner.
(iii) It is free from examination system as conducted at present.

Limitations

(i) It is quite expensive.

(ii) The knowledge that is acquired by the student, by this method, is not quite systematic.

(iii) The teaching by this method becomes quite mechanical.

6. Problem Method

As defined by C.V. Good, "The problem method is a method of instruction by which learning is stimulated by the creation of challenging situations that demand solution. It is a specific procedure by which a major problem is solved through the combined solution of a Dumber of smaller related problems".

This method consists in training the pupils to solve problems. This method is based upon the process of finding out the results by attaching a problem in a number of definite steps. In this method the student is involved in rinding out the answer to a given problem and terms actually it is a discovery method. In the words of Yoakam and Simpson, "a problem occurs in a situation in which a felt-difficulty to act is realised. It is a difficulty that is clearly present and recognised by the thinker. It may be purely mental difficulty or it may be physical and involve the manipulation of data. The distinguishing thing about a problem, however, is that it impresses the individual who meets it as needing a solution".

Procedure

The method proceeds in various steps discussed in the following lines:

1. *Recognising the problem.* First of all, we sense the presence of a problem and then identify the problem.
2. *Defining the problem.* The problem is then defined very precisely and accurately.
3. *Collecting relevent data.* Then all sorts or relevant data, which can be helpful in solving the problem, are collected and arranged in proper order.

4. *Organising the data.* Then the data is then organised in such a way that it can lead to the solution of the problem.
5. *Formulating the tentative solution.* On the basis of the organised data, the student formulates tentative solutions of the problem.
6. *Arriving at the correct solution.* Out of the tentative solutions, a correct solution is found out by a process of reasoning.

Merits

(i) It prepares the students in problem-solving. This training is solving-problem is quite useful in solving problem in actual life.

(ii) It stimulates thinking, reasoning and imagination of the students.

(iii) It develops, a habit of doing work independently, in the students.

(iv) This method of teaching is quite suitable for history.

(v) It stimulates intellectual curiosity and motivates the students to exert further.

(vi) In this method there is ample scope for individual work as a student is free to solve as many problems as he likes.

(vii) It develops in the student a habit of self-study.

(viii) While learning by this method the student learns by doing and so the information is retained by him for a longer period of time.

(ix) There is a close teacher-pupil contact.

(x) It develops qualities such a patience, co-operation, self-confidence etc.

(xi) It provides to students a training in technique of information processing.

(xii) It helps to develop intellectual honesty in students.

(xiii) It develops inquisitiveness in students and make them a good reasearcher.

Demerits

(i) It is a long drawn out and time consuming method.

(ii) It is not suitable for all topics in history.

(iii) This method is suitable only for bright and creative students.

(iv) This method is not suitable for students in lower classes.

(v) This method requires special preparation on the part of the teacher. An average teacher may find it difficult to adopt this method.

(vi) The content of history can not be organised according to requirements of this method.

(vii) Suitable text-books for use of this method are not available.

Applicability

This method trains the pupils in problem-solving. They learn to sense, analyse, reflect, organise and solve the problems. It helps us at every step in our teaching-learning process. The teacher should carefully select the problems which are real and have definite educational values. The teacher should also prepare himself well for the success of the problem-solving method.

7. Project Method

This method was given by Dewey—the American philosopher, psychologist and practical teacher. The project method is direct outcome of his philosophy. According to Dr. Kilpatrick, "A project is a unit of whole hearted purposeful activity carried on preferably, in its natural setting". According to Stevenson "A project is problematic act carried to its completion in its natural setting". According to Bollard,"

A project is a bit of real life that has been incorporated into the school".

The project method is not totally new. Project equivalent are advocated for the adolescent period by Rousseau in Emile (BK-III). A project plan is modified form of an old method called "concentration-of-studies." The main features of "concentration-of-studies plan" is that some subject is taken as the core or centre and all other school subjects as they arise are studied in connection with it.

Project method is based on the following principles:

(i) Learning by doing.
(ii) Learning by living.
(iii) Children learn better through association, co-operation and activity.

In this method, a project is taken which is then completed in a natural and social setting. As the project is carried to completion, the students learn so many things.

Procedure. Project method generally involves the following steps:

(i) *Providing a Situation.* The teacher provides a situation wherein the student feel like working on certain projects.
(ii) *Choosing.* Then the pupils are helped to choose project that islinked to their need.
(iii) *Planning.* Pupils then discuss how that project is to be executed? Steps of the procedure are planned and noted down.
(iv) *Executing.* The project is then executed as planned. Everybody contributes his share of work.
(v) *Evaluating.* The project is then evəluated and possible knowledge is reviewed.
(vi) *Recording.* The knowledge gained is then recorded for future reference.

I. Providing a Situation

A project should arise out of a need felt by pupils and it should never be forced on them. It should be purposeful and significant. It should look important and must be interesting. For this the teacher should always be on a look out to find situations that arise discuss them with students to discover their interests. Situations may be provided by different methods. Some such methods may include talking to students on topics of common interest, e.g., how did they spend their holidays, what did they are in Delhi etc.

II. Choosing and Proposing

From various definitions of an educational project we get the same underlying ideas (a) School tasks are to be real and as purposeful as the tasks of wider life beyond the school walls. (b) They are of such a nature that the pupil is generally eager to carry them out in order to achieve a desirable and clearly realised aim.

According to Kilpatrick," the part of the pupil and the part of the teacher, in most of the school work, depends largely or who does the proposing." The teacher should refrain from proposing by project otherwise the whole purpose of the method would be defeated. Teacher should only tempt the students for a particular project by providing a situation but the proposal for the project should finally come from the students. The teacher must exercise guidance in selection of the project and if the students make an unwise choice, the teacher should tactfully guide them for a better project. The essentials of a good project are:

(i) It should have evident worth for the individual or the group that undertakes them.

(ii) The project must have a bearing on a great number of subject and the knowledge acquired through it may be applicable in a variety of ways.

(iii) The project should be timely.

(iv) The project should be challenging.

(v) The project should be feasible.

It is for the teacher to see that the purpose of the project is clearly defined and understood.

III. Planning

The students be encouraged by the teacher to plan out the details of the project. In the process of planning teacher has to act only as a guide and he should give suggestions at times but actual planning, be left to the students.

IV. Execution

Once the project has been chosen and details of the project have been planned, the teacher should help the students in executing the project according to the plan. Since execution of a project is the largest step in the project method so it needs a lot of patience on the part of the students and the teacher. During this step the teacher should carefully supervise the pupils in manipulative skills to present waste of material and to guard accidents. The teacher should assign work to different students in accordance with their testes, interests, aptitudes and capabilities. Teacher should see that every member of the group gets a chance to do some thing. Teacher should constantly check up the relation between the chalked out plans and developing project and as far as possible 'at the spot' changes and modification be avoided. However, it such changes become unavoidable these should be noted and reasons explained for future guidance.

V. Evaluation

The evaluation of the project should be done both by the pupils and the teacher. The pupils should estimate the qualities of what they have done before the teacher gives his evaluation. The evaluation of the project has to be done in the light of plans, difficulties in the execution and achieved results. Let the students have self-criticism and look through their own feelings and findings. This step is very useful because as a result of the project, the pupils can know the values of the information, interest, skills and attitudes that have been modified by the project.

VI. Record

A complete record of the project be kept by the students. The record should include every thing about the project. It should include the proposal, plan and its discussion, duties allotted to different students and bow far were they carried out by them. It should also include the details of the places visited etc.

Role of Teacher

(i) In project method of teaching the role of it is that of a guide, friend and philosopher.

(ii) He helps the students in solving their problems just like an elder brother.

(iii) He encourages his students to seek collectively, amicably in the groups.

(iv) He also helps his students to avoid mistakes.

(v) He makes it a point that each member of the group contributes some thing to the completion of the project and in this process helps the sky and weaker students to work along with their classmates.

(vi) If the students face failure during execution of some steps of the project the teacher should not execute any portion of the project but should only explain to his students the reasons of their failure and should suggest them some better methods or techniques that may be used by them next time for the success of the project.

(vii) During the execution step teacher also learns something.

(viii) Teacher should always remain alert and active during execution step and see that the project goes to completion successfully.

(ix) During execution of the project teacher should maintain a democratic atmosphere.

(x) The teacher must be well read and well informed so that he can help the students to the successful completion of the project.

Main Features of a Good and Successful Project

1. *Usefulness.* The project must be individually and socially valuable and must have a practical aim.
2. *Maximum Number of Activities,* It should provide many-activities of various types. These should be quite suitable to pupils undertaking the project and should be able to draw the best from them.
3. *Availability of Resources.* The material connected with the project, should be readily available in or in the neighbourhood of the school. The pupils should be able to handle it without difficulty.
4. *Economy.* The project should not be expensive. It should give the best of results in the shortest possible time and with the least possible expense.
5. *Beat Experience.* It should provide experiences of a very high standard, including social contacts and character training. It must fulfill some educational purpose.

There are unlimited examples of projects that can possibly be used in teaching history. These may include field trips, school elections, making card-board, clay or wood models of various objects, writing plays based upon a period of history, preparing scripts for radio programmes, writing a song or a poem inspired by a historical event, dramatising events, making displays for the bulletin board, preparing pageants, arranging community surveys and starting a collection of old coins, stamps, specimens and other such things for the scrap-books and for the school museum.

Advantages of Project Method

(i) The facts learnt are easily remembered.

(ii) It arouses interest of the pupils.

(iii) It provides knowledge in the integrated form.

(iv) There is an opportunity for mutual exchange of view.

(v) In this method the students is free to work according to his capacity.

(vi) It teaches the student the dignity of labour.

(vii) The project is not forced on the student nature it is chosen by him so they are motivated to learn.

(viii) It helps in developing self-confidence and self-discipline in the student.

Disadvantages of Project Method

(i) It does not suit the fixed curriculum.

(ii) It does not provide the necessary drill work which is essential to have mastery of the topic.

(iii) It is quite lengthy, time consuming and expensive method.

(iv) In this method there is a chance that some students may shirk work.

(v) Since each student has to perform certain specified duties for the completion of the project, the learning will not be uniform.

8. Lecture Method

It is the most commonly used method of teaching history. "It involves teaching by means of the spoken word." This method can be used at all levels of teaching.

This method is not quite suitable to realise the real aim of teaching history. In this method only teacher talks and the students are passive listeners. It is a teacher controlled method. The student is provided with a ready-made knowledge and because of this spoon feeding student loses interest and his powers of reasoning and observation get no stimulus. It shall be wise for the teacher to punctuate this method with question-answer method. He may put questions to the students sometimes as the material taught to them. This will keep the students alive to the subject-matter that is being taught to them.

Advantages of Lecture Method

Lecture method commands certain merits. They are:

(i) It is less expensive.
(ii) It is time saving.
(iii) It is effective in providing information.
(iv) It is much inspiring.
(v) It is best toot for motivation.
(vi) It gives a sense of satisfaction to the students as well as the teacher. It gives them a feeling that they have learnt something.

Disadvantages of Lecture Method

Lecture method suffers from the following defects:

(i) It ignores the basic principle of learning by doing.
(ii) It is oral and verbal.
(iii) It is teacher centered and not a students centered method.
(iv) It does not develop scientific attitude and skill.
(v) There is no built in feed back.
(vi) It does not fulfill the needs and abilities of the individual students.
(vii) In this method ideas follow each other very rapidly

and so it is not easy for students to comprehend the chain of the ideas properly, if their attention is diverted a little and if they miss one idea, they may not understand the whole topic at all.

(viii) This method does not keep teacher in contact with the students. There is no room for individual attention.

(ix) In this method the experimental side is totally neglected by the teacher.

(x) It is a kind of spoon-feeding and several faculties of students such as observation, independent thinking etc., get a little or no opportunity to grow.

9. Self-study Method

The basic aim of this method is to develop in pupils the habit of self-study. The teacher may ask the students to read a specific period or event of history and then he may ask questions on that lesson in the class. This helps the students in acquiring the knowledge independently. This is found to be a suitable method for teaching of history.

10. Discussion Method

The present age is an age of discussion. We arrive at a definite conclusion after thorough discussion. Discussion has now come to challenge the authoritarian methods through which education was imported in the old days "Discussion may take the form of a conference, a symposium or seminar. However, it should always be remembered that discussion is quite difficult and dangerous too. After a subject has been put to discussion it cannot be withdrawn. The main aim of discussion is to inculcate in students a habit of "group thinking" and "collective decision."

The essential parts of a discussion are:

(i) A leader,
(ii) A group,

(iii) A problem, and
(iv) A content.

We shall take up these one by one.

(i) The Leader. In our case the teacher is the leader. He has to prepare and conduct the discussion. For this he is required to put in a lot of labour and planning. Once the discussion has been initiated the teacher should act as a co-worker and a co-sharer. He should carefully watch the discussion while it is going on and should act as a prompt guide in case his pupils face any difficulty.

(ii) The Group. Students of the class of history form the group. All types of students (e.g., brilliant, average, below average etc.) are included in such a group. Teacher should make all out efforts to see that every member of this heterogeneous group participates in discussion.

(iii) The Problem. The topic under discussion in the class is the problem. It should be carefully selected and it should be made precise and exact. It should be such a topic that it is liked by the students and they consider it their own topic. For this end it is always advisable to involve the maximum number of students in the process of selection of topic for discussion. The topic selected must be real and functional and must be within the capacity and comprehension of the pupils.

(iv) The Content. It is the material of study and includes maps, charts, picture, visual aids etc. Facts can be discussed only to prove them true or false "Statements about rvalue" can be discussed to establish their truth. It is about there statements that difference of opinion arises and discussion takes place.

Evaluation

Before closing the discussion each one participating in. the discussion should evaluate to find if the discussion has added any thing to his knowledge or information, brought about any changes in his existing views, attitudes and prejudices etc. It is expected that after a successful discussion same changes must occur to make the participant a more active citizen.

Nature of Discussion

Discussion is neither a debate nor a declamation, its purpose is to share and weigh all conflicting interests or values. The participants in a discussion are "inter-related in a process of competitive co-operation" and "Agreement" is the declared purpose of discussion. Discussion is always organised in a disciplined atmosphere. A good discussion is actually a well planned and well mannered conversation and for this those participating in discussion are expected to the courteous, clear, good-natured, tolerant and scincere. To get desirable results from a discussion a healthy and informal climate during discussion is a must.

Advantages

(i) It helps in collective decision-making.
(ii) It gives deep knowledge of the topic under discussion.
(iii) It inculcates the spirit of tolerance.
(iv) It leads to self-evaluation.
(v) It represents intellectual team-work.

This method of teaching history is useful at all levels. It is a very useful method because it enables the students to respect opinions and ideas of others, separate truth from falsehood, understand the topics, evaluate the findings and summarise the results. For this method to the successful it is essential that we have such teachers who are capable of providing guidance to the students.

11. Unit Method

In the teaching of history, unit has become the most popular form of organisation and the different ways of teaching it, are known as *unit method.* Unit method generally incorporates the use to both (problem and project) procedures.

In this method a particular topic is started in a particular class and finished over there, however, this method has failed to get approval from a majority of educational thinkers. In their opinion if this method is used, many irrelevant things may creep in and many relevant this may be left out. The students may be forced to study such things which are of no immediate importance to them. Moreover, if this method is adopted only a few tolrics will find a place in any particular class because all types of problems on that topic shall have to be solved by the students in one class. In the opinion of such educationists the *special method* of organisation of curriculum is preferable. In the spiral method a topic is divided into a number of small independent units to be dealt with in different classes that suit the mental capacities of the pupils. In there opinion such a method is more natural and less tiring to the students. To support it they argue that in such a method student loses nothing in accuracy and gains a lot of power of application of the general rules to particular problems.

The criterion of difficulty lays more emphasis on the fact that topics should be arranged in order of difficulty. But to take the topic as a unit is not a good arrangement. Topical arrangement is based on the unity of the topic i.e., exhaustion of the topic at the same time or at a stretch. However, it is unnatural and also impracticable to take a topic and exhaust all its possible portions and problems, simple as also complex, in the same class. For a good arrangement the following be kept in view:

(i) Every topic should be divided into parts.
(ii) These parts should be graded according to difficulty.
(iii) Each part should be introduced at a proper stage.

These different portions be allotted to be taught in

different classes according to their difficulty and maturity of minds of pupils. Such an approach is called a *special approach*.

A portion is introduced when a sufficient background has been prepared for it. The remaining more tedious portions are left, for being taken up later on. Every thing is taken up at its proper stage and there is enough opportunity for revision. The precaution to be observed is that the portion should neither be too long nor too short.

Presently "Topical Method" is more a system of arrangement of subject matter than a method of teaching. The topics is to be taught a a stretch, without a break or gap, continuous teaching of topic not only will save the students from divided attention and will also ensure their full and whole hearted concentration on the topic in hand. Thus, a natural link will exist in the day-to-day work in the class room.

Formation of Units

Units are formed to facilitate learning. Their function is to guide the student through a learning experience. Like most learning devices the unit is a growth, an evolution, rather than a creation. The following points should be remembered while forming units:

1. Units for lower classes should be shorter than those meant for higher classes. So due consideration to class, grade and time be given while forming units.
2. Children's needs, interests, capacities and capabilities should always be kept in mind while selecting units for them. Thud, units should not be big enough to confuse children with factual material. They should, rather, centre round the children's expanding interests.
3. A unit must have relationship to the whole course.

4. A unit must be comprehensive enough on which sufficient material may be available for its complete understanding.
5. A good unit should provide for the intellectual, social and emotional development of children, through the integration and correlation of their learning activities.
6. A good unit should be evolutionary and functional, moving towards some definite goal.
7. Each unit should be further split up into sub-units for the sake of clarity. For example, the unit "How British Traders became Rulers of India" may be divided into the following sub-units:

   (i) Early European settlements and emergence of the British as the leading power.
   (ii) Decline of the Mughal Empire.
   (iii) Rise and Fall of the Marathas.
   (iv) Rise and Fall of Hyder Ali & Tippu.
   (v) Rise and Fall of the Sikhs.

Procedure in Unit Plan

Dr. H.C. Morrison has set up a procedure that according to him will enable the pupils to accomplish the mastery of the unit His procedure remains even today the most accepted. Like Harbartain steps, Morrison's procedure also consists of five formal steps which are under:

(i) Exploration. In this step, the teacher discovers what the pupils know about the proposed unit. This can be done by a formal written test or an informal class discussion. This step orients the teacher and motivates the pupils. It brings out the perceptive background of the pupils in the subject and prepares them for the new material.

(ii) Presentation. The teacher, presents to the class a complete outline of the unit through a short and well-

planned talk. After the presentation, a test is given to find out whether the pupils have understood the idea of the unit. The talk is repeated for the seconder even for the third time. If the teacher feels that the students have not understood the outline thoroughly.

(iii) Assimilation. This step needs the pupils to engage themselves in reading, studying, writing, talking with one another and consulting the teacher. They are guided by the teacher through study-sheets, containing references, assignments, projects, problems and other such material that teacher in view of teacher will help the pupils to achieve mastery of the unit.

(iv) Organisation. Each pupil is required to write a logical and systematic outline of the facts, he has gathered about that unit. It will demonstrate that he has understood the unit.

(v) Recitation. The pupils are now ready to recite and give a systematic oral account of all or of significant portions of the unit. This step is meant to afford training in speaking.

Importance

It becomes quite clear that in his procedure, Dr. Morrison has tried to utilise the best in modem educational theory and practice. The system may not be perfect, but "it does provide for individual differences remedial procedures, a scientific system of testing with follow-up work, the use of the sound method of supervised study under laboratory conditions, and to some extent, socialised procedure."

Advantages

1. *Gives a Variety of Outcomes.* If the unit procedure is well-planned and skilfully executed, it gives a variety of outcomes. The extension of knowledge and the development of skills, abilities and attitudes are some of the possible outcomes. Many of the traits that history teachers wish to

develop in their pupils, are especially promoted through the unit procedure, e.g. co-operation, courtesy, leadership, loyalty and respect for good workmanship, opportunities for reading, problem solving, project work, discussion and personal interviewing etc.

2. *Provides Flexibility for Adapting Instruction to Individual Differences of Children.* The unit procedure does not aim at fixed and uniform standard of achievement for all pupils. It rather focuses attention on the individual child, his problem and his interests. Well-planned units keep different standards of achievement in case of different children in order to meet the educational needs of individual pupils. This makes learning functional because units are based on the needs and interests of different types of children.

3. *Provides a Natural Situation for Teaching Skills.* If opportunities are not provided for development of skills, "the units become little more than chapters in hooks or logically organised segments of subject-matter." In order to enable children to learn how to work in groups, it is essential that group situations be provided. This is possible through the unit-procedure which provides such situations.

4. *Effective use of Supplementary Materials.* In the unit procedure pupils make use of text-books, source books, encyclopaedias, literature, pamphlets and periodicals etc. A well-planned unit stimulates the use of these and many other types of supplementary material.

5. *Encourages Progressive Measures in Teaching-Learning Process.* In the educational field today, curriculum, correlation, fusion and integration are frequently mentioned. The unit, method not only combines air these progressive measures but also encourages them.

6. *Exemplifies Democracy in the Class-Room.* The unit procedure exemplifies democracy as an ideal, in the best

possible manner, in the class-room. Through this procedure, democracy is not only taught in spirit but can also be made the subject of the unit of study.

REVIEW QUESTIONS

1. Discuss briefly the advantages and disadvantages of the Text-book Method of teaching History.
2. Discuss the main characteristics of the Lecture Method of teaching History.
3. What is the key-idea, underlying the Unit Method of teaching History. Discuss this method with all its merits.
4. Select one lesson for the 10th class which you would like to teach through the Source method. What steps would you follow for the successful utilisation of the method?
5. Differentiate between the Problem and the Project methods of teaching History.
6. How would you use any one of the following methods in senior classes for increasing effective participation by your pupils: (i) Source Method, (ii) Project Method.
7. What is the Source Method of teaching History? Indicate its advantages and disadvantages.
8. What is the value of utilising original sources in the teaching of History? Mention the main difficulties in the way of following this method in our schools.
8. Name the different categories of sources that can be utilised with advantage, while teaching, history in our schools.
10 What is Story-telling method of teaching History? How do you distinguish it from the Discussion Method?

6

Golden Tips for Effective History Teaching

> A man may fall many times but he won't be a failure until he says that someone pushed him.
>
> —*Elmer G. Letterman*

Tip One: Enthusiasm!

Enthusiasm is the first and most important way to bring life to any classroom. Your own enthusiasm for the topic and teaching is the key to success. Any lack of enthusiasm is unfair to the students. What is enthusiasm? Traced back to its ancient Greek origins, it means the spirit with or in you. In other words, enthusiasm is "something inspiring zeal or fervor." Teachers need to be inspired and they need to inspire their students. To be inspired, you must love what you teach. You need to know your subject and learn something more about it each day. And you must make what you teach a part of you. When your students see and understand these qualities, they should be inspired and enthusiastic about learning American history.

Tip Two: Rely Less on Textbooks

Too many history textbooks tend to be dull, boring, and bland. You cannot really eliminate the textbook entirely, but you should not make it your sole authority. Let the textbook guide the outline for the course, but teach from other sources, especially primary sources, as well. Pick the best historical sources that are a pleasure to read. For example, when you study American slavery, have your students read *Narrative of Frederick Douglass, An American Slave* and/or Harriet Jacobs's *Incidents in the Life of a Slave Girl*. Jacob Riis's *How the Other Half Lives*, Ida B. Wells's *Southern Horrors*, and W.E.B. Du Bois's *Souls of Black Folks* shed much light on post-Civil War America while Melba Patillo Beal's *Warriors Don't Cry* provides a very moving account of an African American high school student's experience of integrating Little Rock's Central High School. These are all primary sources and there are plenty of other great examples you can use. You should choose sources that have had the greatest impact on you. Not only will they inspire the students, but you can also teach them with passion.

Preparation is the key to making the most of these sources. Give students questions that will get them to look for important ideas and points while they read.

Tip Three: Use Well-written Secondary Sources

Secondary sources are critical for contextualizing and making sense of those rich firsthand sources. Although you may or may not assign these works, it is your job to prepare your students by giving them the background they need to fully understand the primary sources. And secondary sources provide that framework or context.

Tip Four: Look at the Things That Matter Today

Stop thinking of history as battles and wars, kings and presidents and start thinking in terms of race, class, and gender. Today, these things matter very much in our lives. Sexuality and geography or location are equally important. This is how we identify ourselves. If we are going to teach tolerance, we are going to have to teach respect for different races, classes, genders, and sexualities. With older high school students, you may even be able to introduce the idea of how we construct these categories.

Tip Five: Use Generous Amounts of Local History to Teach World History

Some historical development may make a lot more sense to a student if he or she can see a local manifestation of it. For example, teaching the three phases of Reconstruction — Presidential, Radical, and Redemption — could really bore students if not done well. If you happen to be teaching in the South, try handing out a copy of a contract signed by a local planter and his former slaves the summer after emancipation. This exercise does several things: it demonstrates a primary source; it shows what Reconstruction meant to ordinary people—a planter and freedpersons on his plantation; and it gets the students to interact with the past. These historical figures are real flesh and blood folks right there in the county in which you teach. I guarantee students will remember Reconstruction a lot better than if they had just read about it in the textbook.

Alternatively, ask students to read local newspaper accounts of Reconstruction. What did the editor think of the changes accompanying emancipation? What impact did it have on his or her readers' everyday lives?

You can even use local history in teaching world history. Several years ago, when I taught world history in Georgia, we focused on the new consumerism in the 1920s by looking at advertising, especially by department stores. First, I provided a brief history of the department store and the ways in which these stores created the desire for their goods through newspaper ads—leading to a democratization of desire. How do you get people to buy things? What are their values? How do the ad men appeal to them? We used *Discovering the Global Past: A Look at the Evidence* by Merry E. Wiesner, William Bruce Wheeler, Frederick M.

Doeringer, and Melvin E. Page (Boston: Houghton Mifflin Company, 1997, 2:320-42) which included department store ads from newspapers in the United States, Great Britain, France, Brazil, Canada, Australia, and South Africa. The commonalities in advertising in all these countries were clearly visible in the ads.

So I assigned each student a year in the 1920s and asked them to go to the public library to look for department store ads in the local newspaper, the *Albany Herald*. They had to bring a photocopy of a typical ad to class; explain it; and determine what it was trying to sell and to what values it was trying to appeal (e.g., thrift, status, etc.). Sometimes you will encounter unexpected results. As we looked at the ads, we noticed those in the early 1920s seemed to target men, while the ones in the late 1920s tended to target women. So we discussed what that suggested about changes in advertising and in culture.

You can use local newspapers in a variety of ways. How did local people deal with World War II on the homefront? How did the war affect advertising? What values were important in the 1940s compared to the 1920s? You might have them locate the issue of the local paper for the day they were born—or the day their mother or father was born. What was the important news of that day? What were merchants advertising? What were the values visible in the ads?

Tip Six: Use Music and Film to Appeal to Those Senses not Necessarily Stimulated by Reading

Music can touch the emotions in a unique way. Starting a discussion with a song can break the ice we so often struggle with in starting a class discussion. Help the students develop their listening skills by printing out the lyrics of the songs for them. It demonstrates how important those words are to you and it especially helps them to understand songs sung in a different dialect. Do not hesitate to play different versions of a song to illustrate how people can take a song from one context and reshape it for another purpose. A good example of that is the labor movement song, "Which Side Are You On?" which was altered to become an important song of the civil rights movement. Other civil rights songs came straight out of the black church, illustrating the link between that institution and the movement. Songs can also convey very different feelings if they are performed for an audience at a concert as opposed to be being captured on tape as part of a mass meeting.

Film, too, can be a powerful way to get your students' attention. But be careful not to use films to replace teaching. Instead, teach the film! Tell your students what to look for in the film. Stop the film at critical points and get feedback from them. Do not feel compelled to show the film in its entirety. Use the film as you would any other source. Some films you want to teach in their entirety, just as you would assign the entire brief autobiography of Frederick Douglass. You may wish to use only portions of other films just as you would have them read parts of newspapers and magazines rather than the entire issue. Remember, the film is a tool to help you better convey a deeper understanding of the historical period you are teaching.

Tip Seven: Become More Computer Literate

Learn about the ways in which the Internet can enrich your teaching. Sign up for a listserv in your field. There are listservs for history teachers, for American history, world history, and every imaginable branch of the field. Find out the best web sites for the topics you are teaching and pass them on to your students and then discuss what they are learning on those sites. Just as you teach them how to discriminate between useful and poor historical printed sources, you must teach them to use the same discrimination with electronic sources. For years, we taught our students that just because it is printed in a book does not make it true. Now we have to make very clear that just because it is on the Internet does not make it true. What is the source of the information? Is it reliable? How can you tell? Not only will they have a better understanding of the past, but they are learning a skill they can use in other aspects of their lives.

When you make history exciting for your students, they are motivated to learn more and thus develop a deeper understanding of the meaning of the past. So start or continue incorporating Enthusiasm, Primary Sources, well-written Secondary Sources, Current Issues, Local History, Music and Film, and the New Technology into your teaching—your students will be grateful for the challenging stimuli you provide them.

[Courtesy: *Lee Formwalt, executive director of the Organization of American Historians.* © 2002 Organization of American Historian.]

7

Principles of Teaching History

> An open mind is all very well in its way, but it ought to be so open that there is no keeping anything in or out of it. It should be capable of shutting its doors sometimes, or it may be found a little draughty.
>
> —*Samuel Butler*

To equip oneself with concrete knowledge of fundamentals of the subject is the first prerequisite of a teacher. While teaching history, it is desirable for the teacher to keep following points in his mind.

(i) Teacher's entire attention remains focussed on the child.

(ii) He should be clear about the subject matter being taught.

(iii) He should use a proper teaching method for presenting the subject matter.

There is no any one method in history teaching that may be suitable for all topics and all levels. In the absence of it the teacher has to use his own judgment to select the most suitable method. Further history is an ever growing subject and every day now material is added to its subject matter. Thus teacher has to take extra pairs to collect teaching aids, he is required to use different teaching method at every different stage. This situation can be described, as under, in the words of an eminent scholar: "History perhaps beats over other subjects in the intensity of discussion and the heated argument that has centered round its teaching method in recent times.

GENERAL PRINCIPLES OF TEACHING HISTORY

In spite of all the changes that have taken place in the course of history, it cannot be denied that there are certain basic principles on which the teaching of history rests. Some general principles are as under:

(1) From Concrete to Abstract. While teaching history, the teacher should *proceed from concrete to abstract.* In the lower classes, concrete facts should be presented. With the growth in the mental age of the students, the teacher can resort to presentation of abstract facts. He should proceed from easy to complex, keeping in view the mental age of the students.

(2) From Known to Unknown. The *second maxim of the teaching* is that the teacher should proceed *from known to unknown.* The teacher tries to take advantage of what the students know and then tries to relate the new experiences with the old ones. In this process, the teacher should take reverse course. He should try to present the known facts to the students first and then take them to unknown areas.

(3) Chronological Order. To make subject intelligible to the students, *the facts should be presented in their chronological* order. This is all the more important in the teaching of history. Since history has a scientific outlook so it is necessary that the facts of history should be presented in a systematic and chronological manner.

(4) Correlation of Facts and Events. Facts of history should not be presented independently and in an isolated manner. An attempt should be made to present various facts in a cor-related and co-ordinated manner with the events so that it may look like a chain of events. Every

event and fact should be based on the 'Law of Cause and Effect'. Such a presentation is intelligible and understandable to the students.

(5) Perfection. All the facts that are presented before the students should be perfect in themselves. It is not sufficient to present an outline only. All the events should be presented in their full form. This does not mean that the students should be burdened with informations only. They should be given only that much which is necessary. These events should be presented in a scientific manner and systematic order. An attempt should be made to shift the important from the unimportant and present what is actually needed.

(6) Pendulum Method. This method is useful at every stage of education. The pendulum moves backward and then forward. In other words, it establishes the connection of the past with the present. Similarly, the teacher of history should try to connect the past events and experiences with the present circumstances. If teacher succeeds in coordinating the past with the present, his teachings shall be interesting and successful.

(7) Aids. Teacher should make a balanced use of the teaching aids at every stage of education. Pictures, charts, maps, etc., are the life blood of the teaching of history. They make the history teaching effective and interesting. At no stage should the teacher try to discard these things.

(8) Master the Subject. The teacher should have perfect command over the topic that he is teaching. He should have prepared the lesson thoroughly well so that he may present it before the students is an interesting and attractive manner. On the other hand, the students should also be kept active. They should not be made passive partners in the game. Occasional question and dramatisation will do good.

(9) Dry and Terse Matter must be Avoided. History has certain uninteresting and dry elements in it. Dates, names of rulers, places of events, etc., are not at all interesting to the students. The teacher should, therefore, try to make the subject interesting to the students and, if possible, do away with the unnecessary dates and names.

(10) Time Sense. At every stage of education, the students of history should be given time sense. Unless the students have developed a proper sense of time, it shall not be possible for them to co-ordinate and cor-relate knowledge of various subjects that they have acquired. In the absence of the 'Sense of Time', their knowledge shall be lopsided. It shall neither be completed nor systematised.

(11) Oral Teaching. In elementary or junior classes especially, oral teaching is very useful. At this stage, text-books are not very much needed. In this respect, a scholar has aptly remarked: "In the junior stage especially, the oral lecture is the chief factor in presentation, as text-book is not essential. In the middle and senior secondary stages, there is definitely a need for the text-book because at this stage solid facts are given to the students."

(12) Question and Answer. In the present methods of teaching, question and answer method is supposed to be good and interesting. The teacher should try to apply this method and make the teaching interesting. If the questions are put up to the students, they shall remain active and try to grasp the matter. The questions should be framed in an artistic manner. They should be framed that they awaken the curiosity in the students and inspire them to come forward with the answer.

REVIEW QUESTIONS

1. What important points an emphatic teacher must observe while teaching history.

2. What are the main principles of history teaching ?
3. Give an outline of general principles of history teaching.
4. Can oral teaching be useful in present day context?
5. What is pendulum method of teaching history

8
Curriculum Development

> Teachers of today just go on repeating things in a rigmarole fashion, annoy the students with questions, and say the same things over and over again. They do not try to find out what the student's natural inclinations are, nor do they try to bring out the best in their talents. Only through education does one come to be dissatisfied with his own knowledge, and only through teaching does one come to realize the uncomfortable inadequacy of his own knowledge.
>
> —*Attributed to Confucius and written over 2400 years ago*

History occupies an important place in the school curriculum. Till 1950's history was taught as one subject history and geography under the head general knowledge.

The construction of curriculum of history is a difficult task, however, it would be easier to construct a syllabi in history if we keep certain points in mind, while constructing the curriculum in history.

The syllabus of mainly bound by two considerations.

(i) *Structure of the subject:* The structure of the subject, in most cases, requires that a wide range of elementary rules and techniques be mastered before studying the rest of the subject.

(ii) *Limited and maturing abilities of the pupils:* The consideration of limited and maturing abilities of students decides the order in which the contents of the subject are to be arranged.

The problem of selection arises because knowledge cannot be imparted to the pupils within the short span of their school life. Thus the actual problem is to compress so many facts and details in history syllabus. In our country, in the pre-independence days, the history syllabus suffered from the defect of poor selection and deficient grading. The same facts were repeated in different grades putting under emphasis on political "outlines" to the total neglect of social and cultural life.

We may conclude that a ruthless selection of relevant facts should be our guiding principle in syllabus construction. Here we face a problem of selection of events and the problem of their historical explanation.

There is the problem of "selection of periods", i.e., which particular periods of history are more worthy of study than other? Another problem is related to the "Aspect history", i.e., are some aspects of history more important than others? One more problem of selection relates to the conflicting claims of world history and the history of a country. Are we free to choose between them ? Or, has the history of the particular country any special claims to be taught ?

In the light of problems cited above, we have to make a fair selection of materials. While doing so, we should take note of the various forces, spiritual, material, the great religious, the achievements of science, the arts, vast range of social customs, family life, festivals, amusements, great deeds of heroism and kindness and love.

Cultural Epoch Theory

This theory was one of the earliest attempts of frame history syllabus on psychological foundations. It held away in the educational world during nineteenth century. Its major implication is that the "childhood of history is best for the child, the boyhood of history for the boy, the youthhood of history for the youth and manhood of history for the man." Its basic idea is that ancient history is suitable for elementary stages, mediaeval history for the middle stage and modern history for the high school stage.

The importance of this theory lies in the fact that it lays more stress on social and economic events and problems pertaining to humanity. According to this theory, the student shall know about the various stages of development of the culture of human race, and when they have finished their education, they shall be having full idea of the development of human civilisation.

Critics of the theory point out that human progress did not occur in an orderly way. The progress at every stage was not at all systematic. Human society did not come down like a flight of stars. There were various turns and ups and downs in the path of progress of human race. Unless we have an idea of all these things, we shall not be able to have an idea of the development of human race. It cannot be said that the last stage of the development of human race is most complex.

In the modern history, the language is easy as compared to the language of ancient history. If the curriculum is organised on the basis of this, it shall be difficult to arrange various military events. In the ancient history, political and military events are most important and it is not possible to have an idea of the history without having a thorough knowledge of these.

Biological Theory

This theory has influenced the selection of materials, at least, for the elementary stage. It is claimed that general history is beyond the comprehension of the children below

12 or 13 years. Therefore, they should be introduced to great men of our country and of the world in a strictly chronological sequence. This idea originated in the great man theory of historical explanation propounded by Carlyle. He believed, "The history of what man has accomplished in this world is at bottom the history of the great men who have worked here".

The proponents of this theory think that great men represent their times. They are the noblest creation of God. So the preliminary study of their lives will equip the student to have an insight into the history. Their biographies will form the basis for further study of movements at a later stage.

The critics of this theory point out that it does not recognise the collective life of the community. It also does not take into account the role to collective social endeavour. Instead, it harps on the personality of the great heroes and advocates hero-worship. Actually, the so-called great men do not represent their time. They are far above the average humanity of their age. They do not symbolise the various aspects, of the life of the community.

Whatever the critics may point out, the theory has greatly influenced teaching in schools and has supplied suitable material for the beginners. Even Pt. Nehru was highly impressed by the value of biographies. He pertinently remarked. "I cannot remove from the gallery of my mind the pictures of persons and events which I hung there is my boyhood and youth. These pictures have coloured my outlook on history".

The value of the approach lies in the selection of right personalities. Not only the great men and women of our own country but great personalities from different parts of world should find a place in the syllabus. Along with the heroes, warriors, statesmen who have shaped the destiny of our nation, men of science, explores, inventors, fighters for freedom, leaders of peace, men of letters, artists and a host of others should be included in the history syllabus.

Psychological Theory (Spiral Theory)

This theory is mainly aimed at meeting the psychological needs and requirements of the children. The subject-matter of the history should be so selected and organised that the students may find satisfaction in fulfilment of their mental needs.

This theory, subject-matter of the history at the *elementary stage or the primary stage,* should be concrete. Abstract material shall be difficult for the students of this stage of education. They should be acquainted with the various elements of history through local history. Past experiences and the lives of great men may be presented before them in a systematic and orderly manner. It has rightly been remarked in this connection:

The earliest stage being presented in nature, history will he made as concrete, as possible: Then comes the *next stage.* The subject matter of history at this stage of education, should be so organised that it may lead to the development of the power of imagination. The students should also be trained to keep the historical facts in their mind. The following quotation presents this well:

> History of the representative type, will be, planned at the disposal of the child in the second stage, in accordance with his representative period which characterised by retention of facts and strong imagination.

Then we reach the third stage. At this stage, such events should be presented before the students that may make them to understand their meanings. In this regard the following quotation is worth mentioning:

> This theory of history which aims at giving deeper understanding of the movements that were taught at the

earlier stages in developing cause and effect, sequence of facts and which help pupils to draw inferences and verify conclusions, will be taught in the third stage of child's development.

For selecting the subject matter of history, the views of Prof. Ghat are very important. He has laid it down in the following works:

(i) Select one central idea or a group of associated ideas to build up the structure round it at junior stage.

(ii) Select facts which will bear interpretation and will fit in with a scheme of human development of progress.

(iii) Select facts which will provide continuity and unity in their treatment of history in chronological order.

(iv) Select facts which well, in one way or the other, explain the present day world.

PRINCIPLES OF SYLLABUS CONSTRUCTION

The following are the broad principles that should be observed while making a selection of historical facts.

(i) The syllabus should be based on the present needs, requirements and the circumstances of the child. The child needs experiences more than instructions, i.e., the syllabus should be child oriented.

(ii) The syllabus must meet the aims and objectives of teaching history.

(iii) The syllabus should be community centred. Since the child is to be educated thorough the society in which he is born so the good of individual and good of society cannot be separated.

(iv) The syllabus should be based on the principle of integration. It means that the activities carried on in a school, should not be treated in water-tight compartments, but should be so conducted as to lead the whole child to a functional unity with the environment.

(v) The syllabus be framed on the principle of flexibility.

(vi) While framing the syllabus forward-looking principle should be kept in mind.

(vii) It should present an over all, balanced plan for growth in human relationship.

(viii) It should be broad based.

CONTENTS OF THE HISTORY SYLLABUS

If we look at the history syllabus being following in different countries we find that these have been desired to meet the requirements of their own national outlook. In our own country we want to develop in our children a sense of appreciation of our cultural heritage and also to faster in them a world outlook. A balance has to be made between these two i.e., the claims of our own society and the claim of world community. The history syllabus in our schools should, therefore, be selected from the following fields:

(i) *Early History.* It includes the history of man in stone age.

(ii) *World History.* It is essential to understand the contributions of different people to the development of human society. It includes the story of ancient civilisation, the origin and growth of great religions, life, of middle ages. Renaissance and Reformation etc.

(iii) *National History.* It should form the core of our history syllabus. To that core, the history of other peoples and civilisations must be organically related.

(iv) *Local History.* It should form an important part of syllabus in history for the beginners.

(v) *Social, Economical and Cultural History.* Topics

selected for social economic and cultural history will supplement the pupil's study in political history.

SUBJECT-MATTER ORGANISATION IN HISTORY

Selection is subject-matter is not enough it has to be organised in some proper way. Without proper organisation the purpose will not be achieved. An effort be made to present the subject-matter, before the children, in such a way that they feel interested in the study of history. For this purpose the following plans and theories act as guides.

1. The Concrete System of Plan

In this system the child is first acquainted with those things that are already known to him. Such things that have a bearing on creative activities of the child. Afterwards the subject-matter be made more comprehensive and organised in accordance with the age and mental capacity of the child. This plan is based on the principle *of whole to part.* In it the teacher proceeds from *simple to complex.*

The main criticism against this theory is that it lays too much stress and repeated references to the events, creates impediments in the natural flow of interest of children.

2. Periodic Method

In this method we divide the history into various periods and then these are studied in chronological order. It has been remarked that *chronology is the essential skeleton of history* and so the whole skeleton is studied in various parts of these periods.

Johnson says, "History for schools had begun as a chronological survey, and when it become a continuous study from year to year of school course, it remained a chronological survey".

In this method the ground once covered is never repeated. The whole course is divided into several well-marked stages. In the pre-independence days. Indian history was divided into Hindu period. Muslim period, British period etc.

Its supports recommend this method on the following grounds:

1. It utilises the natural order of events and thereby enables the pupils to grasp the idea of 'time factor' in history. They can witness the long array of events on the canvass of succeeding generations and in the process, develop a chronological outlook.
2. Another advantage is that during the successive years of school instruction, students are introduced to new periods—periods efflorescent with new problems—and so their interest in the subject is sustained. Every time a fresh ground is covered and, therefore, there is no room for dullness and monotony to set in the process of instruction.
3. Moreover, the syllabus formed on chronological lines accords most naturally with the way in which history itself has developed.

Limitations

There are certain defects in this theory as well. They are being enumerated below :

(a) It is wrong to say that by this method, we become acquainted, with the various stages of the development of the mind.

(b) Events of the ancient history are so difficult and complicated that it is difficult for the students of tender age to follow them.

(c) If the teacher of history is not efficient, and does not prefer to repeat the various facts already taught by him, then the students will find it difficult to remember what they have learnt in the past.

(d) Those students, who leave the studies in between, do not have any idea about all events of history. Their knowledge of history remains incomplete.

Apart from the above the following points are also raised in this connection.

1. The critics of the chronological method point out that there is "no principle of selection except that of the order of occurrence of events. There are no themes around which facts, are grouped".
2. In such a treatment as Professor Jeffreys pertinently remarks, "it is difficult to give the pupil a sense of purpose or direction. He is not working for anything except for the end of the chapter".
3. It allows the development of human history and not the child's mind to determine the outline at least, what history is taught to pupils at particular age levels.
4. A syllabus based on the chronological order of presentation, remarks Burston, "would only meet pedagogical criteria if the remote periods were simple and elementary, and if history gradually became more difficult as it became more recent. Some might maintain that this was so, but most would argue that all periods have aspects which are too difficult for junior forms and so a chronological syllabus is only possible at the cost of study of some difficult aspects in the early periods".
5. It involves the learning of dates and ultimately forges into drudgery.

3. Topical Method

In this method the subject matter of history is divided into various topics. It facilitates class-room teaching. This method was introduced by comenius to overcome the difficulties inherent in chronological method.

While dividing the syllabus into topics we should keep in mind that the whole subject may not be taught in isolation. As remarked by an eminent scholar, "A topic, should not be an isolated incident or episode but should present a factor which influence the main current of history". According to Prof. Walsh, each topic contains several events, but they are logically and intelligently inter-related as being part of the same movement or policy.

Merits

(i) This method provides a solution for dealing with vast historical material.

(ii) It can be adopted according, to the age, ability and aptitude of the children. This flexibility is significant in case of projects such as about transport, trade, houses etc.

(iii) Study of history through this method imparts a sense of purpose to the pupils.

(iv) It enables the teacher to control the subject matter and adapt it to the varying needs of the children.

Demerits

(i) It lays more emphasis on social aspect of history at the cost of other aspects of human life.

(ii) In it emphasis is laid on past and present and the past is supposed to provide a background for the development of present institutions and ideas.

4. Regressive Method

In this method of teaching history we move from present

to the past. This is based on the theory that past should be studied as an explanation of the present. We give below an opinion about this method: "The teacher chooses certain vital, social or economical problems of today as a stoning point or introduction, goes back to the remote past which has laid this problem or the state of things, again comes back, to the period that immediately concerns him and follows the chronological order. Thus, the teacher regresses to come forward again. This plan is based on the mechanism go from the known to the unknown".

Merits

(i) Teaching by this method, we can establish in the mind of the students, an essential relationship between the past and the present.

(ii) It inculcates in students an interest in the history of the present

(iii) It helps in liberalising the attitude of the children and their activity is enlisted almost at every point.

Limitations

(i) It lays too much emphasis on the events and problems of present and their background in past and neglects the future.

(ii) It reverses the chronological order.

(iii) It is unpsychological.

(iv) It is burdensome for the students.

5. The 'Patch' Method

The method which has become quite popular in modern times was given by Miss Majorie Reeves. In this method the teacher does not make any attempt to make his pupils acquire in the school any detailed chronological outline of knowledge, nor does he ask them to go over the same course again and again in successive grades. He also does not proceed by topics. Instead he chooses short but significant epochs in man's history such as 'India in the Sixth century B.C.', 'the Gupta period, 'the Elizabethan age' and uses these as the basis of study. The idea is to allow the pupils to "soak themselves in the atmosphere of these periods, finding out of how people lived and earned their living, how they fed themselves, what they wore, what their amusements were, what they believed in, what sort of government they had, and so on.

Merits

1. The advocates of this system claim that the value of historical study in school lies precisely in the process of 'getting, under the skin' of a particular age and this system provides opportunity to delve deeply.
2. Another value claimed for the patch system is that its study gives "practice in that most salutary art, the art of entering in to an entirely different atmosphere and point of view of one's own", because the patch being studied, may have no obvious or continuous connection with any present day institutions of pre-conceptions.

Demerits

Despite the above advantages claimed, the opponents of the system point out that it does not provide a comprehensive system of grading historical material. It is bound to leave great gaps in their knowledge and give them a confused picture of chronology.

STAGE-WISE CONTENTS OF HISTORY

I. Primary Stage

At the primary stage the history be closely related to the abilities and characteristics of the age of children. The work should start with the realities which are near to the children in space and time. They be introduced to *local traditions,* the problems faced by their fore-fathers etc.

They should also be given a glimpse of the life of the earliest man. At this stage children should also be made aware of the contributions of great men in different fields of life. To achieve it the syllabus should have stories about heroes of war and prophets of peace, men of letters and pioneers of science, saints and sages, artists and patriots etc.

Children should also be given a glimpse into the social conditions and elements of daily social life of ancient times. It will remind them of the value of daily work of ordinary people and will make them aware of the change in the order of things with the progress of time.

II. Secondary Stage

The content of history at this stage of education, as suggested by C.P. Hill, should consist of *national history* with special emphasis on those topics which help to an understanding of present day problems or which enable the students to note the differences the similarities between life in earlier times and life today.

In addition to national history some topics about the history of the countries, geographically contiguous and culturally related should also be included in syllabus. C.P. Hill says, "National history should always be taught against international background.... Developments at home should be related to external events... the cultural relationships between different nations and areas should be made clear.... There should be frequent comparisons of social change...."

There are teachers who prefer one independent outline course in world history at this stage. A group of others may like to introduce topics or problems such as the development of government and history of religions, the story of tolerance, the ideas of liberty and law while a different kind of proposal comes from third group of teachers. They want in addition to learning their own national history pupils should study in some detail the history of nations and regions which are dissimilar to their own land. Thus as C.P. Hill suggests we can weave around the core of national history, the fabric of social history, religious history, man's struggle for toleration and peace international cooperation, etc.

III. History Syllabus as Recommended by Ministry of Education

The Ministry of Education, Government of India, has published the contents of history in Indian schools for grades one to eleven. A brief enumeration of these contents will not be out of place here.

Class I. The students should be introduced to the following facts at this stage:

1. *Local Traditions*—stories relating to local social workers saints religious places, historical places, local fairs, etc.
2. *Stories of the ancient man*—stories about food, utensils, tools, ways of living of the cave man and the people of stone age and the copper age.
3. *Practical work*— (a) visit to local places like museums, etc., and (b) making clay models of historical utensils, toys and tools.

Class II. At this stage local traditions and stories about ancient culture should be included in the syllabus. For example—a broad view of the local traditions, taught in class I; stories about Babylon, Mohenjo-Daro, Arkpolis, Pyramids, etc.; life of the pupils in Ashramas and its comparison with Chinese, Greek and Roman life.

Practical work. As in the first grade. Besides, preparation of models, coins of clay and album of historical pictures should be done at this age.

Class III. Stories for ancient India, for example, Rama, Krishna, Buddha, Mahavir, Alexander, Ashoka, Kanishka, Chandragupta, Vikramaditya etc. These stories are to be presented in achronological order.

Practical work—Pupils should be helped to understand distance and direction and initiated in map-drawing. They should be taught how to make an album of historical pictures, dramatise events and do craft work.

Class IV. Stories from medieval India, e.g., Prophet Muhammad, Muslim invasions on India, Prithviraj, All-ud din Khilji, Feroz Tuglaq. Chaitanya, Nanak, Kabir, Krishna Devrai, Akbar, Chandbibi, Maharana Pratap, Aurangzeb, Shivaji, Nadir Shah, Baji Rao I and Baji Rao II, etc.

Practical work. As in class III, children's albums should contain pictures of art and architecture of the Mughal period.

Class V. Stories from modern India; Clive, Mir Qasim, Tipu Sultan, Nana Fadnavis, Ranjit Singh, Jhansi ki Rani, Martyrs of First War of Independence, Raja Ram Mohan Roy, Syed Ahmed Khan, Vivekanand, Annie Besant, Pheroze Shah Mehta, Surendra Nath Banerjee, Motilal Nehru, Mahatma Gandhi, Subhash Chandra Bose, Jawahar Lal Nehru, Sardar Patel, etc.

Practical work. As in above grades.

Class VI. Evolution of Indian society from ancient period to the Sultanate with emphasis on economic, social, religious and political aspects. The following topics may be included.

1. Sources of Indian History;
2. Indus Valley Civilisation;
3. Aryan Civilisation;

4. Epic Age;
5. Jainism & Buddhism;
6. Alexander's invasion, the Nandas, the Mauryas.
7. Maurya-Sythian Civilisation;
8. Kushan empire;
9. Gupta empire—Gupta periods-why a golden age?
10. Invasion of the Huns;
11. History of South India;
12. Colonial and cultural expansion;
13. Rise of Islam;
14. The Slave dynasty;
15. The Khalji dynasty:
16. The Tughlaq dynasty;
17. Bahmani and Vijaynagar Kingdoms;
18. The Syed dynasty;
19. The Lodi dynasty; and
20. Culture of the Sultanate period and its impact on Indian life.

Practical work. Drawing of time-lines, historical maps, charts, sketches; dramatisation; tour of historical places and visit to museums. Preparation of clay models.

Class VII. Development of Indian Society from the Mughal period to the Company rule.

Topics:

1. Invasions of Babur and establishment of Mughal empire;
2. Humayun and Sher Shah;
3. Akbar;
4. Jehangir and Shah Jehan;
5. Shah Jehan's reign—way a golden age?
6. Aurangzed and his policy;

7. Rise of the Marathas;
8. Coming of the Europeans;
9. Expansion of British power;
10. Rise of the Sikhs;
11. The East India Company-power struggle;
12. First War of Independence;
13. Cultural history of the Mughal period; and
14. State of culture, educational, religious and social reforms during the East India Company's rule.

Practical work. As in Class VI.

Class VIII. Modern India. The following topics, should be included.

1. Constitutional history;
2. Development of Indian Administration;
3. History of freedom struggle;
4. History of education;
5. History of Local-self Government;
6. Economic history;
7. New India—(history of Post-Independence era.); and
8. Indian Constitution.

Practical Work— As in the above grades.

Classes IX, X, XI

1. Critical study of Indian history;
2. World history, and
3. Important movements in the west;

    (a) Renaissance and Reformation;
    (b) French Revolution;
    (c) Nationalism in Europe;

(d) Industrial Revolution;
(e) Rise of Socialism;
(f) International organisation—the League of Nations and the U.N.O.
(g) Development of Science.

4. History of Eastern and South Eastern countries;
   (a) China;
   (b) Afghanistan;
   (c) Japan;
   (d) Indonesia;
   (e) Burma and Tibet.

5. Present problems in India;
   (a) History of the progress of science in India;
   (b) History of Indian agriculture and its problems;
   (c) Industrial Problems;
   (d) Language Problem;
   (e) Social Problems;
   (f) Economic Problems;
   (g) Problems of Education.

Practical Work.

(a) Drawing of maps;
(b) Use of sources;
(c) Use of newspapers;
(d) Use of historical journals, magazines and papers;
(e) Tour of historical places;
(f) Collection of coins and historical albums;
(g) Drawing of time charts, sketches, and pictorial graphs, etc.

SUBJECT MATTER PRESENTATION

Having selected the subject matter and have arranged it in proper order the next question that arises is of persecuting it before students. Teacher can use any one or methods of presentation in accordance with the age of students and their class. The following fundamentals should, however, be always kept in mind while presenting the subject-matter before the students.

1. In the classroom, the teacher should try to present fact in a simple, intelligible and effective manner. Preciseness always pays.
2. There is very little scope for discussion and presentation of the differences of opinion in the lower classes. It may be useful in higher classes.
3. The teacher should invariably proceed from 'simple to complex and concrete to abstract'. He should try to localise the subject-matter with the help of maps and charts etc.
4. The time sense of the students should be developed by and by. In the beginning, the students should be acquainted with the events of the present and then an attempt should be made to take them back to the past.
5. The law of cause and effect must be utilised in teaching at every stage of education.
6. An attempt should be made to correlate the present experiences with the past.
7. While teaching history, effect should be made to throw light on the various aspects of the history. Unnecessary and irrelevant materials should be discarded.
8. Dramatisation and other activity methods make history interesting and real.
9. The facts should be treated fully at the time of presentation.

I. At Primary Stage of Education

This stage of education runs up to fifth class where children between the age group of 6-11 years come for study. This is the stage when children are very fond of listening to stories. These stories may deal with any part of the world or any part of the life.

The teacher of history should try to present the subject-matter in the form of stories. These stories should encourage the activities of the children. The stories should also be told in an interesting manner. In order to be a successful story-teller, the teacher should have perfect command over the subject-matter. He should also be well aware of the psychology of the students.

The stories should be so arranged that they may continue to awaken the curiosity of the students, to know things by saying and doing, and also get on with the historical materials. It is also recommended that teacher, at this stage of education, should use to the maximum possible extent various teaching aids such as pictures, charts, models, maps etc. He should also put special attention to the use of black-board, text-books etc.

II. At the Junior Stage of Education

The teaching of history at this stage of education should be organised on the psychological principles as enumerated below:

1. Stress can be laid on the element of characterisation in the subject-matter.
2. The facts should be properly explained before the students. An attempt may be made to assess their value in the light of the problems of the present-day.
3. Time sense should be developed further.

At Junior stage the teacher should try to present facts

and events of history in a systematic and chronological order but is an interesting way: He should keep in mind the maxim of "proceeding from concrete to abstract." An attempt should also be made by the teacher to correlate the events of history with problems of society as they exist-to-day. At the stage of elation the text-books be used to a larger extent and the black-board shall be used quite often. An outline of the subject matter may be put up on the black-board and the students be asked to develop these outlines at home. The students should also be given home-task and asked to do written work. In addition to the use of maps and charts, the students may be asked to dramatise and enact the various scenes of history. Teacher can ask the students to draw maps and may be asked to fill in the places of historical importance in maps, these things may also be given as home-task.

III. At the Secondary Stage of Education

At Secondary stage of education the teaching should be so organised that it may meet the requirements of adolescence. At this stage of education the teacher should try to present certain problems and encourage the students to solve them. The text-books and black-board be used freely at this stage. Sketches may be drawn on the black-board and the subject-matter may be explained with the help of these sketches class-room discussion can be arrived to discuss certain topics and places of historical importance. Students be encouraged to do written work and for this they may be green home-work. The teacher should check, the home-work and give her suggestions to improve their working. He should ask the students to organise voluntary bodies so as to encourage the teaching of history.

REVIEW QUESTIONS

1. What is the importance of various methods of grading history?

2. What are the merits and limitations of chronological method of organising facts?
3. Write short notes on :
   (a) Patch system.
   (b) Topical method.

REFERENCES

1. Burston W.H. (1963), *Principles* of *History Teacing* Macmillan and Co. Ltd., pp. 110-111.
2. Burston and Green (1962), *Handbook for History Teachers.* Methuen & Co., p. 8.
3. IAAM (1952). *The Teaching of History.* C.U.B., p. 20.
4. Jeffevs, M.V.C. (1939), *History in Schools.* Landon, Pitman, p. 32.
5. Johnson, H. (1940), *Teaching of History* New York, The Macmillan Company.
6. *Teaching History.* Pamphlet No 23 HMSO. p. 18.
7. Vajreshwari, R., A *Handbook for History Teachers,* Allied Publishers p. 161.

9

Teaching History for Citizenship in the Elementary School

> Men often oppose a thing merely because they have had no agency in planning it, or because it may have been planned by those whom they dislike.
>
> —*Alexander Hamilton, The Federalist*

A substantial amount of research and curriculum development completed over the past two decades can be used to improve the teaching of history to young children. This ERIC Digest discusses (1) insights from recent research, (2) insights from recent curriculum development, and (3) connections of research to curriculum development. A list of Web sites which may be used to enhance elementary teachers' history-for-citizenship lessons is provided.

Insights from Recent Research

Recent studies on the teaching of history to young children have investigated the development of children's conceptions of historical time (e.g., Barton and Levstik, 1996; Hoge, 1991), children's ability to construct historical narratives (Barton, 1997; Levstik and Pappas, 1987), and their explanations of historical change over time and their ability to interpret, sequence, and date historical events and images (Barton and Levstik, 1996; Foster, Hoge and Rosch, 1999). The following are generalizations selected from the conclusions of this body of research.

Brophy and VanSledright (1997, 23) found that even the youngest elementary students have a sense of history and often bring prior conceptions of the past into the classroom. They note that young students typically have trouble retaining historical information that has not been situated within a context and linked to a prior understanding. They conclude that a barren, textbook-centered approach that treats history as a thin narrative of events that simply happened may prevent students from "developing the critical, interpretive, and synthetic thinking abilities required for cultivating historical understanding."

Barton's research (1997, 13-16) also revealed that young students, even kindergartners, possess some accurate historical knowledge; for example, that covered wagons came before cars. Older elementary students demonstrate similar understandings — often gained without formal history instruction — about clothing, technology, and architecture. Barton determined, however, that pre-fifth grade students "have a very limited understanding of the nature and purpose of the government, politics, and economic institutions." He also found that even when students in the intermediate grades do study these topics, "They tend to interpret them solely in terms of the actions and desires of individuals, and to misunderstand or ignore the role of government and economics." Barton notes that elementary-grade-level students typically know very little about the methods used by historians in the creation of their narratives and, perhaps as a result, uncritically accept printed historical accounts as the truth.

Many of the aforementioned themes are echoed in Wilson's (2001, 530) review of research on history instruction which concludes, among other things, that students generally find traditional history teaching dry and largely senseless, resulting in "little intellectual engagement, a dominance of teachers and textbooks, and minimal problem solving or critical thinking." Wilson also noted that even teachers who know more about history and historical methods often abandon their more sophisticated understandings and the goal of creating greater student engagement under the pressures of coverage, high-stakes testing, scheduling, and parents' expectations.

Wineburg's comprehensive review of research on history instruction (1996) led him to conclude (a) that despite a lack of school-based instruction, students are hardly blank slates when it comes to historical knowledge, (b) that the historical and conceptual background knowledge of fifth graders is typically quite sketchy, (c) that adolescents can develop a sophisticated form of historical understanding, (d) that there has been little appreciable change in the level of students' historical knowledge over the past 80 years, (e) that historical knowledge develops slowly and comes from sources other than just school, and (f) that discrete and unrelated bits of historical knowledge often get incorrectly conflated. Wineburg's later research (2001) showed that historical thinking was not a natural process and that it would not arise automatically from normal cognitive development.

Insights from Recent Curriculum Development

Over the past two decades, educators identified national curriculum standards for all subject areas and the development of history instruction standards took center stage in the effort to strengthen K-12 social studies instruction. The Center for History in the Schools' (1996) standards begin with a statement on the importance of teaching history for the development of citizenship, a theme that dominates all of their widely circulated and often emulated curriculum documents. In addition, the National Standards for Civics and Government (1994) refer to history as a means of educating America's youth for their future demanding roles as citizens of a modern democracy. Key scholars such as R. Freeman Butts and Paul Gagnon also have stressed the importance of powerfully taught history as an essential subject in the schools of any nation that wishes to be called and to remain a democracy.

Connecting Research and Curriculum Development

A common theme running through these organizations' and experts' authoritative endorsements is that teachers need to do more than simply transmit factual knowledge about the past. Powerful history instruction involves helping students (a) acquire a meaningful understanding of key historical themes and important people and events from local, state, and national history, (b) build experience-based knowledge of the methods and limitations of history, and (c) confront multiple perspectives — including mainstream interpretations — of the past. These may be thought of as the fundamentals of good history instruction. Furthermore, while employing the fundamentals of good history instruction, teachers must offer students substantial and recurring opportunities to think analytically about a variety of democratic values, principles, issues, and tensions, using historical referents as a basis for such lessons. This type of history learning requires more than mere exposure and memorization, it demands active manipulation of the concepts through learning mechanisms such as dramatization activities (e.g., role playing an interview with a famous American, acting in skits or plays that recreate famous events); advocacy activities (e.g., making posters that use historical precedents as support for positions on contemporary issues, writing letters about community needs to public officials); community service projects (e.g., helping to restore the condition of a local monument, using oral history techniques to create a school history) and issues-oriented discussions (e.g., were the courts right in declaring separate public schools for black and white children to be illegal?).

Internet Resources for History Teachers

The following Web sites provide an array of easy-to-use history teaching materials:

The Web site of the National Initiative on American History, Civics, and Service provides access to many original documents: <http://www.ourdocuments.gov/>

The History Net provides articles on history from leading writers and historians: <http://www.thehistorynet.com/>

The National Council for History Education's "History Links" page links to a variety of history-related Web sites: <http://www.history.org/nche/>

The official National Endowment for the Humanities (NEH) Web site offers history/social science lesson plans and resources available through its subject catalogue and extensive list of links: <http://edsitement.neh.gov/>

[*Courtesy: John D. Hoge*]

10

Techniques of History Teaching

> The perfect teacher has the education of a college president, executive ability of a financier, humility of a deacon, discipline of a demon, adaptability of a chameleon, hope of an optimist, courage of a hero, wisdom of a serpent gentleness of a dove, patience of job, and persistence of the devil.

Basically, Techniques of teaching should serve the ends and objectives of the society. India is a democratic country and in this country the teaching of history be conducted on democratic lines. Prof. M.P. Muffut is of the opinion, "All techniques should be in line with democratic process and relate to the goods desired in the study of a topic. Techniques are employed for getting the learning underway with guidance from the teacher. They should be selected as a means of serving the best purpose of a particular time with the result of growth for the individual."

DIFFERENT TECHNIQUES OF TEACHING

The following are some of the techniques used by teachers of history:

I. Narration Technique

In this technique, the teacher narrates the topic and the students try to acquire knowledge through the narration. This narration is made with an eye on the interest, objectives and attitudes of the pupils. Teacher makes an all out effort to present the subject-matter in a simple, interesting and intelligible way. Many a times this technique is adopted to supplement the question-answer technique.

The teacher must keep the following points in mind while, using this technique.

(a) The narration should be in accordance with mental and physical age of the children.
(b) The narration should not be too lengthy.
(c) While using this technique the teacher should supplement it with question answer technique.
(d) An effort be made to make proper use of various teaching aids.

II. Drill Technique

It is the most widely used technique of teaching. It was originally introduced by *Thorndike*. It has become very popular among teachers because it can be used quite easily. This technique is based on the assumption that if a particular learning is revised several times, it becomes stable and permanent. Drill is not a mere repetition of an act for the purpose of attaining perfection, but it is a serious work activity for obtaining perfection, formation of habit or fixing of specific facts for easy and effortless recall, *"Drill"* is sometimes used as a synonym for *"Practice."*

The Drill technique can be used only in some specific aspects in teaching of history. It is quite useful in learning the dates and names of events.

How to Make Drill Effective

To get best results the teacher should put in a lot of thinking while preparing the task. He should select and phrase questions which are brief and concise, on the unit or topic that has been studied. The teacher may try competitive exercise instead of asking questions in a straight forward manner. The contest is very appealing to the students but the real contest will depend upon teacher's planning.

Values of Effective Drill-work

(i) It aids in achieving complete mastery of the subject-matter.

(ii) It helps in isolating the most important points from those of lesser importance.

(iii) It helps in ascertaining the effectiveness of class-room work.

(iv) It helps pupils to prepare themselves for testing and evaluation.

(v) It increase employment by class-room work.

III. Examination Technique

In this technique, the teacher examines his students about the knowledge of the topics learnt by them. By this technique teacher can ascertain how far the students have assimilated the subject taught to them.

This method helps the teacher ascertain how far he has been able to teach the lesson successfully.

While applying this technique the teacher should keep the following points in mind:

(i) Only objective type tests be given and the questions asked should be short and to the point.

(ii) Teacher should remove the difficulties of the students.

(iii) Question be set in such a way that whole of the field of learning is covered.

(iv) While evaluating the test, teacher should remain impartial.

IV. Question-answer Technique

As in other subjects, it is very important technique in the teaching of history. Through the use of this technique teacher makes an attempt to ascertain and evaluate the knowledge of his students about the subject. This technique is used to incite and awaken the curiosity in the students, and then using this curiosity and attempt is made to improve their knowledge.

In history this technique is useful for preparing unit plans, study guides and work sheets etc. For success of this technique it is essential that teacher knows the technique of formulating questions which stimulate and rouse the pupil's desire to learn.

Characteristics of Good Questions

(i) They should be such as can be easily and clearly understood.

(ii) They should be put in the simplest possible language.

(iii) Question should require specific answers and not general ones.

(iv) A good question should stimulate thinking on the part of all pupils, even though it may be addressed to only one of them.

(v) A good question is one that is definite and concise.

(iv) The question asked should be suited, in language and in the desired response, to the ability and maturity of the pupils.

While making use of this technique the teacher should bear the following points in mind:

(i) The questions be asked in a pleasant manner.

(ii) The question be stated first and then the students be called upon to answer it.

(iii) Questions should be distributed all over the class in such a way that the majority of students in the class take part in discussion.

(iv) Questions should not be asked very rapidly without giving sufficient time to pupils for thought.

(v) The needless repetition of questions should be avoided.

(vi) In handling the pupil's answers, the teachers must make every effort to be fair so that the pupils may feel free to respond and are encouraged rather than discouraged by the teacher's comments.

This technique is helpful in developing the power of expression of the students. This is also helpful in ascertaining their personal difficulties. On the basis of knowledge acquired an attempt may be made to remove the difficulties of the students.

V. Illustration Technique

While using this technique some illustrations are shown to the students so as to make the subject matter interesting and intelligible. The illustrations depicted should be scientific and should have a direct bearing on the content material. Various types of illustrations are in use e.g. maps, sketches, models, charts, graphs etc.

VI. Drama Technique

In this technique an attempt is made by the teacher to present different historical events in the form of a drama. He asks the students to enact scenes of history by dialogues and by wearing the dresses.

The use of this technique helps to keep active. Various sense organs of the students. It develops a creative element in the students and also helps in establishing a co-ordination between the head and the hand. It also removes the shyness of the students and so the technique is quite useful for the healthy growth of the personality of the child.

VII. Assignment

Literally Assignment means "giving out of a task or job by a person in authority". However, as a technique of teaching assignment is a planning and organising period. In this period the teacher outlines tentatively the activities of the pupils in preparation for the study.

The modern approach to assignment stresses directed learning and co-operative planning. Each individual pupil or a group of pupil is given a task, related to the topic under study and the students are expected to complete it with the help of work-books, text-books etc. For achieving progressive improvement proper guidance and direction are essential. All out efforts be made by the teacher to arouse pupil's interest in the assignments.

Salient Features

(i) It should be stated in clear and simple terms.

(ii) It should help to remove difficulties and main misunderstandings.

(iii) It should be stimulating and interesting.

(iv) It should recognise individual differences.

(v) It should be co-operative and must emphasise the "we" spirit.

(vi) It should be such as to develop insight and understanding amongst the students.

Importance

Assignments provides proper guidance and direction to the activities of the pupils. It arouses their interest, provides motivation, prevents failures and prepares a sure ground for independent study. It is also helpful to the teacher as it helps him to improve his technique of teaching.

Evaluation

To evaluate an assignment is a must to find if the students have shown any progress in their study periods and have shown more interest in the subject of history. No doubt, it is not possible to measure the definite effectiveness of an assignment but it can be made to certain extent making use of good check lists. Evaluation hare is concerned not only with academic achievements of students but is also concerned with their development in terms of desirable behaviour changes in relation to their feelings, thinking and actions. It is in this broader conception of evaluation that we should measure the effectiveness of the assignments technique.

VIII. Review

It is used to master those facts and skills which are considered very essential both in school and life. It consists of a recall of facts for the purpose of renewing those facts with a view to attain a mastery over them.

Review is different from drill in that it is a new view of previously learned facts and skills and not a mere repetition of them. It is a reorganisation of material from a different point of view. The review is a more broader and more inclusive term than drill.

Importance

(i) All the modern procedures of teaching make good use of this technique, e.g., it is used in Dalton laboratory plan. The problem, the project and the unit methods of teaching.

(ii) It stimulates pupils interest in activity.

(iii) It helps in understanding the cause and effect relationships.

IX. Supervised Study

It is an important technique for teaching of history. This implies Supervision of the teacher or a group of class of pupils, as they work at their desks or around their tables". While supervising his students the teacher is available to his students whenever they find any difficulty. He is always ready to help and assist them when asked to do so. "Supervised study is the effective direction and over-sight of the silent study and laboratory activities of the pupils."

Pupil's silent study may consist of reading, interpreting or writing activities and laboratory work. It may involve the collection or selection of reference material, preparation of illustrative aids, debates, discussions etc. It is thus clear that "supervised study is an activity period in which both teacher and the pupils work together to accomplish desirable goals." A supervised study can make the teacher to note various deficiencies of his pupils and he can then plan to make them up. Now educationists are of the firm opinion that school is the only place where a pupil can do much more work in a better way and lesser time. However, the work to be done under the supervision of a teacher must be interesting and enjoyable for the pupil.

Plans of Supervised Study

The following plans are formed to be more helpful.

(i) *The Conference Plan:* Under this plan the teacher remains in the class-room for another extra period and provides individual help to such students who lag behind in their studies. It is quite helpful for weak students to make up their deficiencies.

(ii) *The Special Teacher Plan:* The special teacher appointed to help students must be very kind hearted, sympathetic and should possess a wide knowledge of many subjects. He must also have a sound knowledge of child psychology.

(iii) *The Study Hall Plan:* A room set apart for supervised study is referred to as *Study Hall.* The students work in Study Hall and may get help from other pupils or from the teacher In case of difficulties. However, perfect discipline has to be maintained in the Study Hall.

For the purpose of class recitation, the following types of plans are used.

(i) *The Divided-Period Plan.* In this plan the class-period time is divided between the usual class recitation and the supervised study. For this division the teacher provides the necessary direction and guidance. With such an arrangement students get ample opportunities for independent study under the direct supervision of the class-teacher.

(ii) *The Double-Period Plan.* It is quite similar to divided-period plan except that two complete periods are set apart for his purpose instead of one.

(iii) *The Fixed Study-Period Plan.* A number of head-masters recommend a fixed period for supervised study. It may be extra period added to school time-table or one hour a week, for supervised study in each subject.

Advantages

(i) The teacher can detect the slow workers and can guide them into effective learning experiences, which are meaningful to them.

(ii) It meets individual differences.

(iii) It promotes better pupil-teacher relationship.

(iv) It develops the senses of belongingness and achievement.

(v) It helps in developing certain important skills, e.g., age of maps, charts, atlases etc.

(vi) By this plan a more efficient use of sources and materials becomes possible.

Limitations

(i) It does not help bright students.

(ii) It destroys self-reliance on the part of the pupils.

Supervised study plan will, however, depend upon circumstances. But whenever it is possible, the history teacher must utilise this important technique of directing his pupil's learning.

REVIEW QUESTIONS

1. Why should assignment grow out of the activities and interests of pupils?
2. Enumerate the characteristics of good questions.
3. How can the reading programme in history be unproved through Supervised Study?
4. Name the different techniques which a history teacher should employ with different age groups, during the course of teaching.
5. Discuss the various plans of Supervised Study.
6. Why should we emphasise the need for effective assignment technique?
7. What are the chief outcomes of questioning?
8. What is Supervised Study technique? What purpose does it serve in History?
9. How does the review differ from drill?
10. How should a teacher deal with pupil's questions?
11. Mention the various review activities for a history class.
12. Discuss the limitations of Supervised Study Technique.
13. What are the essential characteristics of a good assignment?
14. How can we make use of questioning technique in history in an effective manner?
15. What are the purposes involved in the use of notebooks by history teachers?

11

Lesson Planning & Time Sense in History

> Pure hero-worship is health. It stimulates the young to deeds of heroism, stirs the old to unselfish efforts, and gives the masses models of mankind that tend to life humanity above the common-place meanness of ordinary life.
>
> —*Don Piatt,*
> *Memories of Men Who Saved the Union*

I

Lesson planning is the most important task in emphatic teaching of any subject. Thus, a proper planning of lessons is the key to effective teaching. The teacher must know in advance the subject-matter and mode of its delivery in the class-room. This planning will give the teacher idea of how to introduce the topic, how to develop the key concepts, how to correlate the concepts to real life situations and how to conclude the lesson.

L.B. Stands conceives a lesson plan as "Plan of action" implemented by the teacher in the class-room.

As stated by Bossing, "Lesson plan is the title given to the statement of the achievements to be realised and the specific means by which these are to be attained as a result of the activities engaged in, during the period".

G.H. Green is of the opinion says," the teacher who

has planned his lesson wisely related to his topic and to his class will be in a position to enter the class-room without any anxiety, ready to embark with confidence upon a job he understands and prepared to carry it to a workmanable conclusion. He has far seen the difficulties that are likely to arise, and prepared himself to deal with them. He knows the aims, his lesson is intended to fulfil, and he has marshelled his own resources for the purpose, and because he is free of anxiety, he will be able cooly to estimate the value of his work as the lesson proceeds, equally aware of failure and success and prepared to learn from both.

Though a syllabus is prescribed for each class yet the teacher is at liberty to draw up his own teaching syllabus. It is best to organise the teaching syllabus around a few broad areas of experience of pupils. For this purpose the syllabus is divided into a number of units.

UNIT PLANNING

A *unit* is a related learning segment made up of a few lessons along with an outline of its execution in the class-room. Thus a unit will consist of both the subject matter and methodology of its delivery to students.

Hoover defines unit as," the teaching unit is a group of related concepts from which a given set of instructional and educational experiences is desired. Unit normally range for these to six weeks long". In view of Preston, a unit is a large chunk or a block of related subject-matter as can be overviewed by the learner.

After having divided the syllabus into a number of teaching units the teacher will decide the time that could be allocated to each unit. After that he could break up each unit into a number of lessons and each lesson should be complete in itself. After that the teacher will enter in his diary the scheme of work under the headings.

Advantages of Unit Planning

(i) It provides a basic course structure around which specific class activities" can be organised.

(ii) It enables the teacher to break away from traditional text-book teaching.

(iii) It provides an opportunity to the teacher to keep a balance between various dimensions of the prescribed course.

(iv) It enables the teacher to integrate the basic, course concepts and those of related areas into various teaching experiences.

LESSON PLANNING

Like planning of other activities, planning of lesson is also needed. Without proper planning of the lesson, it is not possible for the teacher to cany out the teaching successfully. It has been rightly remarked: "Without planning the teacher is just like a ship moving in the sea without any aim and destination."

Main Advantages

Some of the advantages of lesson planning are as under:

(i) Lesson planning makes the work regular, organised and more systematic.

(ii) It induces confidence in the teacher.

(iii) It makes teacher quite conscious of the aim which makes him conscious of attitudes he wants to develop in his students.

(iv) It saves a lot of time.

(v) It helps in making correlation between the concepts with the pupils environment.

(vi) It stimulates the teacher to ask striking questions.

(vii) It provides more freedom in teaching.

(viii) It makes possible for the teacher to move in a scientific manner.

Characteristics of a Lesson Plan

Some important features of a lesson-plan are as under:

1. Objectives

All the cognitive objective that are intended to be fulfilled should be listed in the lesson-plan. Objectives should be formulated in terms of changes desired in behaviour of students. Objectives, as we know, have two specifications; the content specification and the competence specification. We have to mention clearly what type of changes we are going to bring in different domains cognitive, affective and psychomotor of students behaviour within a particular type of content.

The objective should be written in specific behavioural terms stating exactly what the learner will be doing, or saying when he demonstrates that he has achieved the aims of an instructional sequence. Walbesser while constructing behavioural objectives, listed four requirements for the construction of objectives:

1. Words denoting the stimulus situation which initiates the performance should appear in the description of the objective.
2. An action verb which denotes observable behaviour must be contained in the description.
3. A word denoting the object acted upon, must be contained in the description.
4. A phrase which indicates the characteristics of the performance that determines its correctness or acceptability must be included in the description of the objectives.

In selecting the objectives for a particular lesson in

history, the teacher, first of all, should see that they are worthwhile learning out-comes, pertinent to the course. Secondly, the teacher should be clear and definite in his mind about the desired learning outcomes. Lastly, the objective should be feasible. In other words, it should be attained by the procedure followed and within the time allotted for it.

2. Content

The subject-matter that is intended to be covered should be limited to the prescribed time. The matter must be interesting and it should be related to pupils previous knowledges. It should be related to daily life situations.

3. Methods

The most appropriate method be chosen by the teacher. The method chosen should be suitable to the subject-matter to be taught. Suitable teaching aids must also be identified by the teacher. Teacher may also use supplementary aids to make his lesson more effective.

4. Evaluation

Teacher must evaluate his lesson to find the extent to which he has achieved the aim of his lesson. Evaluation can be done even by recapitulation of subject-matter through suitable questions.

In writing a lesson plan the following points be written down:

(i) Date,
(ii) Period,
(iii) Class,
(iv) Duration,
(v) Subject,
(vi) Topic,
(vii) General objectives,

(viii) Specific objectives,
(ix) Previous knowledge of the students,
(x) Teaching aids and materials to be used,
(xi) Introduction,
(xii) Statement of object
(xiii) Presentation,
(xiv) Generalisations,
(xv) Recapitulations,
(xvi) Black-board summary,
(xvii) Hand-work.

Steps in Lesson Planning

Formal Steps in lesson planning are discribed as follows:

(i) Introduction: It pertains to preparing and motivating children to the lesson content by linking it to the previous knowledge of the students, by arousing curiosity of the children and by making an appeal to their senses. This prepares the child's mind to receive new knowledge. This steps though so important must be brief. It may involve testing of pervious knowledge of the child. Sometimes the curiosity of the pupil can be aroused by some chart, model, story or even by some useful discussion. It serves as the bridge between what the students know and what they are going to learn.

(ii) Statement of Aim: After the introduction which is necessarily based on students previous knowledge, the teacher states the aim of the lesson he is going to teach. It should be stated in clear and precise terms so that it brings home to the pupils the importance of the lesson.

(iii) Presentation: It involves the stating of the object of lesson and exposure of students to new information. The actual lesson begins and both teacher and students participate. Teacher should make use of different teaching

aids to make his lesson effective. Teacher should draw as much as is possible from students making use of judicious questions. In selecting the method the teacher should keep in mind the age and competence of the pupils. Story-telling method may be used in primary and upper primary classes, source method in secondary and higher secondary classes.

(iv) Association: It is always desirable that new ideas or knowledge be associated to the daily life situations by citing suitable examples and by drawing comparison with the related concepts. This steps is all the more important when we are establishing principle or generalising definitions.

(v) Generalisation: In this step teacher makes an effort so that the students draw the conclusion themselves.

(vi) Application and Recapitulation: Recapitulation means asking the pupils to reproduce what they have learnt. As we have already stated, recapitulation at the end of the lesson, also serves the purpose of application. Recapitulation is looking back and surveying briefly the path that has been just covered or travelled. It is connecting up all the essential parts of the lesson, in an orderly and systematic way in a few minutes. Recapitulation will not be possible unless and until the pupils have thoroughly understood the lesson in all its essential parts and details. Thus, recapitulation is a very valuable mental exercise which makes studies more efficient and gives increased mastery of the subject-matter.

It is to be noted that the above steps are only guidelines and in many lessons it is not possible to follow all these steps.

There is another way of lesson planning that is gaining currency these days. It is known as *Glover Plan.* This plan has four steps as follows:

(i) Questioning. Teacher must introduce and develop his lesson through related and sequential questions. Start the lesson by asking questions about previous knowledge of the students. The questions should then lead to new knowledge under consideration.

Lesson can also be introduced with the help of some teaching aid like picture, chart, or model etc. The introduction can also be made by describing a situations or by telling a short story.

However, teacher should bear in mind that introduction in brief and interesting.

(ii) Discussion. For discussion the class be divided into smaller groups and in such groups students be encouraged to express their ideas and opinions freely this helps the students in removal of their difficulties.

(iii) Investigation. The students are encouraged to do a project or investigation on the lesson topic either individually or in small groups by processing information.

(iv) Expression. It concerns the strategy in which the students and teachers communication of ideas through observation and listening (passive expression) or through doing (active expression) or by arranging learning situations (organisational expression).

In developing a lesson a teacher must keep in mind the following psychological principles:

(i) Principle of Section and Division. The teacher should wisely select and divide the learning material into smaller segments. It is also for the teacher to decide about the questions of subject-matter to be covered by him and that which has to be illicited from the students.

(ii) Principle of Successive Clarity. It is for the teacher to see that the different learning segments of lesson are

well structured, sequenced and connected. Teacher must ensure, at each segment, that students leave grasped the subject-matter given to them.

(iii) Principle of Integration. Teacher should conclude his lesson only after combining various learning segments to produce some generalisations.

Writing a Lesson Plan

The style given below is adopted for writing a lesson plan

Class: Date:

Subject: Duration:

Topic:

Instructional Material: ....

General objectives: ....

Specific objectives: ....

Previous knowledge: ....

Questions:

1. .... ?

2. .... ?

3. .... ?

Introduction: ....

Questions:

1. .... ?

2. .... ?

Announcement of Aim: ....

Presentation:

Matter	Method	B.B. Summary

Conclusions: . . . .

Applications: . . . .

Recapitulations: . . . .

1. ....?

2. ....?

Home Task: . . . .

SOME MODEL LESSON PLANS

Lesson Plan-1

Class: VI — Time: 40 minutes
Date: Nov. 6, 1994 — Period: IV

Subject: Indian History

Topic: Life of Maharana Pratap

General Aims

(i) To inculcate in pupils a sense of patriotism by acquainting them with the great deeds and lives of great men of their country.

(ii) To develop in the students the qualities of chivalry and bravery and to encourage them to become great.

(iii) To develop in students the curiosity to know more and more about history.

(iv) To develop in students the right attitudes of fellow feeling, friendliness, co-operation, toleration and international understanding.

Specific Aims

(i) To make students familiar with the life and administration of Rana Pratap.

(ii) To develop in the students, the spirit of patriotism and love for motherland in the students.

Teaching Aids

(i) A full size picture of Rana Pratap

(ii) A map of India (political) showing the boundaries of the territory under the rule of Rana Pratap.

Previous Knowledge

Students are already familiar with the names of Lord Rama, Lord Krishna, Ashoka the great etc.

Introduction

The lesson will be introduced by asking the following questions:

(i) Name a few historical personalities born in India.

Ans. Rama, Krishna. Ashoka etc.

(ii) Name the Rajput personality who struggled hard for keeping India free from Mughal domination.

Not getting a proper reply, the teacher will announce the name of Shivaji and will also announce the topic for the day.

Recapitulation

The teacher will ask the following questions:

1. When was Shivaji born?
2. What was Shivaji's father.
3. What was the main aim, of Marahattas at that time?

Home Work

Write down an outline of the life of Shivaji.

II

TEACHING OF TIME SENSE IN HISTORY

A history teacher finds the task of cultivation of time and space sense and imagination development amongst his pupils as the most complicated and a difficult problem. Time and space being two most abstract concepts in history. All the events of history have occurred at a definite place and a definite time so history devoid of the sense of time and place is nothing but a story, similarly, development of historical imagination is also an equally important task. A history teacher should therefore try to develop among the pupils the capacity to see every historical event in its time perspective.

Time sense refers to the capacity through which we are able to establish a lively relationship between the various events. In fact, time is focal point or some definite point. It helps in understanding the flow of various events of society in the order they come to pass.

Elements of Time Sense

Location, distance and duration are the three elements which constitute time relations.

(a) The Location of Time: Most of the historical facts are localised and not indefinite. Location of an event refers to its placing on the long line of time so that it may enable as to measure its distance from us. By location we mean determining the events with the help of dates and periods. For having a time sense we have following agencies: (i) Time chart, (ii) Time line, and (iii) Time graph.

(b) Time Chart: It consists of a list of pictures pasted on it (paper or chart) indicating the description of a particular dynasty. Following lines clarify this point:

"The main use of time chart is to provide a chronological framework within which events and developments may be recorded and to guard against the vagueness of time sense which may result from teaching arranged, often necessarily by 'topics' rather than by 'reigns'.

Panorama charts depicts one event of one century e.g.

To depicts 19th century we may depicts First War for independence, of 1857.

Time charts be drown on certain scale, they should be attractive and drawn in a scientific manner.

(c) Time Line: It is quite helpful in developing time sense in an effective and easy way. It provides the pupils a scientific knowledge about the dates of history.

Time line be prepared to represent a few dates carefully selected. Time lines may be either *progressive time line or Regressive time line.*

To draw a time line following procedure is generally followed:

Draw a line 20 centimeters long to represent a century and divide it into ten equal parts which will indicate units often years.

The figure for each unit of 10 years will be written on the left side of the line. On the right side, the dates which are considered most important will be marked at suitable points.

(d) Time Graph: It is also used for development of time sense. It can be used for making a comparative study of certain events. It can also be used to show the comparative down fall of two dynasties.

In drawing a time graph, we may take a line of 3 to 4 centimetres in length. Each centimetre may indicate 10 years and so this line shall indicate 3 to 4 centuries. We can sort out certain dates on this line. On special dates and places, certain straight or perpendicular lines may be drawn. They should be indicative of the development of the English Rule in the Indian sub-continent.

Requisites of time line and time graph. Following are the requisites of time line and time graph:

1. Time line and time graphs should be drawn with great caution. An attempt should be made to see that the dates are accurate. While drawing graphs, it should be borne in mind that the line does not go very high.
2. Time line and time graph should be artistically drawn. III-drawn figures shall scare away the students from history. If these graphs are nicely drawn, the students shall be attracted towards them and they shall try to look at them carefully.
3. The students should be associated with drawing, of these figures.
4. These things should be explained elaborately to the students. Their explanation is difficult than their drawing. Aims of these things is to develop time sense in the students and therefore, their explanation should be properly done.

Since this is a difficult task, only those teachers who are interested in the teaching of history can do these things properly.

Walls of the history class or the 'history laboratory' should be decorated with these time charts and time graphs. They shall provide decorative as well as study material for the students.

The teachers should put questions to the students in regard to these devices.

Forms of the Time Line Charts. Time line charts may be of the following forms: (i) Prependicular form, (ii) Circular form, (iii) Straight line form, and (iv) Peak form.

MEANING OF SPACE SENSE

Space sense refers to the capacity of the individual to comprehend the place relations of historical phenomenon.

It is an understanding of the places located on the surface of the earth or on other planets where man on his long march down the ages, has settled, cultivated the soil, fought battles, etc. The *location, direction* and *distance* from the basic elements of our space sense.

The cultivation of space sense is comparatively easier than the time sense. The place relation of historical facts offer more tangible things to work with their time relationship. Johnson say, "the experience of seeing or walking a mile down the road has a line of physical reality denied to the thirty minutes which it may take a child to walk a mile down". The teaching of place relations will, however, require ingenuity and strenuous effort on the part of the teacher. For this purpose he can make use of various devices such as maps, place charts, layer charts etc.

Maps

Map is the most commonly used symbol for the representation of space. It shows location, direction, distance; extent, area, land and water forms. It conveys information about distribution of people, animal and vegetable life, climate, economic resources, etc. It also indicates the extent of territories, areas of political control, routes of movement of armies, travels, and so on. It also helps us in visualising important historical happenings which would not have been possible for us to understand the appreciate properly from their oral and written accounts. Thus maps are the sure means of concretising historical happenings and help in the understanding of the historical phenomena with reference to their place of occurrence.

From their very birth children being to experience persons and objects around them. They note their size, location, differences and relationships and meanings in order to deal with them successfully. Maps give expression to these through visual symbols. From, the very beginning of their school instruction pupils should be initiated in the art of drawing maps. First of all the teacher should try to make the pupil familiar with general lay out of the map drawing. He should give them the idea of directions, scale and other symbols. After this preliminary knowledge pupils should be asked to draw map of their own locality and in this way as the area of their experience widens they will take to the drawing of the sketch maps of their town, their province, their country and finally of the world. But at every stage the need is that they got a clear understanding of location' distance and direction.

Place Charts

The concept of distance and direction can be greatly clarified by drawing lines from their home town or from a particular place of historical occurrence. We may call this resulting diagram a place chart. It may be constructed within a blackboard or on the outline map of a country or of the world or as lines without any map. Exercises of this kind help the pupils to have an idea of the distances and directions of the places mentioned in the history lesson. They also help the pupils to have an idea of "Where he is in history while he is there".

Layer Charts

It is an interesting device for showing the growth of a kingdom or an empire. For this a thick paper of the same size of the map is taken and the portion under each rule is cut. These papers may be pinned or stitched in one side, one over the other and thereby will show the territories under each ruler over the other. By lifting each sheet and then allowing it to fall, the pupils would get a good idea of the addition made by a ruler or the loss suffered by him in regard to territories.

Cultivation of Historical Imagination

History is the study of past human actions and more

particularly with the motives, intentions, purposes, designs and policies which prompted human beings to behave in a particular way. The human actions of the past societies are not available for direct observation. They can simply be inferred or apprehended through the imaginative powers of mind.

Historical imagination refers to the capacity of an individual to visualise scenes and incidents as narrated to him through spoken or written word. It is also the capacity of an individual to draw inferences about past events to form mental pictures of the past happenings and to try to find the meaning hidden behind past human actions. The essence of history teaching lies in the encouragement of the powers of historical imagination of the pupils who are anxious to know about other people, about their lives, personalities, deeds and ideas. It can help them to visualise an atmosphere, entirely different from their own. It can awaken in them an imaginative wonder and excitement about the lives and actions of the people down the ages. And finally, it will help them to create an abiding interest and reverence in all things which are the relics of the past ages.

The cultivation of historical imagination is a difficult task. He should also see that his descriptions of places, persons and things are graphic and are communicated through vivid word-pictures. In fact at this stage of life children usually possess a riotous imagination. The need is to channelise this imagination in desired direction.

REVIEW QUESTIONS

1. What do you understand by lesson planning?
2. What are the chief characteristics of lesson planning?
3. Give a categorical account of various steps in lesson planning?
4. What do you understand by Time Sense in history? What will you do to cultivate time sense in the pupils?

5. What is the meaning of Space Sense? How can it be developed in the students?
6. What are the basic constituents of Time Sense? Explain them with examples.
7. What is the Historical Imagination? How will you cultivate historical imagination among your pupils?

12

History Library & Role of Text Books

> Hammers and tongs instead of library cards would have been needed in medieval times to "borrow" a library book. In the 15th century library books were laid on the desk and chained to a horizontal bar. Chains were still in use for this purpose in church libraries in England down to the early part of the 18th century.

I

Library, the treasure house of knowledge is of utmost use for academics as well as laymen. Its utility in teaching and learning of any subject can not be ignored. History library is quite useful to the students. When students read or consult some books from the library, their doubts become clear. Moreover, the study of library books acquaints them with new exercises or problems and prepares them better for the examination. A good history library also helps inculcating proper attitudes, interests and appreciations in the students. It can acquaint them with historical background of different topic and the contributions of various personalities.

Library Facilities in Schools

Generally the two types of libraries are found.

(a) General School Library

In most of our schools there is a general school library which contains books and magazines an all subjects. Then there should be separate sections for history books. For the teachers there should be good books on methodology of teaching, contributions of various historians and important historical personalities. For students there should be books on recreational activities, well selected text-books, some reference books and other historical books.

(b) History Department Library

Subject to the availability of resources there should be a separate history library. It may be housed in the history room. The librarian or the person incharge of it should classify the books properly so that students do not find and difficulty in getting the books issued. History teacher himself should remain in touch with latest books or magazines on the subject and make additions in the library. A number of copies of good books should be purchased. A few copies of prescribed text-books may be purchased for the use of poor students.

Importance of History Library

Library has a key role in scheme of education. Class-room teaching must be supplemented with the dissemination of knowledge through library. Different types of books in history library can be quite helpful to the students in completing the work assigned to them and to tackle all types of problems emerging from different topics prescribed in their syllabus. Class-room teaching many a times leaves many gaps and doubts. They can be removed if students work use of good books available in the library. History teacher can help the students in the selection of good books in the library.

A history library, is not only a source of learning and inspiration for students but also serves the need of the teachers. A teacher must keep his knowledge ever fresh and up-to-date, this is possible by making a free use of mathematics library. He can also learn latest methods of teaching history from the new books available in the library. Thus a good history library helps to keep the lamp of historical knowledge burning so as to kindle light in the minds of the students as also the teachers.

Need for Separate History Library

The general library help in encouraging the students to make use of library services; but the students cannot get proper guidance for removing their deficiencies in a particular subject. For this a separate library of subject concerned is essential. A separate library for history is a great necessity for rendering proper help to needy students. Such a library can be housed in history room and can be put under the charge of history teacher. There should be a period of library reading in the time-table so as to enable the students of every class to make use of library. A separate history is essential because of the following reasons:

- (i) It helps to bring efficiency in organisation of library service.
- (ii) History teacher remains in constant touch with the latest books in history.
- (iii) It provides a sense of separate identity to history and helps to inculcate interest in the subject.
- (iv) The students get better library facilities.
- (v) It helps the activities of history club.
- (vi) It can be of a help to gifted and bright students.

Thus, it is essential that all out efforts be made to establish a separate history library in every school.

Utilising Library Resources

Library is a resource centre which is extensively used by all members of the school family. It helps the teacher to enrich curriculum and facilitates personal and professional reading. It helps the students to gain meaningful experiences in reading thinking and forming independent judgements.

To the community, it provides for recreational and hobby interests. Library can thus justify its, position as a basic tool for instructional programme. Because of the above reasons library occupies a unique position in modern school and it cannot be replaced by any other agency.

The important functions of library are:

(i) It provides material for instructions and for reading.
(ii) It stimulates reading for recreation and enjoyment.
(iii) It teaches the technique of using the library effectively.
(iv) It provides the opportunities to students to assume responsibility.

IDEAL MATERIALS

History library should contain useful audio-visual aids required for teaching of history. The educational pictures, charts, maps, posters about history be displayed on the walls of library room.

In history library there should be a good collection of history books. The history teacher should be responsible for making a wise selection of books for the library. These books should be of the following types:

1. Text-books

A number of good text-books on various periods of Indian History as also history of the world and history of other important countries, must be made available in the library. It is also very important to note that keeping in view in the excavations in different parts of our country and also in other parts of the world and because of rapidly changing human life in the modern age, new and revised editions of standard text-books should continually be purchased for the school library, with a view to supply up-to-date knowledge and information to teachers and students.

2. Reference Materials

These include reference books, encyclopaedias, dictionaries, year books, biographies, atlases, bibliographies, directories, old manuscripts, old coins and other excavated material, Govt. Gazetteers and the like.

3. Literary Materials

These include biographies autobiographies, fiction, folklore, short-stories, travel books, books of adventure, herostories, romance, drama and poetry. This type of material provides reading for enjoyment and pleasure.

4. Source Materials

These include source books, manuscripts, original accounts of travellers and contemporary historian diaries, proclamations, original letters and dispatches of kings governors and viceroys, treaties, old monuments, historical buildings, sites, old tools, weapons, armours, coins etc.

In addition to the book resources (stated earliar) a good history library be supplemented by periodical, pamphlets, newspapers, magazines etc. This material can be easily and inexpensively used as teaching aid in the teaching of history.

Motivating Pupils to Utilise Library Resources

With the commencemtn of new session, minimum amount of supplementary reading should be fixed by the teacher for each pupil. It may be different for different classes, according to their standard. Even in the case of bright students and poor readers, lists of different types of books, both fiction and non-fiction particularly related with history, should be prepared by the teacher in consultation with the librarian. These lists should be provided to all pupils and they may be asked to read the required number of books, out of which no more than half may be fiction.

To motivate pupils to read, the teacher should set apart some marks in his subject for supplementary reading of this type. They may be added to the total number of marks, the child receives in history at the end of the session. In this way the pupils will definitely be motivated to read. Moreover, at the time of periodical or monthly tests, at least one compulsory question out of supplementary readers with adequate choice for different categories of pupils, should be given in the question paper. Such a programme should, however, be made known to pupils before hand.

Further, the teacher while teaching a certain unit about a particular period in history should bring with him such books as contain interesting accounts of living conditions prevailing in those periods and read out a few paragraphs in the class from those books. He should, also give to his pupils the names of the books, the names of the authors and those of their publishers and ask them to collect material therefrom, connected with the unit, under study. After a day or two he may ask a pupils who has gone through a certain book and prepared reports and notes, to stand up and read out what he has collected, pertaining to the lesson in hand. In this way, pupils can be motivated to read library books.

Pupils may be asked to collect form different writers, the different views upon a single topic. This is very important because in stead of relying upon only one source, the pupils are encouraged to draw upon several sources of information. This is perhaps the most valuable lesson that can be learned in the library.

Teacher's Role

The teacher will be able to motivate his pupils for extra reading, if he himself is a wide reader and is familiar with all the books published in his field. He should see that all those books are made available to students from the school library. In addition to books, he should also be a regular reader of newspapers and periodicals. The present day emphasis on current events in the teaching of history demands a good selection of news papers and magazines for the school library. Pupils can only of encouraged to make use of this material if the teacher has himself formed a habit of reading a daily newspaper and at least one or two magazines, related to history and making current-events a basis of study of some important unit in history.

II

ROLE OF TEXT-BOOKS IN TEACHING OF HISTORY

Place of Text-Book in the Teaching of History

About the importance and the place of text-books in the teaching of history. Some scholars have opined that as far as possible, text-books should not be used in the teaching of history. Some educationists are of the view that teaching should be conducted through the medium of textbooks; Johnson says, "The most important aid in the teaching of history is the text-book. It is indeed more than an aid." Both these views are at extremes. Actually, it is a 'golden means' that should be resorted to. Thus, we can say that text-books should be used that but sparingly and economically. They should be used, for strengthening the experiences of the students. They should not be taught like reading, books or supplementary books in the classroom. These books should be with the students and they should be asked to use them at home for revising the lesson that they have been taught in the class. They may also be encouraged to take help from these text-books for preparing the answers to various questions of home task.

Main utility of text-books lies in the fact that they develop self-confidence in the students and help them to learn to work in a systematic and scientific manner. In addition providing them historical data, they also help the students to learn and draw charts and tables.

It is al so suggested that a history text-book should be used in a way that it promotes historical thinking among the pupils. It should also help them in realising the specific aims and objective set forth in a particular lesson.

Thus, we conclude by saying that "whatever method or methods may be used, the overall effect in the use of text-book should be to achieve the objectives of the teaching of history. This should stimulate the pupils historical imagination to know more of history and to rationalise casual relationship, relating to different historical events. The use of history text-books most be followed by a series of well-graded and thought-provoking questions which make the text-books not an end in itself but a means to realise desirable objective. History text-books, when used effectively, not only vitalise instruction in the class but also give a new meaning to history teaching and learning.[1]

Types of History Text-books

Johnson, in his boom " The Teaching of History in Elementary and Secondary School," has given the following categories of history textbooks.

(a) Precise Text-books. Precise text-books are those which are of a brief and short nature. They present only a skeleton or frame-work of the facts of history. They are not written in a detailed form.

(b) Manuals. Manuals are those text-books which are written in a detailed form. They present a detailed account of the facts and the data. They are just the opposite of the precise text-books, although they leave some room for further development.

(c) Course. Course are those text-books which present the subject-matter in complete details of the facts and the

data. There is no likelihood for further development. In these text-books, ,each topic is treated so well that it is quite intelligible without further description.

All the above mentioned types of history text-books, must have the following essentialities:

1. Diction of the Test-book should be According to the Age and Standard of Pupils

Good text-books on history must be suited to the age, ability and interests of the pupils for whom these are written. Thus they should be child centred and should reflect the stage the child has reached.

2. Text-books should Give a Cause-effect Relationship

Good text-books in history should reveal to the pupils where they are in time, space and society. They should make clear to the pupils the relationship which links the present with the past, the local with the distant and personal and national life with the life and cultures of the people living in the other lands.

3. Text-books should be Course and not Manuals

The two terms *course* and *manuals* are explained below:

Manuals. These are the text-books which are written in a detailed form and they present a detailed account of the facts and the data.

Course. These are the text-books which provide a complete description of the facts and details. There is no likelyhood or their further development/improvement.

4. Text-books should be Well Illustrated

They should contain pictures, maps, charts, time-lines, graphs and sketches of various historical events to make the subject-matter easily understandable and to sustain the interest of the pupils.

5. Text-books should be Written in Clear and Simple Language

The author should write the books in a clear and simple language. It is possible for the author to present the events and thoughts in very clear manner if he has command over the subject. The style adopted in a text-books should be lucid.

6. Free Form Bias

A text-books in history should be free from bias and should tell the truth, the whole truth and nothing but the truth.

7. Good Printing and Get-up

The printing and the get-up of the history text-books should be good, otherwise the students shall not get interested in the text-books.

8. Element of Selectivity

While construction curriculum, the principle of selectivity is to be kept in mind. Only such events and facts are selected for inclusion in the curriculum that are helpful for upholding social values and make progressive step. The principle should be kept in mind while writing text-books of history. Such events should be emphasised in the history text-books that have influenced mankind and are likely to cast greater influence in the present social set-up.

9. List of Contents and Bibliography

There should be a list of contents in the beginning of the book and in the end, there should be a bibliography. List of contents helps the students in finding out the topics which they want to study without wasting much of their time. Bibliography gives them the subject matter for further study of the subject.

10. Psychological and Scientific

Text-books of history should be written on the basis of the principles of psychology. They should be scientifically planned and written.

11. Reasonably Priced and Within the Reach of Common People

Text-books should be reasonably priced. They should be priced such that it may be possible for the common man to purchase them.

12. Questions at the End

At the end of every chapter, there should be certain questions. These questions should be so designed that they may help the students to recapitulate the topic that they have read. These questions should be psychologically planned and scientifically put.

Advantages of a Good Text-Book

1. It Meets the Needs of Students: A good text-book is written from students' point of view recognising their difficulties and limitations. It, therefore, meets their needs by the use of simple headings, sub-headings, questions, exercises, maps, charts, pictures and other illustrative aids.

2. It Helps Developing Study Skills: A good text-book gives a common basis on which the process of reading, analysing, outlining and summarising can be mastered.

3. It Gives an Accurate Account of the Subject: A good text-book gives a reasonably correct account of the subject, field or area in an organised manner. Its treatment of the subject-matter is logical and systematic because it is written according to the latest syllabus, prescribed for the class. It, thus, sets a standard of the minimum essential, to be achieved by students of all categories in the class.

4. It Suggests Application of the Material Read: A good text-book in addition to giving the required subject-matter, suggests application of that material through assignments, drills, questions, projects, problems and other exercises of all sorts— reproductive imaginative, dramatic and manual.

5. It Reflects and Establishes Standards: A good text-book indicates what a teacher is to do to teach and what a pupil is to do to learn. Thus, by its teaching aids, it greatly effects methods as well as reflects and establishes the standards of scholarship.

6. It can Serve as an Organ of National Integration: By co-ordinating various activities in history a text-book can serve as an organ of national integration. Everyone connected or concerned with national co-ordination in India, has emphasised the improvement of inter-cultural friendship in India by giving, a careful consideration to school text-book.

7. It Expands and Limits its Scope and Size According to Needs: A good text-book can expand and delimit its scope, size and content according to the changing requirements of education. Thus, it may sometimes lead and sometimes follow the educational process.

8. It can Serve as Basis for Almost all the Methods: Almost all the methods of teaching can be used with the text-book as a basis of study. Thus, Assignment Procedure of Discussion, Problem, Project and Unit methods can all be used with advantage with the help of the text-book. All these methods and activities are rather suggested in the text-book at the end of each chapter.

REVIEW QUESTIONS

1. What are the important functions of a library?
2. What is the importance and need of a history library?
3. What are the different library resources for teaching history?

4. How can a history teacher encourage his students to read?
5. What is the place and importance of text-book in the teaching of history?
6. It is sometimes argued that good teaching is impossible if the pupil confines himself or herself to a single text-book. How far do you agree to this statement and why?
7. What are the essential qualities of a good text-book of history?
8. Discuss the good ways of using a text-book effectively.
9. What are the advantages of using a good text-books?
10. Discuss the different types of history text-book? Which of these types would you recommend for use by your students and why?

13

The History Teacher and The History Room

A good teacher plays a role model for pupils. It is the teacher on whom the real success or failure of any method, aid, device or procedure depends. It is he who can evaluate how far the aims, and objectives of teaching have been achieved. The history teacher not only deals with the successes and failures of the man in the past but also of the current and recurrent events and happenings of the world of today and so he is of special importance. It is very much apt to quote Lord R. Bryce, "The teacher of history must have the power of realising the date passed in a living present and have a touch of imagination as well as vastly large amount of positive knowledge, then he will attempt to pile upon the memory of his class".

In India the Kothari Commission Report (1966) says, "of all the different factors which influence the quality of education and its contribution to national development, the quality, competence and character of teachers are undoubtedly the most significant".

Dr. S. Radhakrishnan a great philosopher-king and illustrious teacher himself, "The teacher's place in society is of vital importance. He acts as the pivot for transmission of intellectual traditions and technical skill from generation to generation, and helps to keep the lamp of civilisation burning. He not only guides the individual, but also, so to say, the destiny of nation. Teachers have, therefore, to realise their special responsibility to the society. On the other hand, it is incumbent on the society to pay due regard to the teaching profession and to ensure that the teacher is kept above want and given the status which will command respect from his students".

Qualities and Qualifications

A history teacher is expected to possess certain academic qualifications as also certain professional qualifications.

As regards the academic qualifications it is usually a pass in matriculation/senior secondary examination for becoming a history teacher in a primary school. A pass in B.A. examination for being a teacher in history in a middle or high school and a pass in M.A. examination for being a teacher in a senior secondary school (grades 11 and 12). In addition to the above academic qualifications, any one who wish to be appointed as a history teacher has to undergo a teachers training course (i.e., either G.B.T. or B.Ed.). This professional training is all the more important these days when new techniques of teaching, evaluation etc., are being introduced. Trained teachers also require the stimulus of a refresher course to keep themselves informed about the latest methods of teaching and to refresh his knowledge of history. All this is quite essential because a good teacher must always keep him self-informed of the latest development in the field. This aspect of teacher has been brought out in the following words by Dr Rabindra Nath Tagore, "A teacher can never truly teach unless he is still learning himself. A lamp cannot light another lamp unless it continues to burn its own flame".

Characteristics

A successful history teacher must have the following qualities:

1. Mastery over the Subject: Like the teacher of any other subject a history teacher should have a thorough knowledge of the subject. For such a knowledge the teacher should read various reference books in addition to the prescribed text-books. Such a study will help the teacher to grasp the spirit of the subject and study it in a proper perspective. The continuity in study is also essential to keep the knowledge of the subject upto date it is not essential that a secondary school teacher be a specialist of his subject but it is essential that he should be able to present the facts of history in a psychological manner. For such a presentation teacher should be aware of the fact that social sciences are a developing subject.

2. *Faith in Subject:* Unless a teacher has faith in his subject, he will not be able to acquire thorough knowledge of it. This faith also encourages the teacher to learn more and more. This faith also enables the teacher to realise the utility and the value of teaching history.

3. *Knowledge of Child Psychology:* For success in any subject a knowledge of child psychology is essential and so is the case with history teacher. The psychological requirements of child differ from age to age and a teacher must have a thorough knowledge of child psychology if he wish to impart the knowledge of the subject in a proper manner. Thus the knowledge of child psychology and its proper use can contribute a lot in teaching of history.

4. *Knowledge of Different Methods of Teaching:* The knowledge of various methods of teaching is essential because it is only then possible to choose a suitable method according to the requirements of a particular class, e.g., a student at the age of 14 is fond of excursions and travels and a good teacher knowing it can coordinate the two in his teaching method to make the teaching successful.

5. *Knowledge of Regional and Provincial History:* In addition to thorough knowledge of history of our country, a good history teacher must have a good knowledge of

regional and provincial history. While teaching history he should give examples from this history.

6. Knowledge of Current Events: Such a knowledge helps the teacher in making a comparative study of the events of various periods, in the history of different countries of the world.

7. Knowledge of Aims and Objectives of Teaching of History: The history teacher should have clear knowledge of the aims and objectives of the teaching of history. The teacher must also have a faith in these aims and objectives. With such a faith, be becomes interested in the subject and tries to impart knowledge in a scientific and interesting manner to suit the students and society both.

8. Originality: A history teacher should never feel satisfied by reading what others say but should be in a position to form his own independent judgement of men and affairs. He must not have a blind faith, rather he should make it a habit to inquire to Mod the truth. If he possesses such qualities he can face any class-room situation that may arise unexceptionally under various circumstances.

9. Sympathetic, Creative Imagination and Ability to Act: The history teacher should have a sympathetic outlook. It is essential for presenting the historical facts in an impartial and scientific manner without sympathy, it is impossible for the teacher to understand the perspective of the developments of history.

He should also be endowed with 'Creative Imagination'. Creative imagination enables the teacher of history to present the facts and the events in a lively manner to his students. This helps him to have the proper understanding of the facts and enables him to present them in a lively and interesting manner.

Unless the teacher of history has some touch of an

acting in him, he cannot bring to life the past, in the classroom. The teacher has to modulate his voice and present things in such a way that the events may look like real.

10. Broad Outlook and Strong Memory: The teacher of history must have a broad out-look and strong memory, so that be is able to have proper knowledge and assessment of the events and facts of the past. Sharp memory enables him to remember the details. All these things will make the teaching of history interesting and successful. Prof. K.D. Ghosh observed, "Teacher of history is likely to be guided by his personal likes and dislikes. History teacher colours teaching of history, his interpretation of incidents and personality with his own likes or dislikes bom of the religious denominations to which he belongs."

Actually, the teacher of history should try to rise above the situation. If he colours his teaching with his likes and dislikes and with the views of his religion, the teaching of history will lose its value in a Secular state.

11. Responsible Social Worker: Since the history teacher has to serve coming generations with his social service so his role is more or less of a responsible social worker. He can be said to have achieved his task if he has been able to would the lives of young ones in the right direction.

12. Impressive Personality: The teacher of history should have an impressive and interesting personality. If he lacks these then he shall not be able to present the facts in an effective manner. The teacher of history quite often has to play the role of an actor. A person without an impressive and interesting personality shall make himself only a laughing stock if he takes to acting. This element of personality should also be accompanied by certain other traits. According to Prof. K.D. Ghosh: "While an interesting personality is one of the important facts in a successful effective lesson, it is very doubtful if the teacher with personality would have a continuous success in his lesson unless he has a proper grip over the method, i.e., methods of teaching."

According to Bryce: "He has to do as much talking as is necessary for fulfilling his fundamental duty of making things vivid, clear, and kindling a love for the subject."

13. Capacity to Undertake Excursions and Tours: The teaching of history requires that the students should be taken out on tours and execussions to the places of historical importance. It is the teacher of history who has to accompany the students in order to explain the things to them. The teacher of history should be capable of undertaking and understanding things.

14. Capacity to Arrange and Decorate the History Room: A teacher of history, in the words of Prof. E.L. Husluck should have the following qualities: "History requires a teacher who is willing to be ever active, ever inquiring, ever on his guard against the numerous fit falls which beset his path. He may take as his motto that of our 'ducal houses covendo huts."

In the modern education the need of a separate history room or history class has been well-emphasised. A history room cannot be established and furnished unless the teacher of history is anxious to furnish and decorate it. In fact, in the teaching of history, a good deal of importance is given to a history room. The history room should be equipped with black-board, historical pictures, charts and other materials.

15. A Good Story Teller: Story-telling is an art and it is most desirable thing to be possessed by a history teacher. A good history teacher should be capable of framing stories connected with different historical aspects and present such stories to his students in an interesting way. This quality is more desirable in a history teacher teaching lower classes. It makes him a very successful teacher.

Problems Faced by History Teacher

A number of problems baffle an ordinary history teacher. Some are as under:

1. Lacks the Knowledge of World History: Generally history teachers in our schools are found lacking in the knowledge of world history. Due to this lack of knowledge they fail to view the historical facts in their real prospective. Every social or political movement in any part of the world has its effect on the entire world, so it is not possible for anyone to deal with the history of his country quite exclusively. Thus the knowledge of world history is a must for any successful history teacher, without it his teaching will remain imperfect.

2. Scanty Knowledge of History: An ordinary history teacher is generally not much interested in his subject and he is not quite enthusiastic to supplement his knowledge of history that he acquired in the school/college age. He is neither interested in reading nor in excursions. He is not interested to train himself in a scientific way. He generally has wrong notions about historical facts and it leads to a disastrous situation. Such a teacher is likely to present distorted facts to the pupils and thus distort their personality.

3. Religious or Social Bias: Most of the teacher suffer from such a bias and any one suffering from it cannot provide the correct knowledge of history. If a Hindu teacher is fanatic and has racial bias he cannot teach the history of Muslims period correctly and impartially. He shall definitely be dishonest in teaching because it would be quite difficult for him to explain how the Muslims pondered over the Hindu rulers. Similar situation will exist for teacher of other religions.

4. Faulty Method of Teaching: In our country history is generally considered to deal with dead princes and bygone events and such a teaching will become lifeless. However, history is a living subject as it deals with 'drama of the human beings or the stage of the world which is still growing on'. This drama should be presented before the children in a vivid manner in class-room. For this a history teacher should be active and full of life.

5. National Bias: In the teaching of history, national bias is as harmful as the religious or racial bias. "My country, right or wrong" is a condemned slogan. Patriotism has great virtues and one should be patriotic but patriotism and national bias have different meanings. A true patriot sees and confesses the weaknesses of his country while a person who has national bias cannot do this. A teacher of history suffering from national bias shall never explain before the children the weaknesses of his country. If a history teacher in India has national bias, he shall not explain before the children that the Britishers were able to have their rule in this country due to the weaknesses of his own countrymen. On the other hand, he will tell the students that there were no weaknesses in Indian rulers and it was the mere cunningness of Britishers that they dominated over the Indians. A history teacher should be patriotic but he should never have national bias. He should try to develop the international understanding in himself and his people.

How to Make History Teaching Realistic

To inculcate the interest of students in history and to make history teaching realistic, the following points he kept in mind:

1. Correlation with the Other Subjects: In order to make the teaching of history interesting and realistic it is of great importance to correlate the subject with other subjects. Correlation of history with subjects make it interesting and meaningful. Historical novels, if exploited skillful, help us to a great extent in proving the knowledge of history, to the people. They create an atmosphere and environment of the previous ages easily. In the same way, correlation with geography proves useful and helps in understanding the background of most of the historical facts.

2. Excursions to the Sites of Historical Interest: As we have already said that today the world is not as it was about 200 or 400 years ago. However, there are places of historical interests where can get the same atmosphere as it was during old age. So, the execursions to the sites of historical importance are very useful in the teaching of history, and it will make our lessons interesting realistic. Old historical sites, ruins and buildings are the real and original sources of history. They help us a lot in understanding the past and so such excursions are most important for the teaching of history.

3. Dramatisation: Dramatisation is another valuable device which makes the lessons of history interesting and effective. This device fixes the historical events in memory and helps in creating the real atmosphere of by gone ages. The students who had acted as Mahanna Pratap understand the great hero more than an ordinary teacher of history. A student who has seen Chandra Gupta, can leant more about Chandra Gupta than the student who has not seen him inaction.

4. Use of Audio-visual Aids: Use of audio-visual aids can also make the teaching of history interesting and realistic. These aids are meant for making the history teaching lively and useful. Films and cinema, radio, cinema projectors and television can make our subject more realistic, and so a teacher should utilise these aids upto the maximum extent.

5. Maps: Use of maps also make the teaching of history effective. The teacher tries to substantiate his statement with the help of these maps. If he can explain the various places of historical importance and the empires of the various rulers with the help of maps, the lesson becomes more interesting. In fact, map is not merely an aid to history teaching but it is essential and we cannot ignore it.

6. Collateral Reading: Collateral reading should also be encouraged while teaching history. It develops the understanding of the subject. It fills in the gaps in the knowledge.

All the points mentioned above will be of no use if the history teacher lacks the qualities desired in a good history teacher. Actually speaking it is the competent teacher who creates an atmosphere for his pupils to roam in past and thus make the teaching of history interesting.

II

HISTORY ROOM

Essential Equipments for a History Room

Preferably, the history room should be a little bigger than an ordinary class-room. It should then be furnished and provided for carrying out various activities such as instructional work, demonstration, group works etc. For carrying out such activities the following material is essential for every history room.

1. Bulletin Board: It is used to display maps, charts, current events, news-items, paper cuttings, magazine articles etc.

2. Chalk Board: The colour of such a board may be green, yellow, white or even black. This is used to draw outline pictures as also to write summaries etc. It should be located at such a place that it can easily be seen by the students.

3. *Furniture:* Sufficient furniture for seating of the students be provided. It should also be provided with a movable desk or table and a chair for the teacher. In addition to this it should be provided with a table dictionary, desk calender, pen etc., for teachers use.

4. *Audiovisual Teaching Aids:* The history room should be fully equipped with various types of audiovisual teaching aids such as pictures, maps, models, specimens, films, film-strips, globe etc. If possible provision should also be made to have projectors, record player, radio-set and tape recorder in the history room. There teaching aids play an important role in teaching of history.

5. *Books and Book Cases:* Text-books by different authors, current magazines, periodicals, reference books be provided in sufficient numbers so that students have an easy access to the reading material. Open-book shelves may be provided for storing these items.

6. *Collections:* A corner in the history room be reserved for old coins, old clothes, dresses, utencils, historical relics, old paintings, art pictures etc. Such items may be got collected through history students.

Flags of different nations be also exhibited in the history room. It need be a brief history of such flags may also be tagged with the flags.

7. *Cabinets and Files:* Cabinets and files are required to store different materials. The filing system is helpful in locating the needed article at once.

The above points can be summarised as under:

(a) It should be spacious enough as to accommodate the students and have space for demonstrations, models, blackboard and charts etc.

(b) It should also have arrangement for acting certain dramas.

(c) There should be a good arrangement of blackboards. Teaching of history requires a lot of use of blackboards. There may be overlapping boards. Such arrangement would facilitate the drawing of charts and the maps.

(d) There should be a small collection of books in the history room.

(e) The history room should be decorated with the pictures of historical personalities and charts etc. There should also be pictures of the battles and wars and similar events.

(f) There should be arrangement of Epidiascope. There should also be arrangement of globes and project pictures.

Advantages of History Room

Various advantages of a separate history room for the teaching of history are as under:

(1) Scientific Teaching. It helps to make it possible to bring about the scientific teaching of the subject.

(2) It Makes Teaching of History Effective. In the absence of a separate history room, the teacher has to carry the teaching aids and other materials with him. Such steps are not needed when there is a separate history room. It saves the spoiling of the material for the teaching of history, in the transit and also the time.

(3) Proper Atmosphere. It creates an atmosphere suitable and congenial for the teaching of history.

(4) It Develops the Power of Imagination and Observation. In a particularly equipped history room, there are maps, charts and other useful things for the teaching of history. These things help to develop power of observation and imagination of the students.

All these things are possible if the history room is properly equipped.

It shall be useful to have a small historical museum. This museum should consist of the coins, clothes, dresses, utensils etc., of olden days. Models of these things would also serve a good purpose. There should also be devices for developing time sen e in the students.

All these things can be arranged only if the teacher of history is competent and painstaking. Without hard labour on the part of the teacher, the teaching of history cannot be made lively and interesting.

Management

The history room should be the place where a healthy social relationship develops between pupils and pupils and also between teacher and pupils. To achieve it students be given their due share in the management of the history room. Various committees be formed for purchase, collection, arrangement etc., and students be given a training for group leadership and committee co-operation through such committees.

In the words of Moffatt and Howell "Class-room management expresses a business like and orderly approach to the teaching-learning situation. Leadership gives direction and provides for the type of atmosphere so essential for effective instruction. Good organisation for all activities eliminates confusion and possible discipline problems. Pupils should, therefore, be encouraged to develop abilities and attitude commensurate with the democratic sharing of responsibilities in the co-management of their own class-room." Good work should be appreciated and each student should be encouraged to show his worth. Opportunities for self-discipline and self-control, based on cooperation, should be provided to all pupils. This will lead to character building and personal development. If our students assume responsibilities in the true spirit and discharge them to the best of their abilities and capacities, they are receiving effective training for democratic citizenship.

History museum

In every school or college, there should be a museum in which the material of historical importance should be kept. In the lower classes, there is no need for a separate history museum. However, there should be a museum in which old coins, pieces of architecture etc., should be placed along with the other materials. For the higher secondary and degree colleges, there should be a separate room for the history museum in which all the available material of historical importance should be placed.

The museum helps a lot in the teaching of history. The students when visit the museum, are easily acquainted with the historical species which develop their knowledge of history. The students should be encouraged to collect the material for the history museum. However, the teacher should take care that only those things are kept in museum which are really of the historical importance. If the teacher is not conscious in this respect, the whole purpose of the museum will be spoiled and it would not serve the purpose of educating the young ones in the right perspective.

Laboratory-Work in History

Besides regular history periods provided in the school time-table, some periods be allotted for *laboratory work* in history. The basic purpose of laboratory work is to develop skills, original thinking, planning and to develop creative expression among students. In the laboratory-work period students are busy in drawing maps, preparing graphs, charts, time lines, models or pictures, solving problems, working on projects and answering given questions and assignments individually or in groups. Specific instructions are given to students regarding the work to be done and sources from where the material is to be collected. They try to learn through research and exploration. They are given freedom to move about the class-room and make maximum possible use of the material, pertaining to the work in hand. Although time is fixed for the completion of each activity or unit, yet the students are allowed to progress according to their own ability and capacity.

In these work periods the teacher acts as a guide and a director. He gives suggestion, guidance, encouragement and help when the pupils are in difficulty. It is his duty to see that the pupils achieve their goal with the least wastage of time and energy. Laboratory work provides the kind of social relationship in which both the pupils and the teacher plan, work, study and learn together. They may be working individually or in groups, but the feeling is that all engaged in a task leading to a common goal.

REVIEW QUESTIONS

1. Why does history require the highest type of teacher?
2. Write a short essay on "An Ideal History Teacher".
3. Why is general and liberal education necessary for a teacher of history?
4. What should be the essential qualities of a history teacher?
5. What is the need for a history room?
6. Given in brief the management of a history room.
7. List the main equipment of a history room.
8. Write a note on History Museum.
9. Describe the importance of laboratory work in History.

14

Evaluation in History

'When a man's knowledge is not in order, the more of it he has the greater will be his confusion."

—*Herbert Spencer*

Never make a decision yourself, if you don't have to. When one of your men asks you a question, ask him what is the answer. There is only one answer to many questions, and, therefore, this method answers many questions before they are asked. It not only develops your men, but also enables you to measure their ability.

—*Henry L. Doherty*

Basically, 'Evaluation' is a continuous process which is an integral part of teaching. It is not merely a test at the end of history lesson or unit. Instead evaluation goes on constantly during lesson and units and is clearly related to the teacher's goal and points of view on history teaching. The main aim of any teaching-learning programme is to bring about certain desirable change in pupils.

As learning takes place teachers have to ascertain very frequently the growth and change taking place in pupils as a result of teaching learning experiences. This is evaluation. To evaluate means to characterise the work or value of something. It is a method of determining the extent to which previously established goals or objectives have been achieved. It is a "process of making an overlay of the outcomes of an educative experiences against the background of anticipated or stated objectives. To make improvements in any educational programme we need its evaluation. Good evaluation can only be made in relation to the goals of instructions. Thus there is a close relationship between objectives, experiences and evaluation. A good evaluation rests upon: (i) educational objectives, (ii) learning and behaviour changes, and (iii) tools and techniques of evaluation.

To test efficiency of teaching, to judge the progress of students and to discover their achievements and evaluate the whole system we require some sort of measuring tools. These tools are tests or examinations. Tests are essential to grade and rank pupils, however, if evaluation is used merely to indicate areas of subject to which students have been exposed or for classifying and categorising students, a great value is lost. The same loss occurs if evaluation is interpreted only as arriving at numerical or alphabetical ratings for report cards. In this way much of the positive use of evaluation as a means of teaching and learning could be destroyed.

Effective instructional planning and evaluation of students performance have always been stressed on the statement of instructional objectives so that they are of great help to the students. According to Muller, an instructionally usable objective must state the intended outcome in terms of terminal behaviour of students. Terminal behaviour here means the behaviour of the student after class-room instruction and evaluation is possible if the learning outcomes are carefully specified. By combing continuous evaluation with immediate application of what has been learned, the teacher can provide for:

(i) The stimulation of students who learn rapidly to greater growth towards goals be application of advanced works.

(ii) The identification of specific weaknesses and difficulties in functional understanding (concepts, principles, generalisations) and the needed reteaching of varied activities skills or problem solving abilities, and

(iii) The clarification, modification or complete alteration of goals as needed for the unit.

Evaluation, teaching and learning are the three coeners of the education system. *Evaluation* is concerned with finding out how far students have learned as a consequence of teaching. There are two kinds or evaluation depending upon whether the comparison of students is made with some absolute performance standard or with other students of group.

Norm-Referenced Evaluation

It accesses the students performance relative to other students of the group. Students are awarded marks and relative ranks in this method of evaluation.

Criterion-Referenced Evaluation

It assesses the students performance in terms of a specified performance standard or criterion without any mention of the performance levels of the other students of the group. This evaluation method is related to mastery and developmental test.

Aim of Evaulation

The main aim of evaluation is: (i) for determining the teaching-learning process, (ii) for revision of the curriculum, (iii) to provide an objective basis for reporting progress of students, (iv) for securing effective co-operation from the parents and the community, (v) for determining the policies of promotion, and (vi) to provide suitable guidance to pupils, on the basis of their evaluation.

Thus we find that evaluation is an essential part of the educational process. It helps in realising the goals of instructions. It points out the defects in teaching-learning process.

SPECIFIC OBJECTIVES

Following are the specific objectives of evaluation in history:

(a) Diagnosing Weaknesses

Evaluation in history is essential to discover specific weaknesses of the student. Making use of this information teacher can take remedial measures for removal to the weakness.

(b) Measurement of Factual Knowledge

The evaluation is done to determine the extent and rate of pupils growth along the line of aims and objectives of teaching of history. It is expected that each individual pupil will acquire some definite, knowledge, information and concepts. Such a knowledge helps in creating a fellow-feeling and also helps to develop clear thinking and critical judgement. Thus, it becomes essential to measure achievements in this direction.

(c) Future Achievements Prediction

Evaluation helps in determining the potential achievements of pupils. It also helps to discover their special abilities and attitudes. It thus helps to predict the future success of the student and to provide him guidance for future educational opportunities, vocational students etc.

(d) Stimulate Instructions

Evaluation stimulates both teacher and the pupil to work harder so as to attain a higher level.

Characteristics of Good Test in History

A good test in history should have the following characteristics:

1. Validity

The test should be valid. It should fulfil the objectives for which it is meant. For this it should be free from defects that are likely to affect the valid results.

2. Reliability

Any test can be considered reliable if it gives some results every time when it is used for testing the individual's ability under same conditions. An objective test is bound to be reliable.

The reliability of a test is affected by the following factors, thus to be reliable it should be free from:

(a) The whims of the examiner.

(b) The physical and mental condition of the student.

(c) The language of questions—lack of clearness or any ambiguities is statements.

(d) Lack of clear-cut instructions for marking.

(e) Inefficient method of scoring.

A reliable test is not influenced by subjective conditions, it is objective.

3. Comprehensiveness

Any good test should be comprehensive, i.e., it should assess knowledge, skills, abilities, attitudes etc., as adequately as possible. No aspect of the curriculum should be ignored while making evaluation.

4. Administratibility

It should be easy to administer, economical in time and money, easy to score and interpret. The direction of the test should be clear-cut. There should be answer keys for scoring.

5. Capable of Maintaining the Interest of the Student

Any good test should be able to capture the interest of the students and maintain it. Thus it should be interesting for the students. A good test is motivating for the students and stimulates their best effects. It should be neither too easy nor too difficult. It should never be used as a means of punishment.

6. Diagnosticity

A good test is diagnostic. The aim of diagnosis is to analyse the difficulties of a student in a particular phase of work. The aim is to reveal reliable information concerning his weaknesses so as to overcome them by concerted action and remedial teaching. In this way it would help the teacher to guide them properly and adopt remedial measures to eliminate their weak points.

7. Utility

A good test is useful in various ways. For example a test result may be used for improvement of teaching, may be useful to measure some desired quality/ability in the student, useful in finding out deficiencies in pupils so that the remedial measures may be taken up for their removal.

Evaluation and the Traditional Type of Examination

The traditional system of examination in History was mainly based on essay. It measured only the factual knowledge retained by the pupils. Memorisation and cramming were the chief criteria for promotion to next higher class. It was, thus a "one way street" which deprived children of varied abilities, a chance of continuing their studies in the school. Attitudes, emotions, interests and appreciations had no place in the examination programme.

The new idea of evaluation is more comprehensive which includes the testing of both tangible and intangible qualities. It is related to total learning situation. It is a meaningful process, utilising many sources as they apply to the objectives of a democratic and forward-looking educational structure. It takes in to account the growth of the child as a whole individual and in his total environment. In evaluation one has to know where the pupils were at the beginning of the teaching learning process, get a record of changes brought in them and judge how good those changes are in relation to established objectives. Evaluation, therefore, includes many facets. It is both objective and subjective. It comes both from within and without. Evaluation is thus, a continuous and developing process which must form an essential part of educational programme. It must be made part of each problem and each unit of work in history and should relate to the objectives of that unit or problem.

Demerits of Traditional Type of Tests or Examinations

Some of the defects from which traditional type of examination suffer are:

A. Students' Views

(i) Essay type tests are less objective and so they lack Validity. This type of tests can reveal child's cramming capacity only.

(ii) *These tests lack reliability.* A student is compelled to have a selective reading. He depends more on guess papers and so there is an element of chance.

(iii) It keeps the students busy and full of nervous tension. The study does not spread over the whole year and is limited to a short period just before the examinations. Thus a habit of irregular study is developed in the student.

B. Teacher's Views

(i) The teacher covers only a limited and important portion of course because his aim is to see that maximum number of his students pass the examinations.

(ii) The teaching programme of the teacher is wholly examination oriented and the basic principle of teaching his students are given least consideration.

(iii) The teacher is compelled to encourage his students to cramming which is not a psychological method of teaching.

(iv) Since a teacher is judged by the results of his students so every thing becomes subservient to the examinations.

(v) To show good results sometimes the teacher devotes a good deal of his time to indulge in guess work which affects his teaching.

From the above are can conclude that essay type examination is not correct method of evaluation in history. The improvement in system of evaluation is possible if following suggestions are given due consideration.

(a) *Improvement in Essay Type Questions.* The language of the questions should be clear and precise and clear cut directions be given for scoring. Shorter questions spread over the whole course be set.

(b) *Use of Objective Tests.* In addition to essay type tests, some objective type tests be used for evaluation. The objective tests can be of the following type:

   (i) True-false type
   (ii) Completion type
   (iii) Multiple choice type
   (iv) Matching type
   (v) Short answer type

(c) *Assessmentof Regular Work.* For such assessment a record of child's developments should be kept. Such a record may be kept for his home-work, practical work etc., and this should be taken into consideration while assessing a student.

(d) *Use of Oral Tests.* In such oral tests questions are asked and the students answer them orally. Such questions require quick recall and thinking. These tests helps in assessing the ability of the students to apply the knowledge of facts in different situations.

Thus, we find that no single device in enough and a judicious blend of various evaluation tools is the best approach.

Evaluating the Results of History Instructions

A complete evaluation programme in history should include the following instructions:

1. *For evaluating knowledge information and concepts:*

(i) Oral tests, (ii) Essay-type tests, (iii) Objective-type tests, (iv) Testing the pupil's day-to-day work, in the class.

2. *For evaluating skills i.e.,* assessment of the process of work, of actual performance and of furnished product etc.

3. *For evaluating attitudes, interests and values:*

(i) Observation, *(ii)* Conferences and interviews, *(iii)* Anecdotal Records, *(iv)* Diaries and Logs, *(v)* Work Samples, *(vi)* Pupils' Interest Inventories, *(vii)* Sociometry, *(viii)* Objective Standardised Tests, and *(ix)* Cumulative Records.

For evaluation of knowledge, information and concepts. We carry out the: *(i)* Oral Tests, *(ii)* The essay type tests, and *(iii)* Objective type tests.

The oral tests and the essay type tests have already been dealt in previous section and here we take up the discussion of objective type tests.

The objective type tests in common use are:

(i) The standardised tests.

(ii) The non-standardised or teacher made tests.

The standardised tests are the work of experts who, have established their validity and reliability, fixed definite and uniform procedures for using them and providing keys for scoring. A test is said to be standardised if the conditions under which it has to be given are standardised to ensure uniformity of procedure.

The standardised tests are of four types:

(i) Achievement tests.

(ii) Diagnostic tests.

(iii) Intelligence tests.

(iv) Aptitude and personality tests.

Diagnostic and Achievement Tests

The aim of diagnosis is to analyse the difficulties of students in a particular phase of work. The aim is to reveal reliable information concerning his weaknesses in order to overcome them by concerted action and for remedial teaching. It can also be used as an inventory test to find out how much the student knows about a given phase of the subject-matter. Diagnostic tests are used to discover and analyse pupils difficulties with a view to setting up specific remedial measures to correct errors and remove difficulties.

A diagnostic test is different from achievement test in that the main purpose of a diagnostic test is to study the nature of difficulties experienced by pupils. While constructing a diagnostic test. The teacher has to consider the individual difficulties experienced by students in solving problems. The test items should also give due consideration to the varying abilities of pupils in solving different types of problems. The age norm, the grade norm etc., should also be given due consideration. Before constructing such a test a pilot study be conducted over a given area or unit and its results statistically analysed before finalising the test.

The reliability coefficient of the test has to be calculated and then the diagnostic test can be deemed to be fit for administration over a large sample.

Appropriate remedial instructions be given and for this careful planning is essential. The causes of failure on solving a problem are to be hypothesised systematically.

The importance of diagnostic tests is due to the following:

(i) Nature of the subject matter.

(ii) Difficulties experienced by students as a group.

(iii) Difficulties experienced by certain individual.

An *achievement test* is used to measure the degree of mastery of skills, fundamental concepts, processes and general knowledge of the subject, attained by the student The achievement test is valid when it can measure the extent to which the purpose for which it has been constructed.

Importance of Blue-print in Constructing Achievement Test

The blue-print there means the plan that the teacher has in evaluating the performance of the pupils.

The *blue-print* concerns itself to the knowledge acquired by means of study, remembering, thinking, solving problems, formulating hypothesis. It is here that the formulation of instructional objectives and their respective behavioural changes can be clearly identified.

In a blue-print the objectives are listed horizontally. They are knowledge, understanding, application and skill.

Again horizontally forms of test items are indicated. They are essay questions, short answer questions and objective questions.

Vertically we find the subject divided into sub-units. The question paper should cover all the sub-units and all the objective. The score for each type of questions viz. essay, short answer and objective type should be fixed.

It is desirable that most of the final examinations in schools should be achievement tests.

1. Aptitude and Personality Test

These tests are intended to measure the trait of temperament and character. These are in the form of inventories and rating scales. They are more qualitative than quantitative.

2. Non-standardised Tests

They are informal type new tests. They are generally of two main types (a) recognition, and (b) recall.

(a) Recognition type questions include true/false, matching, multiple choice etc.

(b) Recall questions include, i.e., completon type or short answer questions.

This type of objective tests have the following merits:

(i) They have little or no scope of subjectivity.

(ii) They are more reliable.

(iii) These are comprehensive.

(iv) There is no chance element in them.

(v) They are easy to administer and easy to score.

(vi) They are economical in respect to time.

However, they also suffer from certain drawbacks. Some of these are as follows:

(i) They fail to test the organising ability of the child.

(ii) They fail to develop thinking and reasoning power of the students.

(iii) They put more emphasis on factual knowledge and very little importance is given to processes, methods, originality of thought etc.

(iv) They encourage guess work.

(v) These tests are not diagnostic.

(vi) These tests may pose some administrative difficulties as there may be indiscipline in the students. They may use unfair means, whisper answers or make same gestures.

(vii) It needs a lot of time and labour to prepare such a test.

Different Types of Objective Tests

We now take up the discussion of various types of objective tests.

1. *Completion Type of Test or Memory Recall.* This type of test consists of questions that are either sentences or statements, in between the words a blank is left within the body of the material. Sometimes the space is left in the margin which has to be filled in by the students.

2. *True and False Type.* In this type, a number of statements are given. Some of these are true and some are false. The students are required to tick ✓ or write 'yes' before a correct statement.

These tests can cover a wide range of subject-matter and wide sampling of knowledge is possible. There is an objectivity in scoring. Such a test is not difficult to construct but while constructing such a test the care be taken not to put very descriptive statements before the students.

3. *Multiple Choice Tests.* Such tests contain a number

of items, each of which has two or three responses. One of the responses in each item is correct. The students are required to tick the correct response.

This type of test requires memory as also the correct knowledge and a good vocabulary.

4. *Matching Type Test.* In these tests, in each item, there are two columns. Each item in the first column is to be matched with the relevant item of the second column, not given in the same order. To avoid guess work, the items in the second may be more or less in number than items in the first column.

5. *Time-sequence form.* This type of questions contain a list of items and the student is required to arrange them on the basis of chronology.

Requirements of the New Type of Tests

New type tests have to be carefully constructed. The following precautions be taken otherwise these tests are likely to lose the utility.

(a) Determination of the Purpose: The basic purpose of the test should be decided first.

(b) Relation of the Test in Accordance with the Purpose: After purpose has been decided, the test has to be found out which would suit the purpose.

(c) Objective Questions. The questions that are constructed should be objective.

(d) Ability of the Student to be Kept in Mind. The individual differences and the mental ability of the students should be kept in mind, otherwise the purpose shall not be served.

(e) Scoring Key to be Prepared. The scoring key that provides answer to the questions must be prepared. Unless

it is done, the purpose shall not be served. Without it, it shall be different to award marks.

(f) Standardisations. These tests need standardisation. Then only it is possible to do away with the element of subjectivity.

(g) Intelligent Planning. It is not possible for all the teachers to plan these tests. These tests have to be planned and constructed by intelligent teachers as they require intelligent planning.

Precautions

While planning these tests following should be avoided:

(i) Difficult words and sentences should be avoided.

(ii) Text-book sentences should be avoided.

(iii) Ambiguities should be avoided.

(iv) Clues and suggestions should be avoided.

REVIEW QUESTIONS

1. Clarify with examples the need and importance of evaluation in the teaching learning process.
2. What is evaluation? State briefly the difference between evaluation and traditional types of examination.
3. What is the difference between appraisal and measurement?
4. What are the important objectives of evaluation in history? To what extent is the present system of examination based on these objectives?
5. What are objective-type tests? Distinguish between standardised and non-standardised objective-type tests.
6. List the important points a teacher should keep in mind while constructing new-type tests?
7. Suggest remedial steps for evaluation system and traditional pattern of examination.

15

Teaching Aids

> One can no more develop capacity by resting on his job than he can learn to spell by sitting on a dictionary
>
> —*Arthur Dean*

In fact, to teach a subject like history is monotonous in nature. Most often a history teacher to invest pupils to gain an experience of human behaviour in past societies. Through verbal expositions, be this to explain the past happenings but their time appreciation demands that events of past are understood in their casual and sequential relationships. In this respect audiovisual aids, with their various devices, techniques and resources, come to the help of the history teacher. Audiovisual aids are the effective tools that "invest the past with an air of reality." Teaching aids should be used to supplement the process of teaching. Teaching aids make teaching concrete, effective and interesting. By making an appeal to the auditory and visual senses of pupils, audiovisual aids in vest reality to the past, increase pupil's interest in the subject and supplement verbal explanations of the teacher.

SIGNIFICANCE OF TEACHING AIDS

(i) They make the lesson of history interesting.
(ii) They help to stabilise the knowledge of the subject.
(iii) They make the process of learning interesting and practical.
(iv) They help the teacher to proceed 'from concrete to abstract'.

(v) They help the teacher to conduct the teaching efficiently and creditably.

(vi) They are a good substitutes for direct experiences and are a supplement to direct experience.

(vii) They are very helpful for poor readers and slow-learners.

(vii) They help to develop the power of imagination and observation.

(ix) They provide an opportunity for a change in the monotonous atmosphere that generally prevails in the class-room.

(x) They provide an opportunity for a better rapport between the teacher and his pupil.

(xi) They help the pupil to develop a scientific attitude.

(xii) They provide a training in scientific method.

(xiii) They can be used in bigger classes.

(xiv) Use of such aids is based on the principles of psychology.

KINDS OF TEACHING AIDS

For convenience of discussion the teaching aids in history may be grouped as under:

(i) Traditional aids, e.g., Text-books, black-board etc.

(ii) Visual aids, e.g., charts, pictures, graphs, maps and globe, stereoscopes, motion pictures, specimens and models.

(iii) Auditory aids; e.g., Radio, dictaphone, loud speaker, phonograph, gramophone etc.

(iv) Audiovisual aids, e.g., Television, Sound-Motion pictures, Dramatisation, Field trips and school journeys.

A few of these aids will be discussed in detail.

USE OF TEACHING AIDS

Following points are important for use of teaching aids:

(i) They should be woven with class-room teaching and should be used only to supplement the oral and written work being done in the class.

(ii) An effort be made that the teaching aids used in class are in conformity with the intellectual level of the students as is in accordance with the previous experience of the students.

(iii) Only such aids be preferred which provide a stimulus to the students for greater thinking and activity.

(iv) They should be exact, accurate and real as far as possible.

(v) The teacher should use a teaching aid only when he is quite sure about handling a specific teaching aid.

(vi) The teacher should use a teaching aid only after proper planning so that the aid is used exactly at the point, in the process of teaching; when it best fits in the process of teaching.

(vii) Teacher should see that a follow up programme follows the lesson in which a teaching aid has been used.

(viii) Teacher should carry out occasional evaluation about the use, function and effect of a teaching aid on the learning process.

1. Text-books

For various classes text-books are prescribed. They contain the subject-matter prescribed for a class but these books should not be used as reading-books in the class. They should help the students to prepare the lesson at home.

Qualities and Characteristics of the Text-books

The chief qualities and characteristics of the text-books are as follows:

1. Description of the historical events should be presented in the history on the basis of the principle of *cause and effect.*
2. An attempt should be made correlate the events of the post with the present social life.
3. The books should be written in an interesting style.
4. The language and style of the history book should be appropriate for the standard for which the books are meant.
5. While writing the book, the writer should refrain from giving his personal opinion.
6. The books should be well illustrated.
7. The events that are described in the history, books should be selected ones. The author should apply the 'principle of Selectivity' in prescribing the event. Only those, events that have some bearing on the social life or are of interest for the students should be included in the text-books.

   According to Johnson, the history books should be tested on the basis of pictures, maps and visual aids. While testing the quality of text-books, the teacher should keep the following things in mind:

   (a) They should be clearly printed.

   (b) They should be scaled to easy vision. It means that they should be interesting to the eyes of the students.

   (c) They should be related to the text. It means dial they should conform to the course prescribed for the particular class of students.

(d) The sources of the pictures and charts should be indicated. This will make the book authentic.

8. The subject-material of the books should proceed from concrete to obstract and the subject-matter should be arranged on the basis of the 'principle of selectivity' of the organisation of the subject-material.
9. The books should be nicely printed and their get-up, type and paper should be good and attractive.
10. In the beginning of the book, there should be a list of content material.
11. The whole subject-matter should be divided into various chapters. At the end of each chapter, there should be certain questions for recapitulation.
12. The book should be reasonably priced and should be within the reach of common man.
13. The style of the book should be in accordance with the age group of the students. For example, the books meant for the students of primary classes should be written in 'Story method'.

2. Maps

Maps are the universally accepted symbols which represent historical reality in space. They show the location, distance and direction of places connected with historical events. They give information about the distribution of land, water, vegetable life, climate, economic resources which have directly or indirectly shaped the destiny of man. They help to visualise historical realities and supplement their oral and written account. Maps are of various kinds. Globe gives a three dimensional representation of the earth and may be conveniently used in showing historical events like World Wars I and II and other events of universal character. Relief maps are useful in showing the depressions and elevations on the surface of earth which have influenced the course of history. Invasions, military operations, migration of the people and social intercourse, all bear the impact of the inequalities in the surface of the earth. Flat maps showing physical features, political divisions, population, rainfall, temperature, soil, vegetation, means of transport and communication of the world and other countries provide ample opportunities for illustrating a history lesson.

The teacher tries to substantiate his statements and narration with the help of these maps. He tries to explain various places of historical importance with the help of these maps. Empires of various rulers may be indicated with the help of these maps.

The teacher has to use a pointer for indicating things on the maps. The pointer should be quite pointed at the end so that these may not be any confusion with regard to the location of the place, that the teacher wishes to point out.

The maps should be so drawn and coloured that they may be clearly visible to the students. Writing about maps a scholar says, "The map is not merely an aid to history teaching. It is as essential as in the fundamentals in other works are to be understood. Only through the use of maps can the area and relative positions of political units be visualised and make it possible to indicate the development of states. The progress of military campaigns or of exploration or the general distinction of religions and languages".

3. Charts

Various types of charts are drawn by the teacher on black-board while teaching history. Such charts may be classified as: (i) Table charts, (ii) Genealogical charts, (iii) Flow charts etc.

(i) *Table Charts.* They represent historical data in a tabular form and with their help the pupil gains a comprehensive view of the facts at a sight such charts facilitate comparison and contrast between different historical phenomenon.

(ii) *Genealogical Charts.* Such charts are used to represent the growth and development of an empire, a dynasty or such other historical facts. They are quite useful in summarising historical topics.

(iii) *Flow Charts.* Such charts are generally used to represent organisational element and their functional relationship.

4. Black-Board or Chalk Board

It is one of the oldest and an important teaching aid. Black-boards have been in use since a long time but these days chalk boards are extensively used in teaching of history in place of black-boards. Making use of these boards teacher can illustrate many things. In the primary stage they can be used for presenting the subject-matter with illustrations. In the middle and secondary classes, these can be used to present various diagrams, charts, maps etc. It is a convenient and vehicle of illustration etc. Edgar Dale says, "It provides an opportunity for creativity and initiative, as one 'Visualises' an explanation or a 'demonstration'. Its purpose is to visualise curriculum by means of graphic demonstration".

Illustrations. These are the material aids. They are of three types:

(i) *Verbal illustration:* These are the oral examples presented as stories etc.

(ii) *Symbolic illustration:* They are mall structures which are presented as symbols of certain historical facts and events.

(iii) *Visual illustration:* They refers to such things as charts, models, diagrams, pictures etc.

5. Pictures

To understand the physical and social activities of man in the background of his physical and natural environments pictures are quite useful. They give two dimensional representation to historical phenomenon and help in making history real. Besides presenting portraits of great personalities, pictures may be conveniently utilised to represent men and ideas. They can be used to represent the essential facts of history.

In recent years with tremendous developments in the field of science and technology, with the help of projectors, the teacher can create the third dimension illusion, sustain the interest of the pupils in the topic and enable them to understand the past happenings in their true setting.

Various types of pictures in use are:

(a) *Still pictures.* These are projected with the help of opaque projector, film strip projector, magic lantern etc.

(b) *Motion pictures.* They represent historical events in their proper perspective, showing their casual sequence and continuity. The emotional impact of such films is enormous and historical facts and events are remembered easily.

(c) *Films.* There are various types of films such as: (i) Class-room films, (ii) Documentary films etc. These films can bring into class-room such an element of realism which cannot be attained by any other medium of instruction.

(d) *Film strips or Film slides.* These are easy and simple to use. Many a film strips covering various parts of history are available. These are quite helpful to give the students useful knowledge of our history in an interesting way.

6. Models

Since original materials are scarce and rare and even those that exist are beyond the reach of all schools, the history teacher may take the help of models to give as vivid a picture of historical objects as possible. *Model* is nothing but a replica of a thing that we want to present or explain. It makes the teaching of history interesting and gives concrete idea of the abstract things. Models can be used to depict different aspects of human life—political, economic, social, religious and cultural.

Making of models provides an opportunity for 'learning by doing' and enlivens the interest of the pupils in the topic. Models prepared by the students or purchased from the market should be properly labelled, mounted and displayed. Labels should be short and self-explanatory.

Qualities of a Model

(i) It should be simple to understand.

(ii) It should be useful.

(iii) It should be accurately drawn.

7. Magazines and Newspapers

Newspapers and magazines are the means of conveying the information about the current events. They also bring forth informations in regard to certain past events. They present various social and political problems before the people in greater detail.

7tudents of secondary classes must be encouraged to acquaint themselves, with the political and social problems and movements with the help of the newspapers and magazines. They have the following advantages.

(i) Newspapers and magazines broaden the outlook of the students, they develop their power of understanding. They also give them an idea of the systematic representation of the subject-matter.

(ii) They enrich the knowledge of the students and they get fully acquainted with the social and political movements of their state and country.

8. Diagrams

Diagrams represent historical facts and events with the help of visual symbols that convey a number of things within a short space and time. They help to present historical data in an interesting way and captivate attention of the pupils. Many themes such as, sources of history, important battles, administrative systems, comparison and contrast between religions, life in early civilisations may be diagramatically presented.

9. Posters

Posters are generally used for commercial purposes. They show pictures of peoples and objects. They can also give symbolic expression to ideas concerning local history. They can throw light on many aspects of human history.

10. Flash Cards

These are the cards on which written documents are printed in bold letters. Such cards are presented with the help of projector as a flash and students get a glance on them and comprehend the idea given in them. This technique introduces a dramatic element in teaching and captivates the attention of the pupils.

11. Graphs

Graphs are used for representing quantitative data showing comparison, trends, developments and relationships. With the help of simple lines, drawn vertically or horizontally, graphs supply visual imageries for abstract ideas and concepts in history. In the teaching of history the following kinds of graphs may conveniently be used:

(a) Time Line. Time line gives linear representation of

time. Time is the most abstract concept in history. Time line helps the pupils to gain time sense with the help of space symbols. An event happens at a particular time in history and at a particular place. We are interested to know its exact location on the long and unending line of time. In a time line, the length of time is symbolically represented by a line drawn horizontally of vertically. It gives a visual image of the sequence of events and their relative difference in their occurrence in time. It also helps us in comparing and contrasting and showing mutual relationship between events and happening at different places but at the same time.

(b) Hitsogram. Histogram represents an idea with the help of broad lines or narrow rectangles, drawn vertically or horizontally. The scale of values is placed at the bottom in horizontal and at the left in a vertical arrangement. The broad lines of rectangles may be coloured or differentiated in some other ways. Histograms may be used to represent growth and fall of empires or some other historical phenomena.

(c) Pictorial Graph. Pictorial graph expresses an idea or a concept with the help of picture symbols which are self-explanatory and appropriate. The symbols generally used are man, ship, horse, elephants, money, etc., and their total qualities are shown by proper number or multiple of the symbols.

12. Flannel Board

It is also sometimes referred to as flannel graph or felt board. It is made of wood, card board or straw board with colour led flannel or woollen cloth. It can be used as an effective teaching device in teaching of history. It can be used by the teacher to place various objects such as pictures 'cut-outs' from news papers or magazines etc.

Use a Flannel Board

Following points be kept in mind for effective use of flannel board:

(i) The teacher should collect a large number of pictures or wall cut diagrams etc., and make use of these one by one after proper selection.

(ii) Display the material on the flannel board in a sequence to develop the lesson.

(iii) Make proper use of flannel board in a sequence to develop the lesson.

(iv) Change the material on the board as frequently as possible.

(v) Flannel board can be used quite effectively for showing relationship between different parts or steps of a process.

Advantages

Some of the advantages of flannel board are as under:

(i) It is quite economical and easy to handle and operate.

(ii) The pictures or cuttings can be easily fixed and removed when required without spoiling the material. Thus the same material can be used for display many a times.

(iii) Any display material on the board hold the interest of students and arrests their attention.

(iv) Such boards enable a teacher to talk alongwith changing illustrations to develop a lesson.

13. Bulletin Board

It is a display board and has great value for the teaching of history. It is used for displaying pictures, drawings, compositions, posters, photographs, news paper clippings. Such bulletin boards can be specified for specific branches or topics in history. Such a board should be fixed at a conspicuous place in the history room. The material displayed should be directly concerned with the activities of the pupils. An effort be made to change the material on bulletin board as frequently as practicable. Whenever teacher starts a new topic he may ask the students to display the concerned material on the bulletin board and the teacher should specifically mention to the students the display material on the board while teaching a topic to the class. Students be asked to take the charge of bulletin board by rotation.

14. Radio

Radio can serve as an effective aid in teaching of history. The broadcasts from experts can be easily made available to all children. They transcend the limitations of space. All India Radio has in its regular features some programmes meant for school children. In such programmes generally talks on educational matters are broad casted. The topic, date and time of such broadcast are given in advance by A.I.R. They touch many aspects in history of India. They throw light on the life of personalities who have soaped the history of our country. There are also light programmes consisting of music, drama, comics etc. There are also general broadcasts about important speeches and declarations of important personalities on important occasions.

To make a best use of all these talks and broadcasts the following points be kept in mind:

(i) The school broadcasts should be integrated with class-work and class projects.

(ii) Every school broadcast should serve as the starting point of discussion between the teacher and the pupil.

(iii) To derive the maximum benefit, from such a talk, the class should be supplied with ample supporting literature generously illustrated.

Advantages

(i) The radio broadcasts are of high intellectual and educational value and help in ordering the mental horizon of the children.

(ii) It brings dramatic feeling into the class-room.

(iii) It transcends the limitation of time and space.

(iv) It provides an opportunity to the students for coming in contact with great personalities through their voices.

(v) It gives the pupils a sense of participation.

(vi) It facilitates group instructions.

Limitations

(i) When the receiving set is not working satisfactorily a sense of strain prevails in the class-room.

(ii) Some students ate poor listeners and may not be benefited by such talks.

Keeping in view the utility of radio broadcasts UNESCO has recommended that compulsory arrangement for a radio set should be made in every school and radio broadcasts be directed for this purpose.

15. Television

The role of television in the present day world is becoming more and more important as a teaching aid. In it the advantages of radio and film are combined. These days U.G.C. programmes are a regular feature on 'Door Darshan'.

It is "medium of mass communication which far surpasses in effectiveness anything our civilisation has yet known." It accomplishes certain communicative tasks which are incomparable in their effectiveness.

Television, with its two-fold engagement of the eye and the ear, like the motion pictures, can bring us into contact with events in an exciting and clarifying way. It is a "means by which teachers, parents, children, and all citizens may share a common experience at the same time." It is a versatile vehicle to use a beauty of audio-visual materials.

The potentialities of television in history teaching are enormous. It can transport the places and sites of historical importance which the pupils are unable to visit. It can bring the experts in the classroom not only in voice but in person. It can make available to the classroom rare examples of natural or man-made objects.

16. Films and Cinema

Today cinema is a very powerful agency of propagation of ideas and knowledge. Through it, knowledge can be disseminated very effectively. It also brings about recreation and so the students do not feel bored while acquiring knowledge through cinema or films.

In foreign countries, films on historical events and historical places are made and they are exhibited in the classrooms as well as in the picture balls. They are generally called documentaries.

Coins and other historical material can also form the subject-matter of the firms.

17. Cinema Projectors

This is the mechanism through which the films are exhibited. If the History laboratory has a light weight cinema projector, small films may be exhibited in the class and this shall be of great use to the students.

Johnsons has laid good deal of stress on the use of films in the teaching of history. He said: Dozens of historical film have stirred children to ask historical questions and when such questions are brought to school, almost' any teacher is likely to suggest it best to the children 'look it up in some history or encylopaedia'."

Eddison has gone a step further. He thinks, the films in themselves can serve the purpose of the teachers. He has remarked, "Films are inevitable as practically the sole Teaching method".

18. Epidiascope

It is a costly instrument and is used to project opaque objects as well as transparent objects. The pictures projected are much brighter and needs a less powerful light and the need of absolutely dark room is not there.

The name *epidiascope* is given to it because it works as an *episode* when it is used to throw an image of an opaque object. When it is used to project a slide it works as a *diascope* and so *epidiascope* is a combination of the two.

Advantages

(i) It can be operated in a room which may not be absolutely dark.

(ii) It can project the original colours of the pictures or photographs.

(iii) The projection or the screen can be kept for sometime during which teacher can explain it and discuss it in the class.

(iv) It provides the teacher an option to handle the lesson according to himself.

19. Museum

A museum ought to be a very valuable part of history department in school. Museum not only provides necessary help in teaching but also helps in creating the right type of atmosphere in the school. The importance of museum has nicely been summarised by a scholar, "It is true that the wealth of painting, music, sculpture, dress, industry tools and religious outlook, all the significant phases of life that are well-illustrated in the important museums of the land, cannot be adequately represented in the school history museum, but an attempt must be made imagination to picture the life that is gone, and yet at the same time, influences the present in a subtle though in a very real way."

In the organisation of museum both teacher and students have to take an active part. They should help the following points in mind:

(i) Systematic arrangement of various exhibits.

(ii) Clear and complete description of various parts of an exhibit.

For this purpose an ideal arrangement will be that a card of suitable (5" x 4") be attached, to each exhibit, containing the following information typed on it:

(i) Name of the exhibit.

(ii) Place from where the exhibit has been obtained and relevant information.

(iii) Importance of the exhibit.

The language used to provide above information should be simple and all efforts be made to avoid phrases and technical terms in the description of the exhibit.

20. Tours and Excursions

Excursions and trips provide an opportunity for the direct study of original materials inhistory. Visits to places of worship, tombs etc., help to break the monotony of class-room lectures and provide a chance to come in direct contact with historical realities.

It has been said that "History is the action and reaction of nature and thought." In other words, it means that history should be studied in the light of the effrect of various events that have their reaction on the social life.

For organising such trips the teacher should survey

various local possibilities and then should carefully plan all the details of the trip or excursion and then during such a trip he should see that every detail of the plan is adhered to. The trip should be held in an informal atmosphere. During the trip or immediately afterwards the teacher should try to correlate the experiences gained to the history lessons.

An evaluation of the trip is essential. For this teacher should invite comments and remarks. Such as evaluation will provide basis for other trips and help in the removal of their shortcomings.

Advantages

(i) It makes class-room teaching interesting.

(ii) It helps to develop love for cultural heritage.

(iii) It helps to develop a sense of patriotism.

(iv) It helps in the development of the knowledge of local history.

(v) It helps to develop mental faculties and powers.

REVIEW QUESTIONS

1. Prepare a list of the teaching aids, which you consider absolutely essential for the successful teaching of History. Give reasons as well.
2. Mention in detail the devices you would employ in the teaching of History in order to make the past 'real.'
3. Describe the various devices you would use for making the past real in the teaching of history.

16

Salient Features of Ancient Indian History

The study of ancient Indian history is important for several reasons. It tells us how, when and where people developed the earliest cultures in India. It indicates how they started agriculture which made life secure and settled. It shows how the ancient Indians discovered and utilised natural resources, and how they created the means for their livelihood. We come to know how they took to farming, spinning, weaving, metal-working, and so on: how they cleared forests; and how they founded villages, cities, and Anally large kingdoms.

Ancient Indian history is interesting because India proved to be a crucible of numerous races. The pre-Aryans, Indo-Aryans, the Greeks, the Scythians, the Hunas, the Turks, etc., made India their home. Each ethnic group contributed its mite to the making of Indian culture. All these peoples mixed up so inextricably with one another that at present none of them can be identified in their original form.

India has since ancient times been the land of several religions. Ancient India witnessed the birth of Hinduism, Jainism and Buddhism; but all these cultures and religions intermingled and acted and reacted upon one another in such a manner that though people speak differ-ent languages, practise different religions, and observe different social customs, they follow certain common, styles, of life throughout the country. Our country shows a deep underlying unity in spite,of great diversity.

The ancients strove for unity. They looked upon this vast subcontinent as one land. The name *Bharatavarsha* or the land of Bharata was given to the whole country, and the people were called *Bharatasantati* or the descendants of Bharata. Our ancient poets, philosophers and writers viewed,the, country as an integral unit. They spoke of the land stretching from the Himalayas to the sea as the proper domain of a single universal monarch. The kings who tried to establish their authority from the Himalayas to the Cape Comorin and from the valley of the Brahmaputra in the east to the land beyond the Indus in the west were universally praised. They were called *Chakravartins.* This kind of political unity was attained at least twice. In the third century B.C., Asoka extended his empire over the whole country, except for the extreme south. Again, in the fourth century A.D. Samudragupta carried his victorious arms from the Ganga to the borders of the Tamil Land. In the seventh century the Chalukya king, Pulakesin, defeated Harshavardhana who was called the lord of the whole of north India. In spite of lack of political unity political formations all over the country assumed more or less the same shape. The idea that India constituted one single geographical unit persisted in the minds of the conquerors and cultural leaders. The unity of India was also recognised by foreigners. They first came into contact with the people living on the Sindhu or the Indus and so they named the whole country after this river, The word *Hind* is derived from the Sanskrit term *Sindhu,* and in course of time the country came to be known as 'India' in Greek, and 'Hind' in Persian and Arabic languages.

We find continuous efforts for the linguistic and cultural unity of the country. In the third century B.C. Prakrit served as the *lingua franca* of the country. Throughout the length and breadth of India, Asoka's inscriptions were written in the Prakrit language. Later Sanskrit acquired the same position and served as the state language in the remotest parts of the country. The process began in the Gupta period in the fourth century A.D. Although, politically the country was divided into numerous small states in the post-Gupta period, the official documents were written in Sanskrit.

Another notable fact is that the ancient epics, the *Ramayana* and the *Mahabharata,* were studied with the same zeal and devotion in the land of the Tamils as in the intellectual circles of Banaras and Taxila. Originally composed in Sanskrit these epics came to be presented in different local languages. But whatever the form in which Indian cultural values and ideas were expressed, the substance remained the same throughout the country.

Indian history deserves our attention because of a peculiar type of social system which developed in this country. In north India arose the varna caste system which came to prevail almost all over the country. The foreigners who came to India in ancient times were absorbed in one caste or the other. The caste system affected even the Christians and the Muslims. The converts belonged to some caste and even when they left Hinduism to join the new religion they continued to maintain some of their old caste practices.

II. THE STONE AGE

The Old Stone Age

Man has been living in India roughly from 500,000 B.C. He used tools of unpolished, undressed, rough stones, which have been found in south India and in the Soan river valley in north-western India. The chips of Stone were pebbles used for hunting, cutting and other purposes. In this period man barely managed to gather his food and lived on hunting. He had no knowledge of cultivation and house building. This phase generally continue till 8,000 B.C.

Palaeolithic tools, which could be as old as 100,000 B.C., have been found in the Chotanagpur plateau. Such tools belonging to 25,000 B.C. 10,000 B.C. have been found in Kurnool district in Andhra Pradesh about 55 km from Kurnool. In association with them bone implements and animal remains have also been discovered. They show how man lived exclusively on hunting and food gathering in the Old Stone Age. The Puranas speak of people who lived on roots and fruits; some of these people have been living in the old way in the hills and caves till modern times

The Old Stone Age or the Palaeolithic culture of India developed in the Pleistocene period or the Ice Age, which is a geological period. The Pleistocene period comes immediately before the geological period Holocene or recent period, in which we live and which began about 10,000 years ago. We do not know when the Pleistocene period exactly began, but human remains associated with stone tools have been dated in east Africa, as early as 3.5 million years ago. In India the first human occupation, as suggested by stone tools, is not earlier than the Middle Pleistocene, which perhaps began about 500,000 years ago. In the Pleistocene period ice sheets covered a great portion of the earth's surface, particularly in the higher altitudes and their peripheries. But the tropical regions, excepting the mountains, were free from ice. On the other hand they underwent a period of great rainfall.

Phases in the Palaeolithic Age

The Old Stone or the Palaeolithic Age in India is divided into three phases according to the nature of the stones tools used by the people and also according to the nature of change in the climate. These phases are the Early Old Stone Age, the Middle Old Stone Age and the

Upper Old Stone Age. The first is called Early or Lower Palaeolithic, the second, Middle Palaeolithic, and the third, Upper Palaeolithic, The Lower Palaeolithic or the Early Old Stone Age covers the greater part of the Ice Age. Its characteristic feature is the use of hand-axes. These axes found in India are more or less similar to those of Western Asia, Europe and Africa. Stone tools were used mainly for chopping, and hence these tools are called *choppers*. The Early Old Stone Age sites are found in the valley of the river Soan in Punjab, on the banks of the Narmada in central India, at the mouth of the Godavari and also between the Tungabhadra and the Pennar. Hand-axes have been found in a deposit of the time of the second Himalayan glaciation became less humid.

The Middle Old Stone Age or Middle Palaeolithic industries are all based upon flakes. These flakes are found in different parts of India and show regional variations. The principal tools are varieties of scrapers made of flakes. We also find a large number of borers. The Middle Old Stone Age sites in India are found in the Soan valley. Here we notice a crude pebble industry in strata contemporary with the third Himalayan glaciation. The artifacts of this age are also found at several places on the river Narmada, and also at several places south of the Tungabhadra river.

The Upper Palaeolithic phase or the Upper Old Stone Age was less humid. It coincided with the last phase of the Ice Age when climate became comparatively warm. In the world context it is marked by the appearance of new flint industries and of men of the modern type. In India it is marked by the use of blades and burins. These stone tools have been found in, Andhra, Karnataka, Maharashtra, Bhopal and Chotanagpur plateau.

It is difficult to estimate the beginnings of the Palaeolithic Age. It is said that in the world context human remains associated with stone tools are as old as 3.5 million years. But it seems that through several stages the modern human being (*Homo Sapiens*) first appeared in the Upper Palaeolithic Age.

The Late Stone Age

The Upper Palaeolithic Age came to an end with the end of the Ice Age around 8000 B.C., and the climate became warm and dry. Climatic changes brought about changes in fauna and flora and made it possible for human beings to move to new areas. Since then there have not been any major changes in climatic conditions. From 8000 B.C. began an intermediate stage in stone age culture, which is called the Mesolitaic Age. It intervened as a transitional phase between the Palaeolithic Age and the Neolithic or New Stone Age, and is also called the Late Stone Age. In the case of India it started about 8000 B.C. and continued up to about 4000 B.C.

The characteristic tools of the Late Stone Age are microliths. The Late Stone Age sites are found in good numbers in Chotanagpur, central India, and also south of the river Krishna.

It would thus appear that the palaeolithic sites are found in practically all part of the country except the alluvial plains of the Indus and the Ganga and the central and eastern mountains.

So far the finds of the Late Stone Age have not been dated scientifically, but there is no doubt that these finds preceded the Neolithic Age.

The New Stone Age

Although in the world context the New Stone Age began much earlier, in 7000 B.C., neolithic settlements in the Indian sub-continent are not older than 4000 B.C. Some of the settlements which have been found arose as late as the first millenium B.C. insouth India and eastern India.

The people of this age used tools and implemtns of polished stone. They particularly used stone axes, which have been found in large numbers throghout the greater part of the country. This cutting tool was put to various uses by the people, and in ancient legends Parasurama became an important axe-wielding hero.

Based on the types of axes used by the neolithic settlers. We notice three importnat areas of neolithic settlements. One area is to be found in the north in the valley of Kashmir at a place called Burzahom at a distance of about 20 km from Srinagar. The neolithic people lived ther on a plateau in pits, and probably had a hunting and fishing economy. They did not seem to have been acquainted with agriculture or domestication of animals. They used not only polished tools of stone, but what is more interesting, they used numerous tools and weapons made of bone. They only other place which has yielded considerable bone implements in India is Chirand, which is 40 kilometres west of Patna on the northern side of the Ganga. These bone implements have been found in a late neolithic set-up in an area with about 100 cm rainfall. The settlement became possible because of the open land available on account of the joining together of four rivers, Ganga, Son, Gandak and Ghaghra at this place. The people of Burzahom used coarse grey pottery. It is interesting that the Burzahom domestic dogs were buried with their masters in their graves. Pit dwelling and the placing of domestic dogs in the graves of the masters do not seem to be the practice with neolithic people in any other part of India. The earliest date for the Burzahom is about 2400 B.C., but the bones recovered from Chirand cannot be dated earlier than 1600 B.C., and they possibly belong to a stone-copper phase.

The second group of neolithic people lived in south India south of the Godavari river. They usually settled on the tops of granite hills or on plateaus near the river banks. They used stone axes and also some kind of stone blades. Terracota figurines suggest that they kept a large number of cattle. They possessed cattle sheep and goats. They used rubbing stone querns, which shows that they were acquainted with the art of producing grains.

The third area from which neolithic tools have been recovered is in the hills of Assam. Neolithic tools are also found in the Garo hills in Meghalaya on the north-eastern frontier of India. We have ho means of dating them. In addition to this we also find a number of neolithic settlements in Baluchistan which seem to be the oldest.

Some of the important neolithic sites or those with neolithic layers that have been excavated include Maski, Brahmagiri, Hallur, Kodekal, Sanganakallu, T. Narsipur and Takkalakota in Karnataka, and Paiyampalli in Tamil Nadu. Piklihal and Utnur are important neolithic sites in Andhra Pradesh. The neolithic phase seems to have covered the period from about 2500 B.C. to 1000 B.C., although the earliest scientifically determined date for Utnur is 2300 B.C.

The neolithic settlers in Piklihal were cattle-herders. They domesticated cattle, sheep, goats, etc. They set up seasonal camps surrounded by cowpens made with posts and stakes. In these enclosures they accumulated cow dung. Then the entire camping ground was put to fire and cleared for camping in the next season. Both ash mounds and habitation sites have been discovered in Piklihal.

The later neolithic settlers were agnculturists, who lived in circular or rectangular houses made of mud and reed. It is held that the primitive people living in circular houses owned property in common. In any case, these neolithic people led a settled life. They produced *ragi* and horsegram *(kulathi)*. Their polished tools also included microlith blades.

Since in the neolithic phase several settlements came to be acquainted with the cultivation of cereals and the domestication of animals, they needed pots in which they could store their foodgrains and milk. They further needed pots for cooking and eating. Hence hand-made pottery is found in the early stage. Later they used footwheels to turn up pots.

Neolithic celts have also been found in the Orissa hill areas, and it is likely that rice cultivation and small-scale settlements begun in this part of the country quite early.

The period between 7000 B.C. and 3000 B.C. saw the first technological revolution in, history in Western Asia, because the people developed the arts of cultivation, weaving, building houses, domestication of animals, etc. But the Neolithic Age in India began at a later date. Some of the important crops, including wheat and barley, came to be cultivated in the Indian subcontinent in this period, and the first villages also appeared in this part of the world. It appears that the people, were now on the threshold of civilisation.

The people of the Stone Age suffered from one great limitation. Since they had to depend entirely on tools and weapons made of stone, they could not found settlements far away from the hilly areas. They could settle down only in the hilly river valleys. Further, even with great effort they could not produce more than what they needed for their bare subsistence.

III. THE INDUS VALLEY CIVILIZATION (3250 B.C.—2000 B.C.)

Up to the beginning of the twentieth century the general impression among historians was that the secondary stage of culture began in India after the advent of the Aryans about 1500 BC so that Indian culture was regarded as the youngest among the ancient cultures. But in the first quarter of this century the excavations made by the Archaeological Department of India at Harappa in west Punjab and Mohenjodaro in Sind led to the startling discovery that much earlier than that, in the bronze age, there existed in the valley of the Indus a fairly advanced urban civilisation. Later excavations in other parts of the country have so far revealed that in area this culture covered the whole of Punjab, Sind, Baluchistan and a considerable part of Kathiawad extending on one side to west Uttar Pradesh and on the other side along the coastal region on the west to a part of south India. This culture is believed to have reached its zenith about 3000 BC. But it had come into being at least 250 years earlier and must have continued till about 2000 BC when it was destroyed probably by barbarous hordes from the west. So it should be counted among the oldest cultures of the world along with those of Elam, Sumeria, Babylonia, ancient Egypt and ancient China. The Dravidians in south India, who were in close contact with the Sind Valley Civilisation, had by 2000 BC reached a high stage of cultural life and kept the torch of civilisation burning during the centuries preceding the advent of the Aryans when north India was plunged in darkness. So we can rightly say that India has maintained a more or less advanced cultural life since its emergence 5000 years ago. No other country except China affords an example of a civilisation continuing without a break for such a long time.

The ruins of the ancient cities found in Mohenjodaro and Harappa show, according to Sir John Marshall, that the standard of civilised life reached by the people inhabiting these cities was higher than that of the ancient Babylonians and Egyptians and equal to that of the Sumerians. They were big cities with networks of regular wide roads, canals for irrigation and sewers for drainage. This shows that they had not only made fairly good progress in civil engineering but had some idea of town-planning also and that there was some civic body like a municipality or a local board. Among the archaeological finds in Mohenjodaro and Harappa are instruments, weapons and utensils made of earth, copper and bronze. Some of the earthenware are painted. Figures of human beings and animals made of baked clay and bronze hava been found in abundance. The most common among these is the figure of a semi-nude woman wearing a fan-shaped cap. This represents the mother-goddess worshipped by them. But the best specimens of the art of that age are seals bearing pictures of Brahmani bulls, elephants, buffaloes, tigers, etc., or inscribed with pictographs. Ornaments of gold, faience and beads, ivory dice and hairpins bear testimony to the considerable progress which the various industries had made. The gold and silver ornaments in particular were, in the words of Sir John Marshall, 'so well finished and so highly polished that they might have come out of a Bond Street jeweller's of today rather than from a prehistoric house of 5000 years ago'. But the most remarkable thing was that in the valley of the Indus, people had not only learnt to grow cotton but had developed the textile industry which, for centuries afterwards, was unknown in other countries. The discovery of Indus Valley seals in Mesopotamia, Arabia and other countries of West Asia is an indication of commercial and cultural relations which must have existed between these countries and India.

As the pictographs inscribed on the seals of Mohenjodaro and Harappa have not yet been deciphered, we know very little about the mental and spiritual life of the ancient inhabitants of the Indus Valley. All that we can say on the strength of the available material is that their religious beliefs and practices are to some extent reflected in Hinduism. The figures shown on the seals provide ample evidence that they worshipped Shakti or the mother-goddess and sacrificed goats and other animals to her. There is no doubt that the Hindus inherited both these practices from them. Some seals have been found with representations of a god resembling Shiva. In one of these he is shown with three faces wearing a horned head-dress which was replaced later by Hindus with a *trisula* or trident. The worship of rivers, animals and trees and also the *pipal* is traced to that period. Among animals the bull, the buffalo, the tiger and the elephant were possibly regarded as sacred. In Hindu mythology the bull became the vehicle *(vahana)* of Shiva. The use of the swastika and wheel as the symbols of the sun also dates from that period. Some scholars think that the stress laid on belief in spirits and magic in the *Yajurveda* and the *Atharvaveda,* which is not in keeping with the teachings of the *Rigveda,* was due to the influence exercised by traditions of the Indus Valley Civilisation.

Opinions differ about the origin of the builders of this civilisation. Some regard them as immigrant Aryans or Sumerians and some as Dravidians. But most scholars agree that they belonged to the old Austric race with a mixture of the races coming from the Mediterranean coast. But before reaching the level of an urban civilisation they had lived in India for centuries so that their culture was in spite of some resemblance with the Sumerian, on the whole, essentially Indian. It is very likely that when further research reveals to us a complete picture of the Indus Valley Civilisation we shall find in it all the essential features of what later became the common culture of India.

Even now there are strong reasons to believe that the Indus Valley culture was in its last phase closely associated with the Dravidian culture and both had a deep influence on each other. We will find later that the Dravidians made an important contribution to the national culture of India. So if the Indus Valley civilisation has not played a direct role in shaping the present culture of India it has certainly exercised an indirect influence through the Dravidian, culture.

IV. TWO STREAMS: THE DRAVIDIAN CULTURE AND THE VEDIC CULTURE OF THE ARYANS (2000 BC—1000 BC)

About 2000 BC when the Indus Valley civilisation was being destroyed in north-west India by the ravages of wild invaders, the Dravidian Tamil culture in South India had reached a very high level of development. Archaeological finds point to a long period of commercial and cultural exchange between the Indus Valley culture and the Tamil culture. In the Deccan and other parts of south India burial urns and other earthen pots exactly like those which were, used in Mohenjodaro and Harappa have been found. Excavations in the Indus Valley have yielded plenty of shells and pearls which must have come from south India. The presence of nearly fifty per cent Dravidian words in the Brohi language spoken in some parts of Baluchistan is a strong indication that there was a close cultural contact between the Indus Valley and south India in prehistoric times. Obviously this must have been before the destruction of the Indus Valley Civilisation about 2000 BC and by that time the Dravidian culture must have reached a very high level so that it could exercise such a deep linguistic influence over an advanced urban civilisation.

According to tradition, early Tamil literature can be traced as far back as 2500 BC and there is positive evidence that long before 1000 BC south India had had three *Sangams* (academies) at old Madura, Kapadapuram, and modern Madurai. The most prominent member of the first *Sangam* was Agastya who wrote the first Tamil grammar called *Agathiam.* There is a legend that he was an Aryan preacher from the north who had come to south India to propagate the Vedic religion. His twelve disciples wrote a large number of treatises on grammar, literature, music, dance, etc. One of these treatises *Tolkappiam,* written about 1000 BC is still extant. It deals essentially with Tamil grammar but throws valuable light on the cultural life of ancient Dravidians.

In prehistoric times south India, the present home of Dravidian culture, extended very far to the south of the present peninsula. In course of time much of it was submerged under water by continuous violent storms. In one Dravidian community the matriarchal system prevailed and generally mothers were given a high status throughout Dravidian society. There was no rigid caste system. But later, various classes based partly on birth and partly on occupation developed. The most common religious cult was that of the mother-goddess. Various trees, demons, spirits and the snake (Naga Raja) were also worshipped.

The Dravidians had reached a high level of civilisation. They had made considerable progress in agriculture and engineering, put up dams across rivers for irrigation and built cities with walls around them. Their industries, specially the weaving of cotton and woollen cloth, dying, making gold and silver ornaments inlaid with precious stones, were fairly advanced. Trade by land and sea was carried on with the countries of east and west Asia. There is evidence of cultural contact between south India and Egypt about 2000 BC. Dravidians had their own script, numerals and calendar. The progress which they had made in science and literature can be judged by the existence of three academies in an age when the rest of the world had no idea of such institutions.

About 1500 BC while the Dravidian culture was flourishing in the south, the dark period following the destruction of the Indus Valley Civilisation was coming to an end in the north-west and immigrant Aryans were laying the foundations of a new culture infused with vigour and vitality. There is much difference of opinion about the original home of the Aryans. Formerly, the general idea was that they were the inhabitants of Central Asia. But later researches in the field have made some scholars think that they originally belonged to Scandinavia, others that they inhabited the part of Asian Russia to the east of the Urals. But the only thing which can be said with certainty is that they came to India from the north-west. The hymns to their gods, which they composed probably after they had come to India, were later collected in the *Rig Veda*. The *Rig Veda* is not only a holy scripture of Hinduism but also the earliest document of Indian history. Most historians think that the hymns of the *Rig Veda* were composed between 1500 BC and 1000 BC. The religious and cultural life of the Aryans during these 500 years was deeply influenced by the *Rigveda* and it is also the source of all that we know about the period. So it is called the period of Vedic culture.

The hub of this culture was the land between the Sutlej and the Yamuna in east Punjab, and it was gradually spreading eastwards over the Doab or the region between the Yamuna and Ganga. The Aryans had not yet completely subdued the aboriginal tribes whom they called the Dasyus and against whom they were engaged in continuous warfare. They had brought with them a primitive nomadic culture. But their religious ideas and practices, their art of warfare and their poetry were fairly advanced. In India they began to live the settled life of peasants and the various tribes established their little rural democracies.

Representative bodies of tribal chiefs known as the *Sabha* and the *Samiti* ruled under the general control of the raja or king. Kingship was usually hereditary. The main function of the king was to command the army in battle. In this he was assisted by the Commander-in-chief. Next in importance to the king was the Grand Priest *(Purohita)* who presided over sacrificial ceremonies and acted in many cases as the medicine-man curing disease through incantation *(mantra)*.

In the beginning, Aryan society consisted of two classes—the nobles and the common people. But there were no hereditary castes. When the peaceful conditions in India and settled agricultural life had tamed the Aryans, and they had given up fighting the aborigines and wanted to assimilate them in their social system, their pride made them take special precautions that the blood of the Dasyus did not mix with theirs. So the Dasyus were constituted into a separate caste called the Sudras with the lowest position in society and the Aryans were forbidden to intermarry with them. Later, social distinctions became more pronounced and rigid. Among the Aryans themselves the ruling and fighting class (Kshatriyas), the priests (Brahmins) the peasants and traders (Vaishyas), grew into separate hereditary castes with restrictions on intermarriage, etc. This social gradation was given a religious sanction by invoking a verse from the *Rig Veda* to the effect that the Brahmins cams from the face of the Creator, the Kshatriyas from His arms, the Vaishyas from His thighs and the Sudras from the soles of His feet.

The basic unit of society was the family which was governed by the patriarchal system. That is to say the father was regarded as the head of the heritage passed from father to son. The mother was treated with great respect but her position in the household was inferior to that of the father. As a rule monogamy was the most widely practised form of marriage.

The Aryans had taken to agriculture but cattle-breeding still held an important place in their economy and was regarded as an occupation superior to that of tilling the soil. Cattle was priced high and used as a measure of value and medium of exchange. Their flesh was generally eaten by the people. Sheep and goats were also kept and horses were used for drawing war chariots. Houses were built of mud. The art of making bronze utensils and weapons had made great progress. Spinning, weaving, dyeing, and the carpenter's and goldsmith's trade were also common.

Singing and dancing were commonly practised but the most popular pastime was gambling. People drank intoxicating liquors in excess, specially the juice of the *Soma* which acquired a religious significance as seen in the *Samaveda*.

However, the Aryans had not reached any significant level of material civilisation and had not yet learnt to build cities. But their religious consciousness was of a higher order than that of other ancient peoples. They neither built temples nor worshipped images. Their devotion consisted in burning fires in their hearths, singing hymns to their gods and offering rice, milk, *soma* or animals as sacrifice. In this they were guided by the priests. Before coming to India their objects of worship were natural phenomena. Their principal gods were Indra (thunder), Varuna, Mitra, Surya (the sun), Savitra, Pushana, Vishnu, Usha (the dawn), Arti (the earth), Vayu (air), Agni (fire). The *soma* tree was also regarded as sacred because the feeling of exhilaration induced by its intoxicating juice was taken for the state of spiritualbliss.

The Dravidian culture in south India and the Vedic culture of the Aryans in north-west India were in those days two streams flowing apart. But the time was near when the confluence of the two was to give birth to the first national culture of India.

V. THE HARAPPAN CIVILISATION

Geographical Extent

The Indus or the Harappan culture is older than the chalcolithic cultures which have been treated earlier. It arose in the north-western part of the Indian subcontinent. It is called Harappan because this civilisation was discovered first in 1921 at the modern site of Harappa situated in the province of West Panjab in Pakistan. The Harappan culture covered parts of the Punjab, Sindh, Baluchistan, Gujarat, Rajasthan and the fringes of western Uttar Pradesh. It extended from the district of Rupar in the Punjab in the north to the Narmada estuary in the south, and from the Makran coast of Baluchistan in the west to Meerut in the north-east. The area formed a triangle and accounted for about 1,299,600 square kilometres, which is larger than Pakistan and certainly bigger than ancient Egypt and Mesopotamia. No other cultural zone in the third and second millenium B.C in the world was as large as the Harappan zone.

Although over 250 Harappan sites are known, only six can be regarded as cities. Of these the two most important cities were Harappa in the Punjab and Mohenjodaro in Sindh, both forming parts of Pakistan. Situated at a distance of 483 kilometres they were linked together by the Indus. A third city lay at Chanhu-daro about 130 km south of Mohenjodaro in Sindh, and a fourth at Lothal in Gujarat at the head of the Gulf of Cambay. A fifth city lay at Kalibangan in northern Rajasthan. A sixth called Banwali is situated in Hissar district in Haryana. It saw two cultural phases, pre-Harappan and Harappan, similar to that of Kalibangan. To the Harappan period belong the remains of mud-brick platforms and of streets and drains. The Harappan culture is noticeable in its mature and flourishing stage at all these six places; its later phase is found in Rangpur and Rojdi in Gujarat.

Town Planning and Structures

The Harappan culture was distinguished by its system of town-planning. Harappa and Mohenjodaro each had its own citadel or acropolis, which was possibly occupied by members of the ruling class. Below the citadel in each city lay a lower town containing brick houses, which were inhabited by the common people. The remarkable thing about the arrangement of the houses in the cities is that they followed the grid system. Roads cut across one another almost at right angles, and the city was divided into so many blocks.

The most important public place of Mohenjodaro seems to be the Great Bath, comprising the tank which is situated in the citadel mound. It is an example of beautiful brickwork. It measures 11.88 X 7.01 metres and 2.43 metres deep. Flights of steps at either end lead to the surface. There are side rooms for changing clothes. The floor of the Bath was made of burnt bricks. Water was drawn from a large well in an adjacent room, and an outlet from one corner of the Bath led to a drain. It is suggested that the Great Bath served ritual bathing, which was so vital to any religious ceremony in India.

In Mohenjodaro the largest building is a granary, which is 45.71 metres long and 15.23 metres wide. But in the citadel of Harappa we find as many as six granaries. We come across a series of brick platforms which formed the basis for two rows of six granaries. Each granary measured 15.23 metres X 6.09 metres and lay within a few metres of the river's bank. The combined floor space of the twelve units would be about 838.1025 square metres. Approximately it had the same area as the Great Granary at Mohenjodaro. To the sough of the granaries at Harappa lay working floors consisting of the rows of circular brick platforms. These were evidently meant for threshing grain because wheat and barley have been found in the crevices of the floors. At Harappa were also built two-roomed barracks, which possibly accommodated labourers.

At Kalibangan also we notice in the southern part brick platforms, which may have been used for granaries. Thus it would appear that granaries constituted an important part of the Harappan cities.

The use of burnt bricks in the Harappan cities is remarkable, because in the contemporary buildings of Egypt dried bricks were mainly used. We find the use of baked bricks in contemporary Mesopotamia, but they were used to a much larger extent in the Harappan cities.

The drainage system of Mohenjodaro was very impressive. In almost all cities every big or small house and its own courtyard and bathroom. In Kalibangan many houses and their wells. Water flowed from the house to the streets which had drains. Sometimes these streets were covered with bricks and sometimes with stone slabs. The street drains were equipped with manholes. The remains of street and drains have also been found at Banwali. Altogether the drainage system and the quality of the domestic bath-rooms and drains are remarkable, and the drainage system of Harappa is almost unique. Perhaps no other civilisation gave so much attention to health and cleanliness as the Harappan.

Agriculture

Comparatively rainless, the Indus region is not so fertile these days. Its prosperous villages and towns show that it was fertile in ancient times. At present it has only a rainfall of about 15cm. In the fourth century B.C. one of the historians of Alexander informs us that Sindh was a fertile part of the country. In earlier times the Indus possessed more natural vegetation which attracted more rainfall. It supplied timber fuel for baking bricks on a large scale, and also for construction. In course of time, natural vegetation was destroyed by the extension of agriculture, large-scale grazing and supply of fuel. A far more important reason for the fertility of the area seems to have been the annual inundation in the Indus river. Walls made of burnt bricks raised for village defence show that floods took place annually. The Indus carried far more alluvial soil that the Nile in Egypt and deposited it on the flood plains. Just as the Nile created Egypt and supported its people, so also the Indus created Sindh and fed its people. The Indus people sowed seeds in the flood plains in November, when the flood water receded, and reaped their harvests of wheat and barley in April before the advent of the next flood. No hoe or ploughshare has been discovered, but the furrows discovered in the pre-Harappan phase at Kalibangan show that the fields were ploughed in Rajasthan in the Harappan period. The Harappans probably used the wooden ploughshare. We do not know whether the plough was drawn by men or oxen. Stone sickles may have been used for harvesting the crops. *Gabarbands* or *nalas* enclosed by dams for storing water were a feature in parts of Baluchistan and Afghanistan, but channel or canal irrigation seems to have been absent. The Harappan villages, mostly situated near the flood plains, produced sufficient foodgrains not only to feed themselves but also the town people. They must have worked very hard to meet their own requirements as well as those of the artisans, merchants and others, who lived in the city and who were not directly concerned with food producing activities.

The Indus people produced wheat, barley, *rai* peas, etc. They produced two types of wheat and barley. A good quantity of barley has been discovered at Banwali. In addition to this, they produced sesamum and mustard. But the position seems to have been different with the Harappans at Lothal. It seems that as early as 1800 B.C., the people of Lothal used rice, whose remains have been found. Foodgrains were stored in huge granaries in both Mohenjodaro and Harappa, and possibly in Kalibangan. Probably, cereals were received as taxes from peasants, and stored in granary for the payment of wages. This can be said on the analogy of Mesopotamian cities where wages were paid in barley. The Indus people were the earliest people to produce cotton. Because cotton was first produced in this area the Greeks and it *sindon*, which is derived from Sindh.

Domestication of Animals

Although the Harappans practised agriculture, animals were kept on a large scale. Oxen, buffaloes, goats, sheep and pigs were domesticated. The humped bulls were favoured by the Harappans. From the very beginning dogs were regarded as pets. Cats were also domesticated and signs of the feet of both dogs and cats have been noticed. They also kept asses and camels, which were possibly used as beasts of burden. Evidence of the horse comes from a doubtful terracotta figurine from Lothal. The remains of the horse have been reported from Surkotada, situated on the west of Gujarat and belong to around 2000 B.C., but it is clear that this animal was not in regular use in Harappan times. Elephants were well known to the Harappans, who were also acquainted with the rhinoceros. The contemporary Sumerian cities in Mesopotamia practically produced the same foodgrains and domesticated the same animals as the Harappans did. But the Harappan people in Gujarat produced rice and domesticated elephants, which was not the case with the people of Mesopotamian cities.

Technology and Crafts

The Harappan culture belongs to the Bronze Age. The people of Harappa used many tools and implements of stone but they were very well acquainted with the manufacture and use of bronze. Bronze was made by the smiths by mixing tin with copper. Since none of the two metals was easily available to the Harappans, bronze tools are not prolific in Harappa. The impurities of the ores show that copper was obtained from the Khetri copper mines of Rajasthan, although it could also be brought from Baluchistan. Tin was possibly brought with difficulty from Afghanistan and Iran although some tin is also found in Rajasthan. The bronze tools and weapons recovered from the Harappan sites contain a smaller percentage of tin. However, the kit of bronze goods left by the Harappans is considerable, which suggests that the bronzesmiths constituted an important group of artisans in the Harappan society. They produced not only images and utensils but also various tools and weapons such as axes, saws, knives and spears. Several other important crafts flourished in the Harappan towns. A piece of woven cotton has been recovered from Mohenjodaro, and textile impressions found on several objects. Spindle whorls were used for spinning. Weavers wove cloth of wool and cotton. Huge brick structures suggest that brick-laying was an important craft. They also attest the existence of a class of masons. As will be shown later, seal-making and terracotta manufacture were also important crafts. The goldsmiths made jewellery of silver, gold and precious stones; the first two may have been obtained from Afghanistan and the last from south India. The Harappans were also experts in beadmaking.

The porter's wheel was in full use, and the Harappans produced their own characteristic pottery, which were made shining by embroidering them with glass.

Trade

The Harappan cities did not possess the necessary raw material for the commodities they produced. They did not use metallic money. We have no idea about their currency. Most probably they carried on all exchanges through barter. In return for finished goods and possibly foodgrains, they procured metals from the neighbouring areas by boats and bullock carts. They practised navigation on the coast of the Arabian Sea. They knew the use of wheel and carts with solid wheels were in use in Harappa. It also appears that the Harappans used some kind of modern *ekka*.

The Harappans had commercial links with Rajasthan, Afghanistan and Iran. Their cities also carried on commerce with those in the land of the Tigris and Euphrates. Many

Harappan seals have been discovered in Mesopotamia and it seems that the Harappans imitated some cosmetics used by the urban people of Mesopotamia. The Mesopotamian records from about 2350 B.C. refer to trade relations with Meluha, which was the ancient name given to the Indus region. The Mesopotamian texts speak of two intermediate trading stations called Dilmun and Makan, which lay between Mesopotamia and Meluha. Dilmun can probably be identified with Bahrain on the Persian Gulf. Thousands of graves await excavation in that port city.

Political Organisation

We have no clear idea about the political organisation of the Harappans. In sharp contrast to Egypt and Mesopotamia no temples have been found at any Harappan site. We have no religious structures of any kind except the Great bath, which may have been used for ablutions. Therefore it would be wrong to think that priests ruled in Harappa, as they did in the cities of lower Mesopotamia. There are some indications of the practice of fire cult at Lothal in Gujarat in the later phase, but no temples were used for the purpose. Perhaps the Harappan rulers were more concerned with commerce than with conquests, and Harappa was possibly ruled by a class of merchants.

Religious Practices

It Harappa numerous terracotta figurines of women have been found. In one figurine a plant is shown growing out of the embryo of a woman. Probably the image represents the goddess of earth, and it was intimately connected with the origin and growth of plants. The Harappans therefore looked upon the earth as a fertility goddess and worshipped her in the same manner as the Egyptians worshipped the Nile goddess Isis. But we do not know whether the Harappans were a matriarchal people like the Egyptians. In Egypt the daughter inherited the throne or property, but we do not know about the nature of inheritance in the Harappan society.

Some Vedic texts show reverence to the earth goddess, although she is not given any prominence. It took a long time for the worship of the supreme goddess to develop in Hinduism. Only from the sixth century A.D. various mother goddess such as Durga, Amba, Kali, Chandi, etc., came to be regarded as goddesses in the Puranas and in the Tantra literature. In course of time every village came to have its own separate goddess.

The Male Deity in the Indus Valley

The male deity is represented on a seal. This god has three heads and has horns. He is represented in the sitting posture of a *yogi* placing one foot on the other. This god is surrounded by an elephant, a tiger, a rhinoceros, and has a buffalo below his throne. At his feet appear two deer. The seal immediately recalls to our mind the traditional image of Pasupati Mahadeva. The four animals surrounding the god look towards the four directions of the earth. They may have served as vehicles for gods, because in later Hinduism every god is supposed to have his own conveyance for his movements. In addition to the use of the image of Siva, we also come across the prevalence of the phallus worship which became so intimately connected with Siva in later times. Numerous symbols of the phallus and female sex organs made of tone have been found in Harappa. They were possibly meant for worship. The *Rig Veda* speaks of the non-Aryan people, who were phallus worshippers. The phallus worship which started in the days of Harappa came to be recognised as a respectable form of worship in the later Hindu society.

Tree and Animal Worship

The people of the Indus region also worshipped trees. The picture of a god is represented on a seal in the midst of the branches of the *pipal*. This tree continues to be worshipped to this day.

Animals were also worshipped in Harappan times, and many of them are represented on seals. The most important of them is the humped bull. Even today, when such a bull passes in the market streets the pious Indians give way to it. Similarly the animals surrounding Pasupati Mahadeva indicate that these were worshipped. Obviously the inhabitants of the indus region worshipped gods in the form of trees, animals and human beings. But the gods were not placed in temples, a practice which was common in ancient Egypt and Mesopotamia. Nor can we say anything about the religious beliefs of the Harappans without being able to read their script. Amulets have been found in large numbers. Probabaly the Harappans believed that ghosts and evil forces were capable of harming them and therefore used amulets against them. The *Atharva Veda* which is considered to be a non-Aryan work, contains many charms and spells, and recommends amulets for warding off diseases and evil forces.

The Harappan Script

The Harappans invented the art of writing like the people of ancient Mesopotamia. Although the earliest specimen of Harappan script was noticed in 1853 and the complete script discovered by 1923, it has not been deciphered so far. Some try to connect it with the Dravidian or the proto-Dravidian language, others with the Sanskrit language, and still others with the Sumerian language, but none of these readings is satisfactory. As the script has not been deciphered, we cannot judge the Harappan contribution to literature, nor can we say anything about their ideas and beliefs.

Unlike the Egyptians and Mesopotamians, the Harappans did not write long inscriptions. Most inscriptions were recorded on seals, and contain only a few words. These seals may have been used by propertied people to mark and identify their private property. Altogether we have about 250 to 400 pictographs, and in the form of a picture each letter stands for some sound, idea or object. The Harappan script is not alphabetical but mainly pictographic. Attempts have been made to compare it with the contemporary scripts of Mesopotamia and Egypt. But it is the indigenous product of the Indus region, and does not show any connection with the scripts of Western Asia.

Weights and Measures

The knowledge of script must have helped the recording of private property and the keeping of accounts. The urban people of the Indus region also needed and used weights and measures for trade and other transactions. Numerous articles used for weights have been found. They show that in weighting mostly 16 or its multiples were used; for instance, 16, 64, 160, 320 and 640. Interestingly the tradition of 16 has continued in India till modern times, and till recently 16 annas till modern times, and till recently 16 annas made one rupee. The Harappans also knew the art of measurement. We have come across sticks inscribed with measure marks; one of these is made of bronze.

Harappan Pottery

The Harappans were great experts in the use of the potter's wheel. We come across numerous pots painted in various colours. Harappan pots were generally decorated with the designs of trees and circles. The images of men are also found on some pottery fragments.

Seals

The greatest artistic creations of the Harappan culture are the seals. About 2000 seals have been found, and of these a great majority carry short inscriptions with pictures of the one-horned bull, the buffalo, the tiger, the rhinoceros, the goat and the elephant.

Images

The Harappan artisans made beautiful images of metal. A woman dancer made of bronze is the best specimen. Except for a necklace she is naked. We get a few pieces of stone sculptures from Harappa. Of them the images of two human males can be specially noticed. The body of one male is decorated beautifully, and that of the other kept naked.

Terracotta Figurines

We get many figurines made of earthen clay, commonly called *terracotta*. These were either used as toys or objects of worship. They represent birds, dogs, sheep, cattle and monkeys. Men and women also find place, and the second outnumber the first. The seals and images were manufactured with great skill, but the terracotta pieces represent unsophisticated artistic works. The contrast between the two sets indicates the gap between the classes which used them. The first were used by members of the upper classes, and the second by the common people. The Harappan culture is poor in artistic works made of stone. We do not come across any massive work of art in stone as we find in the case of sculptures of ancient Egypt and Mesopotamia.

Origin, Maturity and End

The Harappan culture existed between 2500 B.C and 1750 B.C. Its mature phase lay between 2200 B.C. and 2000 B.C., but throughout the period of its existence we notice the same kind of tools, weapons and houses. The whole style of life seems to be uniform. We notice the same town-planning the same seals, the same terracotta works, and the same long chert blades. But the view stressing changelessness cannot be pushed too far. We do notice changes in the pottery of Mohenjodaro over a period of time. Around 1750 B.C. the two important cities of the

Harappan culture, Harappa and Mohenjodaro, disappeared, but the Harappan culture at other sites faded out gradually and continued in its degenerate phase in the outlying fringes in Gujarat, Rajasthan and western Uttar Pradesh.

It is as difficult to explain the origin of the Harappan culture as its end. Several pre-Harappan settlements have been found in Baluchistan and Kalibangan in Rajasthan, but the connection between them and the mature Harappan culture is not clear, though the Harappan culture may have evolved out of these indigenous settlements. Nor do we have clear proof of outside influence on the Harappan cities. Contact with the Mesopotamian cities may have provided some stimulus to the development of the Harappan culture. But there can be no doubt about the Indianness of the Harappan culture. Certain elements distinguish it from the contemporary cultures in Western Asia. It planned its towns with their chess-board system, grid system, streets, drainage pipes and cess pits. Rectangular houses with brick-lines bathrooms and wells together with their stairways are found in all Harappan cities. Such town-planning is not to be found in the cities of Western Asia. No other people in antiquity had built such as excellent drainage system except perhaps those of Crete in Knosos, nor did the people of Western Asia show such skill in the use of burnt bricks as the Harappans did.

The Harappans produced their own characteristic pottery and seals; the latter represented the local animal world. Above all, they invented their own typical script, which bears no resemblance to the Egyptian and Mesopotamian scripts. Although the Harappan culture was a Bronze Age culture, they used bronze on a very limited scale, and largely continued to use stone implements. Finally, no contemporary culture spread over such a wide area as the Harappan culture did. The structures of Harappa cover 5 km in circuit, and in that way are the largest of their type in the Bronze Age. No urban complex of the Harappan magnitude has been discovered so far.

So far, archaeological evidence of clear contact between the Aryans and the Harappans has been lacking. In the later phases of the Harappan culture, some exotic tools and pottery indicate the slow percolation of new peoples in the Indus basin. A few signs of insecurity and violence appear in the last phase of Mohenjodaro. Hoards of jewellery were buried at places, and skulls were huddled together at one place. We also notice new types of axes. Draggers, knives with mid-ribs and flat tangs appear in the upper levels of Mohenjodaro. Although basically they seem to be India, they may betray some foreign influence. Traces of new peoples appear in a cemetry belonging to the late phase of Harappa, where new kinds of pottery occur in the latest levels. New types of pottery also occur in some Harappan sites in Baluchistan.

All this can be attributed to the barbarian horse-riding people, who may have come from Iran through the hills. But the new peoples did not come in such numbers as to completely overwhelm the Harappan cities in the Punjab and Sindh. Although the Rig Vedic Aryans settled down mostly in the land of the Seven Rivers, in which the Harappan culture once flourished, we have no evidence of any mass-scale confrontation between the Harappans and the Aryans.

VI. THE LATER VEDIC PHASE

The history of the later Vedic period is based mainly on the Vedic texts which were complied after the age of *Rigveda*. The collections of the Vedic hymns or *mantras* were known as the *Samhitas*. The *Rigveda Samhita* is the oldest Vedic text, on the basis of which we have described the early Vedic age. For purposes of singing the prayers of the *Rigveda* were set to tune, and this modified collection was known as the *Samaveda Samhita*. In addition to the *Sama Veda,* in post-Rigvedic times two other collections were composed. These were the *Yajurveda Samhita* and the *Atharvaveda Samhita*. The *Yajurveda* contains not only hymns but also rituals which have to accompany their recitation. The rituals reflect the social and political milieu in which they arose. The *Atharvaveda* contains charms and spells to ward off evils and diseases. Its contents throw light on the beliefs and practices of the non-Aryans. The Vedic *Samhitas* were followed by the composition of a series of texts known as the *Brahmans.* These are full of ritualistic formulae and explain the social and religions aspects of rituals. All these later Vedic texts were complied in the upper Gangetic basin in *circa* 1000-600 B.C. In the same period and in the same area, digging and exploration have brought to light nearly 300 sites inhabited for the first time. These are called Painted Grey Ware (PGW) sites because they were inhabited by people who used earthen bowls and dishes made of painted grey pottery. They also used iron weapons. With the combined evidence from the later Vedic texts and PGW archaeology we can form an idea of the life of the people in the first half of the first millenium B.C., in western Uttar Pradesh and adjoining areas of Punjab, Haryana and Rajasthan.

The texts show that the Aryans expanded from the Punjab over the whole of western Uttar Pradesh covered by the Ganga-Yamuna *doab.* The Bharatas and Purus, the two major tribes, combined and thus formed the Kuru-people. In the beginning they lived between the Sarasvati and the Drishadvati just on the fringe of the *doab.* Soon the Kurus occupied Delhi and the upper portion of the *doab,* the area called Kurukshetra or the land of the Kurus. Gradually they coalesced with a people called the Panchalas, who occupied the middle portion of the *doab.* The authority of the Kuru-Panchala people spread over Delhi and the upper and middle parts of the *doab.* They set up their capital at Hastinapur situated in the district of Meerut. The history of the Kuru tribe is important for the battle of the Bharata, which is the main theme of the great epic called the *Mahabharata*. This war is believed to have been fought around 950 B.C. between the Kauravas and the Pandavas, although both of them belonged to the Kuru clan. As a result practically the whole of the Kuru clan was wiped out.

Excavations at Hastinapur, datable to the period 900 B.C., to 500 B.C. have revealed settlements and faint beginnings of town life. But they do not at all answer the description of Hastinapur in the *Mahabharata* because the epic was finally compiled much later in about the fourth century A.D. when material life had advanced much. In later Vedic times people did not know the use of burnt bricks. The mud structures that have been discovered at Hastinapur could not be imposing and lasting. From traditions we learn that Hastinapur was flooded, and the remnants of the Kuru clan moved to Kausambi near Allahabad.

The Panchala kingdom, which covered the modern districts of Bareiley, Badaun and Farukhabad, is famous for its philosopher kings and brahmana theologians.

Towards the end of the later Vedic period, around 600 B.C. the Aryans spread from the *doab* further east to Kosala in eastern Uttar Pradesh and Videha in north Bihar. Although Kosala is associated with the story of Ramachandra, he is not mentioned in Vedic literature. In Uttar Pradesh and north Bihar the Vedic people had to contend against a people who used copper implements and the black-and-red earthen posts. In western Uttar-Pradesh they possibly came up against the people who used pots of ochre or red colour and copper implements; they had bene living there from about 1800 B.C. The Aryan chiefs succeeded in overcoming their adversaries, whose number in the upper Gangetic basin does not seem to have been large. The Vedic people succeeded in the second phase of their expansion because they used iron weapons and horse drawn chariots.

The PGW Culture and Later Vedic Economy

From around 1000, B.C., iron was used in the Gandhara area in Pakistan. Iron implements buried with dead bodies have been discovered in good numbers. They have also been found in Baluchistan. At about the same time the use of iron appeared in eastern Punjab western, Uttar Pradesh and Rajasthan. Excavations show that iron weapons such as arrow-heads and spear-heads came to be commonly used in western Uttar Pradesh from about 800 B.C. With iron weapons the Vedic people may have defeated the remnants of their copper-using and ochre-coloured pot-using adversaries, who mostly lived in the upper portion of the *doab*. The iron axe may have been used to clear the forests in the upper Gangetic basin, although because of rainfall ranging between 35 cm to 65 cm these forests may not have been so thick. Towards the end of the Vedic period knowledge of iron spread in eastern Uttar Pradesh and Videha. Iron implements have been discovered in this area from the seventh century B.C., and the metal itself is called *syama* or *krishna ayas* in the later Vedic texts.

Although very few agricultural tools made of iron have been found, there is no doubt that agriculture was the chief means of livelihood of the later Vedic people. Some Vedic texts speak of six, eight, twelve and even twenty-four oxen yoked to the plough. This may be an exaggeration. Ploughing was done with the help of the wooden ploughshare, which would possibly work in the light soil of he upper Gangetic basin. Enough bullocks could not be available because of cattle slaughter in sacrifices. Therefore agriculture was primitive, but there is no doubt about its wide prevalence. The *Satapatha Brahmana* speaks at length about the ploughing rituals. According to ancient legends Janaka, the king of Videha and father of Sita, lent his hand to the plough. In those days even kings and princes did not hesitate to take to manual labour. Balarama, the brother of Krishna, is called Haladhara or wielder of the plough. In later times ploughing came to be prohibited for the members of the upper varnas.

The Vedic people continued to produce barley, but during this period rice and wheat became their chief crops. In subsequent times wheat became the staple food of the people in the Punjab and western Uttar Pradesh. For the first time the Vedic people came to be acquainted with rice in the *doab.* It is called *vrihi* in the Vedic texts, and its remains recovered from Hastinapur belong to the eighth century B.C. The use of rice is recommended in rituals, but that of wheat only rarely. Various kinds of lentils were also produced by the later Vedic people.

The later Vedic period saw the rice of diverse arts and crafts. We hear of smiths and smelters, who had certainly to do something with iron working from abut 1000 B.C. Numerous copper tools of the pre-1000 B.C. period found in western Uttar Pradesh and Bihar might suggest the existence of coppersmiths in both Vedic and non-Vedic societies. The Vedic people may have used the copper mines of Khetri in Rajasthan. In any case copper was one of the first metals to be used by the Vedic people. Copper objects have been found in Painted Grey Ware sites. They were used mainly for war and hunting, and also for ornaments.

Weaving was confined to women but was practised on a wide scale. Leather work, pottery, and carpenter's work made great progress. The later Vedic people were acquainted with four types of pottery: black-and-red ware, black-slipped ware, painted grey ware and red ware. The last type of pottery was most popular with them, and has been found almost all over western Uttar Pradesh. However the most distinctive pottery of the period is known as Painted Grey Ware. It consisted of bowls and dishes, which were used either for rituals or for eating or for both, but by the upper orders. Glass hoards and bangles found along with painted grey ware may have also been used by members of the upper orders. On the whole both Vedic texts and excavations indicate the cultivation of specialised crafts. Jewel-workers are also mentioned in later Vedic texts, and they possibly catered to the needs of the richer sections of society.

Agriculture and various crafts enabled the later Vedic people to lead a settled life. Excavations and explorations give us some idea about settlements in later Vedic times. Widespread Painted Grey Ware sites are fund not only in western Uttar Pradesh and Delhi, which was the Kuru-Panchala area, but also in the adjoining parts of the Punjab and Haryana, which was the Madra area, and in those of Rajasthan, which was the Matsya area. Altogether we can count 315 sites, mostly belonging to the upper Gangetic basin. Only a few sites such as Hastinapur. Atranjikhera and Noh have been excavated. Since the thickness of the material remains of habitations ranges from one metre to three metres, it seems that these settlements lasted from one to three centuries. Mostly these were entirely new settlements without having any immediate predecessors. People lived in mud-brick houses or in wattle-and-daub houses erected on wooden poles. Although the structures are poor, ovens and cereals (rice) recovered from the sites show that the Painted Grey Ware people, who seem to be the same as the later Vedic people, were agricultural and led a settled life. But since they cultivated with the wooden ploughshare, the peasants could not spare much for feeding those who were engaged in other occupations. Hence peasants could not contribute much to the rise of towns.

Although the term *nagara* is used in later Vedic texts

we can trace only the faint beginnings of towns towards the end of the later Vedic period. Hastinapur and Kausambi (near Allahabad) can be regarded as primitive towns belonging to the end of the Vedic period. They may be called proto-urban sites. The Vedic texts also refer to the seas and sea voyages. This suggests some kind of commerce, which may have been stimulated by the rise of new arts and drafts.

On the whole the later Vedic phase registered a great advance in the material life of the people. The pastoral and semi-normadic forms of living were relegated to the background. Agriculture became the primary source of livelihood, and life became settled and sedentary Supplemented by diverse arts and crafts the Vedic people now settled down permanently in the upper Gangetic plans. The peasants living in the plains produced enough to maintain themselves, and they could also spare in marginal part of their produce for the support of princes and priests.

Political Organisation

In later Vedic times popular assemblies lost in importance, and royal power increased at their cost. The *vidatha* completely disappeared. The *sabha* and *samiti* continued to hold the ground, but their character changed. They came to be dominated by princes and rich nobles. Women were no longer permitted to sit on the *sabha,* and it was now dominated by nobles and brahmanas.

The formation of wider kingdoms made the more powerful. Tribal authority tended to become territorial. Princes ruled over tribes, but their dominant tribes became identical with territories, which might be inhabited by tribes other than their own. In the beginning each area was named after the tribe which settled there first, but eventually the tribal name became current as the territorial name. At first Panchala was the name of a people, and then it became the name of a region. The term *rashtra,* which indicates territory, first appears in this period.

The king's influence was strengthened by rituals. He performed the *rajasuya* sacrifice, which was supposed to confer supreme power on him. He performed the *asvamedha,* which meant unquestioned control over an area in which the royal horse ran uninterrupted. He also performed the *vajapeya* or the chariot race, in which the royal chariot was made to win the race against his kinsmen. All these rituals impressed the people with the increasing power and prestige of the king.

During this period collection of taxes and tribute seems to have become common. They were probably deposited with an officer called *sangrihitra.* In the discharge of his duties the king was assisted by the priest, the commander, the chief queen and a few other high functionaries. At the lower level the administration was possibly carried on by village assemblies, which may have been controlled by the chiefs of the dominant tribes. These assemblies were also entrusted with the trial of local cases. But even in the later Vedic times the king did not possess a standing army. Tribal units were mustered in times of war, and according to one ritual for success in war, the king had to eat along with his people (*vis*) from the same plate.

Social Organisation

The later Vedic society came to be divided into four varnas called the brahmanas, rajanyas or kshatriyas, vaisyas and studras. The growing cult of sacrifices enormously added to the power of the brahmanas. In the beginning the brahmanas were only one of the sixteen classes of priests, but they gradually overshadowed the other priestly groups and emerged as the most important class. They conducted rituals and sacrifices for their clients and for themselves, and also officiated at the festivals associated with agricultural operations. They prayed for the success of their patron in war, and in return the king pledged not to do any harm to them. Sometimes the brahmanas came into conflict with the rajanyas, who represented the order of the warrior-nobles, for positions of supremacy. But when the two upper orders had to deal with the lower orders they made up their differences. From the end of the later Vedic period it began to be emphasised that the two should cooperate to rule over the rest of society. The vaisyas constituted the common people, and they were assigned the producing functions such as agriculture, cattle-breeding, etc. Some of them also worked as artisans. Towards the end of the Vedic period they began to engage in trade. The vaisyas appear to be the only tribute-payers in later Vedic times and the kshatriyas are represented as living on the tributes collected from the vaisyas. The process of subjugating the mass of the tribesmen to the position of tribute-payers was long and protracted. We have several rituals prescribed for making the refractory people (*vis* or *vaisya*) submissive to the prince (*rajanya*). All the three higher varnas shared one common feature; they were entitled to *upanayana* or investiture with the sacred thread according to the Vedic *mantras.* The fourth varna was deprived of the sacred thread ceremony, and with this began the imposition of disabilities on the sudras.

The prince, who represented the *rajanya* order, tried to assert his power over all the three other varnas. According to the *Aitareya Brahmana,* in relation to the prince the brahmana is described as a seeker or livelihood and an acceptor of gifts, but removable at will. A vaisya is called tribute-paying, meant for being beaten, and to be oppressed at will. The worst description is reserved for the sudra. He is called the servant of another, to be made to work at will by another, and to be beaten at will.

But generally the later Vedic texts draw a line of

demarcation between the three higher orders on the one hand, and the sudras on the other. There were, nevertheless, several public rituals connected with the coronation of the king in which the sudras participated presumably as members of the original tribe. Certain sections of artisans such as *rathakara* or chariot-maker enjoyed a high status, and were entitled to the sacred thread ceremony. Therefore even in later Vedic times varna distinctions had not advanced very far.

In the family we notice the increasing power, of the father, who could even disinherit his son. In princely families the right of primogeniture was getting stronger. Male ancestors came to be worshipped. Women were generally given a lower position. Although some women theologians took part in philosophic discussions and some queens participated in coronation rituals, ordinarily women were thought to be inferior and subordinate to men.

The institution of *gotra* appeared in later Vedic times. Literally it means the cow-pen or the place where cattle belonging to the whole clan are kept, but in course of time it signified descent from a common ancestor. People began to practise *gotra* exogamy. No marriage could take place between persons belonging to the same *gotra* or having the same ancestor.

Asramas or four stages of life were not well established in Vedic times. In the post-Vedic texts we hear of four *asramas;* that of *brahmachari* or student, *grihastha* or house holder, *vanaprastha* or partial retirement, and *sanyasa* or complete retirement from the world. But only three are mentioned in the later Vedic texts; the last or the fourth stage had not been well established in later Vedic times.

Religion and Culture

In the later Vedic period the upper *doab* developed to be the cradle of Aryan culture under brahmanical influence.

The whole of the Vedic literature seems to have been compiled in this area, in the land of the Kuru-Panchalas. The cult of sacrifice was the corner-stone of this culture, and was accompanied by numerous rituals and formulae.

The two outstanding Rigvedic gods, Indra and Agni, lost their former importance. On the other hand Prajapati, the creator, came to occupy the supreme position in the later Vedic pantheon. Some of the other minor gods of the Rigvedic period also came to the forefront. Rudra, the god of animals, became important in later Vedic times, and Vishnu came to be conceived as the preserver and protector of the people, who now led a settled life instead of a semi-nomadic life as they did in Rigvedic times. In addition, some symbolic objects began to be worshipped, and we notice signs of idolatry in later Vedic times. As society became divided into social clauses such as brahmanas, rajanyas, vaisyas and sudras, some of the social orders came to have their own deities. Pushan, who was supposed to look after cattle, came to be regarded as the god of the sudras, although in the age of the *Rigveda* cattle-rearing was the primary occupation of the Aryans.

People worshipped gods for the same material reasons in this period as they did in earlier times. However, the mode of worship changed considerably. Prayers continued to be recited, but they ceased to be the dominant mode of placating the gods. Sacrifices became far more important, and they assumed both public and domestic character. Public sacrifices involved the king and the whole of the community, which was still in many cases identical with the tribe. Private sacrifices were performed by individuals in their houses because in this period the Vedic people led a settled life and maintained well-established households. Individuals offered oblations to Agni, and each one of these took the from of a rituals or sacrifice.

Sacrifices involved the killing of animals on a large scale and especially the destruction of cattle wealth. The guest was known as *goghna* or one who was fed on cattle.

Brahmanas were only one of the sixteen types of priests. The priests who officiated at sacrifices were rewarded generously and given *dakshinas* or gifts.

Sacrifices were accompanied by formulae which had to be carefully pronounced by the sacrificer. The sacrificer was known as the *yajamana,* the performer of *yajna,* and much of his success depended on the magical power of words uttered in the sacrifices. Some rituals performed by the Vedic Aryans are common to the Indo-European peoples, but many rituals seem to have developed on the Indian soil.

These formulae and sacrifices were invented, adopted and elaborated by the priests called the brahmanas. The brahmanas claimed a monopoly of priestly knowledge and expertise. They invented a large number of rituals, some of which were adopted from the non-Aryans. The reason for the invention and elaboration of the rituals is not clear, though mercenary motives cannot be ruled out. We hear that as many as 240,000 cows were given as *dakshina* or gift to the officiating priest in the *rajsuya* sacrifice.

In addition to cows which were usually given as sacrificial gifts, gold, cloth and horses were also given. Sometimes the priests claimed portions of territory as *dakshina,* but the grant of land as sacrificial fee is not well established in the later Vedic period. The *Satapatha Brahmana* states that in the *asvamedha,* north, south, east and west, all should be given to the priest. If this really happened, then what would remain to the king? This therefore merely indicates the desire of the priests to grab as much land as possible. But really considerable transfer of land to priests could not have taken place.

There is a reference where land, which was being given to the priests, refused to be transferred to them.

Towards the end of the Vedic period we notice a strong reaction against priestly domination, against cults and rituals, especially in the land of the Panchalas and Videha where, around 600 B.C., the Upanishads were complied. These philosophical texts criticised the rituals and laid stress on the value of right belief and knowledge. They emphasised that the knowledge of the self or *atma* should be acquired and the relation of *atma* with Brahma should be properly understood. Brahma emerged as the supreme god, comparable to the powerful kings of the period. Some of the kshatriya princes in Panchala and Videha also cultivated this type of thinking and created the atmosphere for the reform of the priest dominated religion.

The later Vedic period saw certain important changes. We find the beginnings of territorial kingdoms. Wars were fought not only for the possession of cattle but also for that of territory. The famous Mahabharata battle, fought between the Kauravas and the Pandavas, is attributed to this period. The predominantly pastoral society of early Vedic times became agricultural. The tribal pastoralists came to be transformed into peasants who could maintain their chief with frequent tributes. Chiefs grew at the expense of the tribal peasantry, and handsomely rewarded the priests who supported their patrons against the common people called the vaisyas. The sudras were still a small serving order. The tribal society broke up into a varna-divided society. But varna distinctions could not be carried too far. In spite of the support of the brahmanas the rajanyas or the kshatriyas could not establish a state system. A state cannot be set up without a regular system of taxes and a standing army, which again depends on taxes. But primitive agriculture did not leave scope for taxes and tributes in sufficient measure.

VII. BUDDHISM AND JAINISM (600 B.C.—200 B.C.)

The common national culture which had developed in the preceding period continued as the main current of cultural life. But during the next eight centuries new currents of religious and philosophical thought sprang up of which Buddhism, Jainism and the six schools of Hindu philosophy are worth mentioning here. Buddhism brought about such a significant change in the life and thought of the people in a large part of the country that it developed into a separate and more or less independent culture—a rival to the main Hindu culture. From the point of view of cultural history this was a period of debate in which Hinduism, Jainism, and Buddhism were struggling to put their stamp on the cultural life of India. Finally it was Hinduism which emerged victorious from the struggle and Buddhism practically disappeared from the country, but it left a deep and lasting impression on the Indian mind and Indian life.

This period marks the beginning of Indian history in the proper sense of the word. About the preceding period, our knowledge is, at the most, semi-historical, because its major source is the Vedic literature which gives us no more than some glimpses here and there of the social and cultural life of the time. On this scanty data it is difficult to base anything like a full account of the period, specially to place the facts chronologically. But as far as the time under discussion is concerned, we have in addition to Hindu, Buddhist and Jain literature another source of information—the writings of the Greeks who had contact with India during this period. The exploitation of the material from all these sources can help, and to some extent has helped, in compiling a more or less authentic historical account.

In the first half of the sixth century the states of Koshala, Magadha and Vatsa still flourished in the region (now called Madhyadesh and Bihar) and a new state of

Avanti (Malwa) had come into existence. Of these, Magadha became the largest and the most important. By the time Alexander the Great invaded India (326 B.C.), it had gradually conquered the neighbouring states and grown into a big empire. During the reign of two great rulers of the Maurya dynasty, Chandragupta Maurya and Asoka, the empire expanded till it comprised the whole of India except a small area in the extreme south. Asoka was a Buddhist and a zealous propagator of Buddhism. Under his patronage the new faith flourished as it had never done before. Even after him Magadha continued to be the capital of a big empire till Pushyamitra Sunga defeated the last Maurya ruler (183 B.C.) and established the Sunga dynasty. The capital was now shifted to Malwa and the empire was reduced to a loose confederation in which the member states paid only normal homage to the centre and were constantly engaged in fighting one another. No lasting empire of the stature of the Maurya empire could be established during the period.

Towards the end of the Maurya empire the Greeks, who had been ruling small states in Bactria for a long time, invaded India from the north-west (190 B.C.) and established their rule over the Indus valley and the Punjab and raided the neighbouring regions to the east. Once during the reign of Menander the raiders reached as far as Pataliputra. At first they were known as Yavanas and regarded as foreigners, but were finally assimilated into Hindu society as Kshatriyas. After the Greeks came the Scythians who were called Sakas in India and set up a state (90 B.C.) extending over the Punjab and Madhyadesh as far as Mathura. They were followed within a short time by the Pallavas whose name indicated their Persian origin. They became rulers of north-western India being, in their turn, displaced by the Kushans, of the Yu-Chi tribe. The greatest of the Kushan rulers was Kanishka whose empire extended from Central Asia to Banaras and beyond. There is much difference of opinion about the date of the beginning of his rule. But most probably he ascended the throne in AD 78, which marks the commencement of the Saka era. Kanishka had embraced the Buddhist religion. He was the sponsor of a new interpretation of Buddha's teaching and the founding of a new sect called the Mahayana. This was the time when Gandhara art flourished. In Orissa about a hundred years before Kanishka, the great conqueror Kharavela, a patron of Jainism, had established a big empire, but it did not last long. About the same time the Andhras or Satavahanas founded on the rums of the Mauryan empire an empire, of their own which continued for 400 years

During these 800 years several new movements, religious and intellectual, arose in India creating storm and stress in the minds of the people and there was a danger that the foundation of national unity laid by the Vedic Hindu culture would be destroyed and the country would be divided into separate cultural zones with nothing common among them. But what actually happened was that this ferment proved to be very beneficial and enriched the Indian mind with a wealth of new and profound ideas. Later, when attempts were made to bring about a synthesis in the various trends of thought, an imposing structure of a new common culture arose on a wider and stronger foundation.

In the later part of the Vedic Hindu period, the religious life of the country had lost its balance. On the one hand popular religion had become a mere set of rites and sacrifices performed with the help of the Brahmins and on the other hand the teachings of the *Upanishads* had totally rejected all ritual and sacrifice and formulated a new system of Hindu religion based on an idealistic philosophy. This philosophical religion was interpreted by the higher classes who had the intellectual capacity to understand it, as an ascetic way of life and they generally lived like ascetics. The caste system had become so rigid that the lower classes of Hindu society were completely cut off from the higher classes and higher culture. So much so that they were forbidden to read the *Vedas*.

At this time (563 to 482 B.C.) came Gautama Buddha who protested against the ritualism of the masses and the asceticism of the higher classes, and most emphatically against racial prejudice and social discrimination. He delivered to the world his message of compassion, move, self-restraint and self-culture. The essence of budhas teaching is the sermon he gave in Banaras after his Enlightenment.

"Listen ye Bhikshus! He who wants to renounce worldliness should avoid both excess and undue abstinence. On the one hand he should not be addicted to things which attract the mind merely through passion, specially through carnal desire. That is the low, vain and worthless life of ignorance fit for none but the blind worshipper of the world. On the other hand, he should not be given to self-mortification. That also is painful, ignoble and useless. There is ye Bhikshus a middle path between the two which the Tathagatha (Buddha) has found. The pursuit of this path opens the eyes and enlightens the mind. This is the way of peace of mind, higher wisdom, illumination and *nirvana*.'

The Buddha looked deep into the human mind and examined the nature of the feeling of pain. He found the roots of the feeling in passions and desires and a sovereign remedy in self-culture, that is, making: our thought and action subservient to a higher purpose by following a strict code of moral life, and a regimen of spiritual exercises. The higher purpose of life is the perfect peace of mind to which Buddha gave the name *nirvana*. He says: "One who attains freedom and peace through the realisation of truth enjoys perfect repose in his thought, word and action." In the famous Banaras sermon the Buddha goes on to speak of his tremendous experience, of the great truth revealed to him and of the pain of life—what it is, how it is born and how it ceases to be—and of the way of life which should be adopted to get rid of it. Here is the gist of the sermon.

"This, ye Bhikshus. is the great truth of the right path by following which pain can be got rid of. It is the eightfold path. (1) right belief, (2) right aspirations, (3) right speech, (4) right conduct,(5) right mode of livelihood, (6) right mindedness, *(7)* right effort, (8) right rapture."

The Buddha showed the way to self-restraint instead of self-mortification, to right action instead of inactivity. What he specially emphasised was that giving up worldiness does not mean giving up the love and service of mankind. On the contrary universal love is essential for attaining peace of mind. This law of love he enunciates in the following words:

"Hatred does not cease by meeting hatred with hatred but by meeting it with love. This is its nature. If one wants to live a happy life one should not hate one's enemies. Conquer resentment with love, evil with good, greed with generosity, and falsehood with truth!"

Gautama Buddha spent the rest of his life in travelling far and wide to preach his faith and after him his followers showed great zeal in the propagation of Buddhism. Still, during the first hundred years the number of his followers was very small and was confined to Koshala and Magadha. The rise of Buddhism began when Asoka embraced it and did his best to propagate it not only throughout India but also in foreign countries.

But owing to the comparatively rapid spread of Buddhism, its organisation could not maintain the compactness and coordination of the earlier days and the

Buddhist community was divided into a number of sects. Of these the Hinayana was the older and perhaps more orthodox sect. Other sects, including the Mahayana with the greatest number of followers, had considerably deviated from the orthodox line. The Mahayana which under the patronage of Kanishka became very popular in India and abroad, believes in gods and regards the Buddha as the greatest of them, and worships them with elaborate ceremonies and rituals. Its emphasis is on devotion, prayer and charity instead of austere self-restraint and self-culture.

By the end of this period, Buddhism had lost some of its popularity in India firstly because the various sects wrangled and quarrelled among themselves, and secondly because the Buddhist Sangha received munificent donations, and the immense wealth which the Bhikshus possessed made them live a life of luxury and led to their moral degeneration.

About the same, time as the Buddha was propagating his faith, Mahavira (522 B.C.-480 B.C.) was preaching a new religion which came to be known as Jainism. The gist of his teaching was that if a man is overcome by violent passions such as anger, self-conceit, greed or blind love, his soul is permeated by matter which binds it with fetters. Its liberation requires that no more matter be allowed to contaminate the soul and that which has already entered it should be completely eliminated.

There are three principles known as three jewels *(triratna):* right faith, right knowledge and right conduct. "Right knowledge consists in a correct understanding of the teachings of omniscient *tirthankaras* (makers of sacred paths). Right faith is the firm belief in the infallibility and competence of the teachers and right conduct consists of strict observance of charity, chastity, renunciation of all worldly interests, honourable conduct like not stealing, not uttering falsehood, and *ahimsa* or non-injury which implies not only the negative act of abstention from all injury to life but positive kindness to all creation."

The Jains share with the Hindus the belief that the chain of *karma* can be broken by vigorous ascetic discipline and advocate self-mortification, even suicide. The man who faithfully observes the principles known as the *triratna* becomes an *arhat* (a perfect one) and attains absolute knowledge and eternal bliss. The Jains do not believe in gods but their idea of an *arhat* is more or less the same as that of a god in Hinduism. They do not, however, regard the *arhats* as objects of devotion but as models of perfection. "They (the *arhats)* do not respond to prayers or lend a helping hand to the struggling spiritual aspirants and the best way of worshipping, them is to follow their example and advice."

Like Buddhism, Jainism flourished for some time and then began to decline. But it was not uprooted from India as it had tried to assimilate itself with Hinduism in many respects and came to be regarded as one of its heterodox sects.

The challenge of Buddhism and Jainism to the Vedic Hindu religion was a stimulating and refreshing inspiration to the minds of Hindu thinkers who now left the beaten track and ventured on new paths of speculation and reasoning.

Orthodox Hindus were still following the line laid down by the *Vedas.* Their practical religious life consisted of (a) the numerous rites and sacrifices performed under the direction of the Brahmins and (b) the duties prescribed for their particular caste under the caste system. For the performance of religious rites and duties, at first the *Sutras,* or gists of the commentaries on the *Vedas* written in short pithy sentences, served as guides. But later these brief hints were amplified in the *Dharmashastras,* or elaborate codes of ritual, prayer and moral conduct prepared in the light of the teachings of the *Vedas.* A separate manual of politics and economics, the *Arthashastra,* said to have been written by Chanakya or Kautilya, the minister of Chandragupta Maurya was an achievement in the field of the theory of government and political institutions. The best known *Dharamashastra* is *Manusmriti* compiled by Manu, probably during the reign of the Sunga dynasty between 200 B.C. and 100 B.C..

Besides, philosophical thinkers made their own original speculation on metaphysical problems and founded their own systems known as the six systems of Hindu philosophy. Four of these, Sankhya, Yoga Nyaya and Vaisheshika were not influenced by the *Vedas.* But the Purva Mimamsa and the Uttara Mimamsa were based on the teachings of the *Upanishads.*

Sankhya philosophy, like the *Upanishads,* rejects the rites and sacrifices introduced by the Brahmins and looks for some other way to peace of mind and salvation. It regards both the body and the soul as real and does not believe in a universal being or God. According to it the soul, as long as it is associated with the body, is subject to passions and desires and afflicted with pain. Even after death the soul is not free but caught in the cycle of rebirth with the body. But if one realises the true nature of the body and the soul one casts off the body and is free from pain.

Sankhya has a fairly high place in philosophical thought and contains valuable contributions to psychology and to the theory of knowledge. But as a code of life it could not make much progress as it had not shown a way to salvation which the common people could follow. This deficiency was made up later by Patanjali's Yoga.

From the theoretical point of view Patanjali's Yoga

has no independent status but is the practical sequel to Sankhya philosophy. All ideas about psychology and the theory of knowledge found in Patanjali are taken from Sankhya philosophy. His aim, like that of Sankhya, is that the human soul should free itself from the bonds of nature, from its own body, from *karma* and *sansar* and attain the realisation of truth and the state of absolute peace of mind which he calls the Yoga. This can be attained by means of prayer and spiritual exercise. In the course of this spiritual training there comes a stage when the *yogi* acquires supernatural powers. He can find out all about the earth and the sky, the past and the future; he can make himself invisible; he can fly in the air and walk on water. But that is not what he is after. His object is to achieve complete detachment, perfect peace.

The Nyaya and Vaisheshika systems also pursue what may be called the common end of all Indian philosophical systems—the attainment of salvation through truth or the knowledge of reality. But in those two systems knowledge does not mean intuitive but scientific knowledge based on observation, reasoning and experiment. Nyaya deals with *pramana* and *pramayya,* i.e. proof and that which is to be proved. The former comprises problems of logic and theory of knowledge and the latter physics. In all these sciences the Indian mind had achieved, about 2500 years ago, a profoundness and precision of thought of which there is no other example except in ancient Greece.

The remaining two systems of Hindu philosophy, i.e. Purva Mimamsa and Uttara Mimamsa differ from the above four in that they derive their inspiration from the teachings of the *Vedas.* Purva. Mimamsa believes that the *Vedas* are revealed and their injunctions must be obeyed. But it does not concern itself either with the theology or the ethics of the *Vedas* but only with the verses dealing with rites and ceremonies, sacrifices, hymns and prayers.

This one-sided trend was probably a reaction against the religious philosophy of the time which had totally rejected all ritual and prayer. While the Purva Mimamsa has stressed one aspect of the teachings of the *Vedas* the Uttara Mimamsa has put emphasis on the other aspect, that is,on the doctrine of Unitism which it has developed into a coherent philosophy. Together, these two schools represent a religious philosophy which aims at vindicating the Vedic Hindu religion against Buddhism on the one hand and Jainism on the other.

But the highest achievement *of* the Hindu mind in this age shows itself in another philosophy expounded in the *Bhagwad Gita.* The *Gita* is not a separate book but a part of the epic *Mahabharata.*

Arjuna asks himself if it is not a sin to bring destruction on God's creatures and to slay his own kith and kin. On the one hand, his Kshatriya *dharma* urges him to do his duty and fight in order to uphold truth and justice and on the other hand, love and fellow-feeling demand that he should not strike against his own brethren. So he is in great distress and does not know what to do. Sri Krishna, the incarnation of Vishnu, disguised as Arjuna's charioteer observes his spiritual predicament and comes to his rescue.

Arjuna's trouble is that his moral duty urges him to act but the consequences of this action seem to be entirely immoral. Sri Krishna resolves this difficulty on the basis of the philosophy of the *Upanishads* and so he has to explain the fundamental principles of this philosophy. The gist of his argument is that to find the right way to moral action it is essential to base morality on religion. Every individual act has to be judged by the standards which religion has laid down. The religious ideal according to the *Upanishads* is the realisation of the unity of Being. It is not mere knowledge but complete absorption in the contemplation of *Brahma* till the illusion of duality is removed and the seeker and the sought become one. At this stage the whole nature of one's action changes. One performs the functions necessary for the preservation of one's own self and of society merely for duty's sale without any consideration for one's personal desire or the consciences of one's action. To Arjuna, Sri Krishna's advice is that he should discharge the duties laid down on him by the Kshatriya caste in a state of spiritual detachment swayed by desire, aid not have the slightest concern with the consequence of his action. He should, in fact, get rid of the feeling that he is acting at all and regard all that is being done as the work of *Brahma,* the real agent. He should realise that his own action, like his existence as an individual, is mere appearance, a mere name.

The *Bhagwad Gita* is not only a commentary on but a supplement to the *Upanishads.* In the *Upanishads* the emphasis is on the theoretical aspect of religion, that is, on the nature of *Brahma* and the *atma* and their identity; in the *Gita* on the practical approach, that is, on the way of the realisation of *Brahma* and the attainment of salvation. The *Gita* has tried to make a synthesis of three ways of attaining salvation—the way of knowledge through speculation and ascetic discipline, the way of faith and devotion, and the way of action. All the three have been mentioned in the *Upanishads* but so much stress has been laid on pure knowledge that the devotional aspect of religion is lost sight of and it looks as if realisation of the truth is something purely intellectual with no scope for love or devotion. Similarly, action is ranked inferior to knowledge. Apparently the *Upanishads* regard action of any kind as a chain impeding the progress of the seeker of truth which has to be broken before knowledge and salvation can be attained. The *Gita* has removed these misunderstandings and made it quite clear that the realisation of *atma* and *Brahma* emphasised in the *Upanishads,* is not mere abstract thought but a spiritual merging of the seeker into the sought involving love and devotion, and that action performed solely from a sense of duty is not an impediment but an effective means to this end.

Hindu thinkers seemed to be trying to reform Hinduism so as to invest it with the moral and spiritual strength to hold its own against Buddhism and regain the status of a national religion. This movement was not confined to religion and philosophy alone but penetrated below the intellectual level into the depths of feeling expressing itself in epic or heroic poetry. The stories of the *Mahabharata* and the *Ramayana* told in various folksongs had been current among the people for many generations. About the middle of this period in the second century B.C. they were compiled and reedited so that the memorable deeds of the heroes of the Vedic Hindu age may remind the people of their great past and stir in their minds the desire for a new and better life. Strictly speaking the *Ramayana* is not a religious poem but may be regarded as the first specimen of secular poetry. But it presents the lofty characters of Rama, Lakshman and Sita in such an attractive and effective way that the readers are inspired with the deepest religious sentiments of love and devotion, and to them it is no less sacred than the holy books of the Hindu religion. On the other hand the *Mahabharata* is, according to ancient tradition, a continuation of the *Yajur Veda* and calls itself the fifth *Veda* as well as a *Dharamashastra.* Religious significance, however, is attributed not to the story of the Kurus and the Pandavas but to those portions of the *Mahabharata* which deal with philosophical problems, specially to the famous discourse of Sri Krishna to which we have referred above.

Against this background of religious thought we have to look at the various aspects of the culture of an age in which religion was not merely a part of life but dominated the whole of it. Social and political organisations, the sciences, fine arts, mode of living, food and dress—everything was cast in the mould of religion.

Though the state was an autocratic one and in matters of administration the will of the raja was law, yet in judicial matters he had to follow the *Dharmashastras*. Generally Brahmins who were known for their learning and piety were employed as advisers to the raja and had a considerable say in matters of state. So it can be said that the state was to some extent subordinate to religion. But with the Buddhist state, at least in Asoka's time, the case was quite the reverse. The raja had come to be regarded as the religious head of the Buddhists. The Hindus enjoyed complete freedom of faith and worship. But as far as moral life was concerned, the state maintained a strict censorship over all its citizens, Hindus as well as Buddhists, and special officers called Dhamma Mahamatras were appointed for the purpose. Apart from this, the general pattern of the state was the same as under Hindu rulers and its most prominent feature was that the raja ruled through a bureaucracy and an executive no less elaborate than we find in a modern state.

The change which Buddhism brought about in the social system was that, though caste distinctions did not disappear, they became less important.

The Buddhist Sangha opened its doors to all castes and thus the religious basis of *varnashram* was weakened. In general social life the hierarchy of the caste system persisted even among the Buddhists and the Jains, but the order of gradation was changed to some extent. The nobles who belonged to the Kshatriya and the traders who belonged to the Vaishya castes were now regarded superior to the Brahmins.

Another important effect of the Buddhist movement was that animal sacrifice, which Asoka had stopped during his reign, was given up forever by the great bulk of Hindu society. Only a small section of the population like the worshippers of Kali continued to observe it. The part played by Jainism in putting an end to animal sacrifice and meat-eating as well as in propagating the doctrine of *ahimsa* in Indian society was no less important than that of Buddhism.

The few sciences which were cultivated at this time had their roots in religion. Philosophy, as we have seen, was intimately connected with religion. Orthography, grammar and prosody had developed in the course of the study of the *Vedas* and were regarded as parts of Vedic lore. The old Indo-Aryan language, generally known as Vedic, was considerably changed and divided into several branches. One of these, current in the middle regions of north India, had developed on a logical pattern and was called Sanskrit. As the language of Hindu religion and philosophy it was studied by the upper classes throughout India. Astrology, which had begun from the study of the movements of stars for determining the time of religious rites and sacrifices was the special preserve of Brahmins.

Buddhism exercised a great influence on education during this age. Before the Buddha the language of science and religion was Sanskrit. All the holy books were in Sanskrit and could be studied by none except the Brahmins and the Kshatriyas. Education, therefore, was confined exclusively to these high castes. The Buddha adopted for the propagation of his message the language of common intercourse instead of Sanskrit. In those days the language spoken in the homeland of the Buddha was the eastern dialect of Indo-Aryan. It was in this dialect that the Buddha preached. By the time of Asoka it had become the religious language of the Buddhists, and spread along with Buddhism throughout India. That is why Asoka used it in his edicts carved on pillars in different parts of the country. As far as knowledge is concerned, the Buddhists generally confined themselves to the study of religious lore. The field of learning continued to be under the sway of the Brahmins throughout the period. So the various systems of philosophy, religious law, political economy and the masterpieces of epic poetry, to which we have referred above, were all works of Brahmin thinkers.

On the other hand, art flourished under Buddhist patronage. In the pre-Buddhist period fine arts were in a primitive stage. Architecture too had made little progress. Houses of one to four storeys were built of wood in cities situated on river-bank or sea-coast and of bricks in those on a higher altitude. They were provided with a large number of windows. Straw and bricks were used for ceilings. Each house had, as a rule, a square courtyard surrounded on all sides by rooms with verandas in front. The cities were generally planned in the form of a square or a rectangle. The main street ran from east to west, side streets from north to south. A separate quarter was set apart for each of the various vocational groups. Temples were situated in the northern part of the city and in each of them there was a chamber of bamboo lattice-work which served as an altar. Even in cities where bricks were used for building houses, temples were generally made of bamboo. The oldest temple which has so far been traced is the Vishnu temple near Chittor. Another belonging to the same period has been found in Bes Nagar.

The use of stone in buildings had begun a little before Asoka's time. But it was he who built stone structures on a large scale. Of these, the royal palaces have been destroyed by the ravages of time. But some *stupas,* pillars and *viharas* (monasteries) are still extant. Specimens of *stupas* can be seen in Sanchi and Barhut. The carvings on their fences and gates deal not with religious but with secular subjects, and present vivid pictures of life in that period. The Asoka pillars cut out of solid stone are from 40 to 60 feet high with a polished surface shining like a mirror. In the upper part there are on a square base a bell-shaped crenate capital and some particular symbolic figures, generally that of a lion. The most famous of them is the pillar in

Sarnath near Banaras with four stately lion-figures bearing the *Dharmachakra*. It is these lions and the sacred wheel that have been adopted as the official emblem of the Indian Republic.

The flower of Buddhist art is seen in the caves of Ajanta and their frescoes. These paintings executed from the second century B.C. to the third century ad present the characteristics of Buddhist art at its best. The first thing to be noticed is that from the point of view of artistic skill and technical perfection, the Ajanta painting had reached such a high standard that it must be regarded as the result of development over centuries. This can only be explained by Jinking the Ajanta art through the Dravidian culture of south India, with the Indus Valley civilisation because the Vedic culture which was the precursor of the Buddhist culture in north India, is not known to have had any painting worth the name.

This hypothesis would account for the fact that these frescoes give as prominent a place to non-Aryan figures like the Nagars, as to the Aryan ones. Another characteristic of these paintings, as of all Buddhist art, is simplicity and restraint that is the avoidance of elaborate decoration and ornamentation as well as that of excessive emotion, which can be regarded as the direct influence of the Buddha's teachings. At the same time the charming Bodhisatva Padampani shows that Buddhist art combined a deep spirituality and inwardness with the capacity to take delight in physical beauty and grace.

VIII. HISTORY OF POLITICAL AND CULTURAL EXPANSION

The Spread of Indian culture was an intellectual conquest through peaceful means. It was, to start with, generally a one-way traffic. While many travellers, especially from China, came to India, there never was any attempt on their part to indoctrinate Indians in the philosophy of Confucius or of any other Chinese thinker. On the other hand, Buddhism secured a footing in China as early as the Ist century A.D. Enterprising merchants, adventurous young princes, and scholars like Kumarajiva, Kásyapa Matanga, Padmasambhava and others undertook this task in a selfless spirit. There is however, no doubt that later india also imbibed foreign culture.

Political expansion in South East Asia was motivated partly by a desire on the part of enterprising princes driven by misfortune to find new homes and kingdoms for themselves and partly to spread Indian culture. A few adventurous men like Kaundinya settled down in the kingdoms explored by them, where they were accepted by the local population as their rulers. These kingdoms also became the repositories of Indian culture in the medieval period when India itself was engulfed in political turmoils. They were not Indian colonies but independent states with little political contact with the motherland. The long war between the Colas and the Sailendras is a pointer in this direction. In the Western and Central Asian spheres, there was contact and possible influence in the filed of religion and philosophy; at the other end in South East Asia it was complete Indianisation of the region. Rulers professing Hinduism or Buddhism set up a socio-political structure on the ancient Indian model and patronised Indian learning, art and architecture. Indian culture dominated in every sphere, although the rulers considered themselves as part and parcel of the indigenous soil. Later on, it was completely submerged in the local culture. This development covers more than a thousand years.

India and Sri Lanka

The earliest historical tradition in Sri Lanka connected with India was the landing of prince Vijaya with seven hundred followers in that island—the first phase of Indian settlement in that pear-shaped island, according to the *Mahavamsa*. Its probable date is about 500 B.C. Political relations between the two countries commenced at the time of Asoka with the arrival of Mahendra and Sanghmitra who were received the king Devanampiya Tissa. Dutthagamani (c. 101-77 B.C or 161-137 B.C) invited *Theras* from different parts of India. Monks of Sri Lanka also visited India. In the time of Samudragupta, King Srimeghavarna (c.A.D, 352-79)sent an envoy with gifts to secure the permission of the Gupta monarch to build a monastery at Buddha Gaya for the residence of Buddhist monks from Sri Lanka. This was readily granted. Sri Lanka's relations with South India, though often strained in the political field, were cordial in other spheres. The Cola rule in Sri Lanka (Ceylon) from c. A.D. 992-93 during the reign of Rajaraja (A.D. 985-1016) was noted for the spread of Hinduism in that island. In the days of Parakramabahu I (c. A.D.1153-86), the Simhalese fought against the Colas as they supported rival candidates for the Pandya throne, and captured Ramesvaram and Madurai, but it was a short-lived victory. Pandyan and Vijayanagar influence continued in Sri Lanka from 13th to the 16th century A.D. and was notable for the establishment of a Tamil kingdom in the north, followed by more than three centuries of foreign rule. Indian cultural influence in the island is traceable in the realms of language, literature, art and architecture; and Buddhism continues to this day to be the binding force.

Early Settlements in Burma, Thailand and Malaya

The march of Indian culture in South East Asia was the outcome of the thirst for reaching the eastern EI Dorado—Kanakapuri—the land of gold. Merchants and adventurous or banished princes, seeking to try their luck in the unknown land, embarked either at the ports of Tamralipti and Paloura or look the land route through dense forests and mountains noticed by the Chinese travellers, Kia-Tan, and also mentioned in Burmese chronicles.

Sri Ksetra

The early history of Burma is shrouded in mystery, but Indians had probably settled in that country since the beginning of the Christian era. The Hinduised Pyus tribe founded the kingdom of Sriksetra (modern Kmawza, old Prome), and their rule lasted till about the 9th century A.D. Excavations at the ancient site of Sriksetra gave brought to light terracotta votive tablets, inscriptions, sculptures and ruins of old buildings. The terracotta tablets, some hundreds from a single mound, contain the figure of the Buddha and scenes from his life nd the well-known Buddhist formula. *ye dharam hetuprahbava* etc., and sometimes short extracts from the *Abhidhamma Pitaka*. The inscriptions are in Sanskrit, Pali and the forgotten language of the Pyus. but in a script similar to the South Indian Pallava-Grantha. Numerous figures of the Buddha in stone, bronze and terracotta have also come to light (A.D. 600-800) and these are all in Indian style. The remnants of the ruined *stupas* at Hmawza also show the common Indian form.

Abhiraja

Tradition has it that Abhiraja, a prince of the Sakya clan of Kapilavastu, founded the city of Sankissa on the upper Irrawaddy from where he ruled as king. Later Aniruddha (A.D. 1044-77) brought about the political unification Burma. He married a Vaisali princess, and their son Kyanzittha was crowned in c. A.D. 1084. He repaired the Buddha Gaya temple and married a Cola princess. Both he and his successor maintained close relations with India. The Mongol invasion in the last quarter of the 13th century spelt political disintegration in Burma.

Indian Colonies in Thailand and Malaya

Thailand and Malaya were colonised by the Indians from the north as sell as from the south Ships touched at Takua Pa in the Malaya Peninsula which was a transit centre for a short cut to Caiya on the Bay of Bandon. Archaeological finds all around bear testimony to the ancient Indian colony. Another port of disembarkation was Tavoy from where travellers could proceed to the Menam delta. The inscriptions from Malaya include those of the famous sailor Buddhagupta found in the north-west of Wellesley province. King Visnu of the Ligor inscription and Visnuvarman of the Perak seal were probably the same person—an early ruler of Malaya. According to a Chinese chronicle, five hundred families of Hu, probably a mercantile class, two hundred Buddhists and more than a thousand Brahmanas of India lived at Tuen-siun in Malaya. Another inscription of the 3rd century A.D. refers to a kingdom called Lin-yang, while Lang-Kia-su is noticed in the *History of the Liang Dynasty*. The former was supposed to be in Central Burma, the latter in Malaya Peninsula was founded about the 2nd century A.D. A ruler named Bhagadatta sent his ambassador Aditya to China in A.D. 515. The Hindu settlement at Pa-hoang welcomed Brahmanas from India and had contacts with China in the 5th century A.D. It is identified with Pahang, and its ruler was Sri Balạvarma, Kan-to-li was another Hindu settlement in the Malaya Peninsula besides many others flourishing in the 4th and 5th centuries A.D. Nakhon Sri.Dhammarat (Ligor) with its great *stupa* surrounded by a large number of temples was a Buddhist settlement of that period. Other Indian settlements in this region were those of Dvaravati and Haripunjaya in Thailand.

Fu-nan

Archaeological funds in places like Sa-huynh in Annam. Samrong-seu in Cambodia, Oc-Eo in Cochin-China and

Sempaga in the island of Celebes (Sulawesi) suggest a sudden change from the Neolithic to the Hindu culture with the arrival of Indian immigrants. either directly from India or through Burma and Malaya. The oldest Hindu kingdom established in the lower valley of the Mekong, the area now included in the Indo-China peninsula-was known as Fu-nan, with its capital at Vyadhapura, probably near Ba Phnom. According to the tradition recorded in inscriptions, it was founded in the Ist century B.C. by a Brahmana named Kaundinya from India who defeated and married the Nagi princess Soma of that place. The second Kaundinya—again a Brahmana from India-reached the place through Pan-pan (Bandon) and was elected king by the people, thus marking the next stage of Indian colonisation. Hinduism took deep root in that country and the rulers bore Indian names and followed Indian religion. The Brahmanical hierarchy was a notable feature in the social order.

Kambuja

Fu-nan lost its importance and was merged in the famous kingdom of Kambuja (Kampuchea) named after Kambu-Svayambhuva, occupying the territory around Vat Phu hill near Bassac in Laos, in the north-east corner of Kampuchea. By about the 6th century A.D., king Bhavavarman founded a new royal family, consolidating his hold over the kingdom of Kambuja and Fu-nan. His successors ruled for a very long time. The later history is that of the empire of Kambuja extending over a period of moire than five centuries.

Campa

The Hinduised kingdom of Campa in the centre of the southern part of Annam was founded at the close of the 2nd century A.D. The kingdom of Siang-lin founded by Kiu-lien in A.D. 192, according to the Chinese Annals, was the nucleus of the Hindu kingdom of Campa. The famous

Vo-chanh inscription (near Nha Trang in the province of Khanh-Hoa in South Vietnam), composed in Sanskrit and written in an Indian script of about the 2nd century A.D., refers to the royal family of Sri Mara who might have been the first historical king, if not the founder of the Hindu dynasty. By the 4th century A.D., Sri Bhadravarman, identified with Fan-Hu-ta, built the temple of Siva at Myson, naming the deity after him, Sri Bhadresvarasvamin. Hindu dynasties and religion (both Hinduism and Buddhism) and Sanskrit language flourished for a long time despite the proximity to and clash with Tonkin then under Chinese occupation. From Sri-Mara of the Vo-canh record to Prakasadharma Vikratavarman in 7th century A.D., the history of Campa is one of incessant struggles against China. This ruler of Campa was related on his mother's side with the Kambuja royal family. In the last phase of Campa's history, the country came into clash with the Annamites and Kambuja. It also offered strong resistance to Kublai Khan, the great Mongol chief. The struggle against the Annamites was a prolonged one, causing loss of territory. A portion of the northern tip passed into enemy hands; and the desire for an Annamite princess costs Jayasimhavarman IV two provinces—this event happened in the 14th century. Campa finally fell before the Annamite onslaught, loosing Amaravati, in A.D. 1402 and Vijaya in the centre in 1471. It was thus reduced to a small principality which was also gone with the ruler seeking refuge in Kambuja.

Early Kingdoms in Indonesia

The Indonesia archipelago containing nearly three thousand island also came under the influence of Hindu culture. The name Yavadvipa, very probably Java, occurs in Valmikis *Ramayana*. The four rock-cut inscriptions found around Jakarta refer to a king named Purnavarman whose capital was the city of Taruma. His father, Rajadhiraja, constructed a canal named Candrabhaga, connecting the royal city with the sea, and another named Gomati. The Indo-Javanese Phase of history in Central Java dates from the 8th century A.D. The Hindus set up kingdoms in Central and Eastern Java, as is evident from the numerous inscriptions and monuments in these regions.

Kingdoms in Java and Sumatra

Besides Java, the neighbouring islands of Sumatra and Borneo were also centres of Hindu settlements. I-tsing refers to the famous kingdom of Sri Vijaya, which in course of time became a great political power in South East Asia. If Po-li of the Chinese text could be identified with Bali, then this small island which has retained its Hindu/character to this day was an early settlement of the Indians. Its ruler's family name was Ca-ri-ya-ka corresponding to Ksatra or Ksatri and the kingdom sent embassies to China from A.D. 518 to 630.

Mulavarman of Borneo

Seven inscriptions recorded on *vupas* and found in the district of Kutei at Muara Kaman, in Borneo, record certain great gifts (*mahadanas*) and religious sacrifices of king Mulavarman, son of Asvavarman, and grandson of Kutlunga. In East Borneo, a large number of images of Hindu gods have been found in the cave of Kombeng, while in West Borneo at various places inscriptions on stone and a number of inscribed gold plates have been found. A Buddha image of the Gupta style and another of the Amaravati style were found at Sambas at Sempaga in the Celebes respectively. It appears that Borso had Hindu settlements, and it is tempting to identify it with the Barhina-dvipa of the *Vayu Purana*. These kingdoms in Malaysia, Indonesia, and Indo-China formed the nucleus of the empire of the Sailendras and the Varmans of Kambuja.

Imperial Phase

Sri Vijaya was probably the first Hindu empire in

South East Asia. I-tsing spent a few years at Palembang, its capital. It was a centre of trade and Buddhist learning. A record dated in the year Saka 606 (A.D.684) mentions Jayanasa or Jayanaga as the ruler of Sri Vijaya. As a leading and powerful state. Sri Vijaya sent several embassies to China between A.D. 670 and A.D. 741. An inscription dated in the year A.D. 75 from Ligor in the Malaya Peninsula refers to the mighty power of the Buddhist king if that place. Sri Vijaya gained power and influence in Malaya and Indonesia and helped trade between the orient and the occident.

The Sailendra Empire

The Sailendras whose origin has been a matter of dispute also ruled in Malaya and Indonesia for nearly five hundred years. The original home of the Sailendras seems to have been in Java where the famous monuments of Barabudur and Candi Mendut are fitting memorials of their munificence as patrons of art. The Nalanda record dated in the year 39 or 35 of the time of king Devapala (c. A.D, 850) records the grant of five villages for the maintenance of a monastery by Balaputradeva, king of Suvarnadvipa. Sri Cudamanivarman and his son Sri Mara Vijayottungavarman, rulers of Kadara or Kataha (Kedda in the Malaya Peninsula) and Sri Vijaya, maintained contacts with the Colas. They were associated with the construction of a Buddhist *Vihara* at Nagapattana (Nagapattinam) on the east coast of India. Cola conquest of Kataha resulted in the overthrow of the sailendras some time before A.D. 1025. The kingdom of San-fo-tsi as called by the Chinese which took its place continued for more than three hundred years till it was destroyed by Java in the 14th century A.D.

The Hindu Kingdom of Eastern Java

Some Hindu rulers figure prominently in the history of Java. King Airlangga, son-in-law of a Javanese king, was formally consecrated ruler in East Java and brought the whole of the island under his control. In his records we have reference to the peoples of Kalinga, Simhala, Dravida, Karnataka, Campa and Khmer who had evidently trade relations with Java. Regarded as an incarnation of Visnu, the fine figure of the deity seated in a Garuda from Belahan is supposed to be his actual representation. The partition of his kingdom between his two sons was the beginning of the decline of his empire. Kadiri, the capital of one, was conquered by the neighbouring ruler of Singhasari named Rajasa who united the whole of Java under his authority. Krtanagara, well up in art and literature., extended his authority over Bali, Sunda (Western Java) Sumatra, Malaya, Borneo and Madura (another island). His egotism and absorption in religious affairs cost him his life and throne. The Mongol ruler Qublai Khan conquered the kingdom in A.D. 1293 but the Mongols did not stay there.

Majapahit

Vijaya, the son-in-law of Krtanagara, founded a new kingdom with Majapahit as his capital, and was known as Krtarajasa Jayavardhana. During the reign of Rajasanagara, who ascended the throne in A.D. 1350, the Majapahit empire included large parts of Malaya and Indonesia. It had contacts with Thailand , Kalinga, Campa and Dharmanagari, and other neighbouring places, and trade relations with Jambudvipa (India), Cina, Karnataka, and Gauda. His death in A.D. 1389 precipitated internal dissensions. Although the kingdom of Majapahit continued for another century, it was of little importance. The influx of Muslim traders, giving Islam a footing in the island, paved the way for its gradual expansion in Indonesia, ultimately enveloping it completely. Only Bali escaped and preserved its old tradition to this day.

Varman Empire in Kambuja Desa

The empire of the Varmans in Kambuja lasted for nearly five centuries. Bhavavarman and his successors

Mahendravarman and Isanavarman had carved out a big kingdom, and in the 7th century A.D. it extended upto Dangrek Mountains in the north, comprising Cochin-China and Cambodia. After a dark period of over a hundred years, when probably the Sailendras dominated there, Jayavarman II ascended the throne in A.D 802 and founded a new dynasty. The kingdom ruled by him and his successor, Jayavarman III, was vast, reaching the frontier of Yunnan in southern China. Indravarman succeeded him and founded a new royal dynasty. He boasted fo his commands being obeyed by rulers of Campa. Cina and Yavadvipa. Yasovarman, who ascended the throne in A.D.889, enhanced the power, prestige and glory of his empire an his family. A distinguished man of letter, he was also a patron of art, and built many temples and his capital at Yasodharapura. During the time of Rajendravarman (c. A.d. 944-68) the empire comprised the vast region to the south of China and east of Burma.

A period of internal trouble soon followed. It was only in the time of Suryavarman II that the dissenting forces were over come, to rise again after his death in or after A.D. 1145. The invasion by the king of Campa, and the sacking of the Kambuja capital shattered its prestige. It was, however, regained by Jayavarman VII who defeated the Chams in a naval engagement in 1190. In the prolonged struggle fortune favoured the Kambuja ruler and the whole of Campa came under his sway. This was the peak period with the Kambuja empire extending from the sea of China to the Bay of Bengal. The city of Angkor Thom was well fortified and well laid out with its enormous buildings and palaces, and the famous temple of Bayon occupying the central portion of the city is regarded as the masterpiece of Kambuja architecture. The last important ruler was Jayavarman VIII whose abdication in A.D. 1295 was followed by internal troubles; and the aggression of the Thais which had begun in the 13th century brought about the downfall of the empire of the Hindu rulers in Indo-China, though the petty kingdom of Cambodia continues till today.

Thailand

Thailand was colonised by the Hindus in the first two centuries of the Christian era. Excavations at Pong Tuk, 32 km, from Pra Pathom, the discovery of a Sanskrit inscription of the 4th century A.D, near Pechaburi, and Saiva and Vaisnava sculptures point to this part being a centre of Hindu culture. After the decline of Fu-nan, of which Thailand had been a part, the Dvaravati kingdom rose into importance. The Hinduised Mons who dominated this kingdom extended their influence in the north as far as Haripunjaya or Lamphun. In the 10th century A.D. the Kambuja empire extended over this region.

Cultural Impact

The Indian immigrants in South East Asia, while setting up their kingdoms, tried to build a social structure on the orthodox Indian model with the traditional four castes (*caturvarnaya*) and the supremacy of the Brahmanas and the Ksatriyas. The distinction between Brahmanas and the Ksatriyas was more apparent than real. Intrer-marriage between the two was not unknown. Agastya, a Brahmana immigrant, married a princess named Yaso mati, and Divakara from Vrindavana in India took the hand of Indralaksmi, daughter of emperor Rajendravarman. Jayavarman VIII's queen hailed from the respectable family of Brahmana Hrsikesa of the Bharadvaja group. In Campa, Rudravarman's father was a famous Brahmana, while his mother was a Ksatriya. So also Prakasadharma's sister married a Brahmana named Satyakausika Svamin, and their son Bhadresvaravarman was a Brahma-Ksatriya. This caste is mentioned in several inscriptions in Kambuja and Campa. The *caturvarnay* also figures in Java and we find a reference to the emergence of caste from Brahma. But the caste system in these regions was not as rigid as in India. The aristocracy and the common people had a sharp line of distinction, specially noticed in their dress, which was scanty in the use of ordinary people but gorgeous and ornamented for the aristocrats. Caste did not interfere in the choice of the avocation. A Kambuja record refers to the members of a Brahmana family being elephant drivers, artisans and priests. In the time of Jayavarman V. certain new castes came into existence. The same inscription refers to seven castes (*saptavarnas*)

Dress and Ornaments

Complete Indianisation was also apparent from the dress of the people as shown in sculptures. The Indian *dhoti* was very commonly used. It was mentioned by Chinese historians. A sculpture at Bayon depicts the king dressed in *dhoti* with a *hara*- jewelled gold garland-round his neck. *The History of the Sui Dynasty* mentions that the king was dressed in purple silk clothes which were embroidered. Inscriptions and sculptures bring out the use of Indian ornaments—diadems (*mukutas*) *ear-pendants (kaudalas)* bracelets (*keyuras*), and wristband (*katakas*).

Family Life and Position of Women

Pastime and recreation included playing on instruments like lyre (*vina*) drum (*mrdanga*) , kettle drum (*bheri*) and cymbal (*panava*). The family life and position of women were similar to those in India. An inscription from Kambuja refers to performance of *pitrtarpana* by the son with water. Joint family was usually in vouge. Some of the rulers traced descent on the mothers side. The food habit of the people was the same ; *tandula* (rice) was the staple food with pulses like *tila* and *mudga*. Likewise *ghrta, dadhi* and *guda* (ghee, curd and molasses) are mentioned in inscriptions.

The contribution of Indians to the economy of the country was no less, as is evident from references to different avocations and the use of coins and weights of several denominations.

Education

Indian influence extended to the field of education and literature as well. We find the progressive use of Indian literature, both Sanskrit and Pali. Prakrt was not unknown, since we have a reference to Gunadhya. The Indian script was retained. There are also references to talented ladies, implying that education was not denied to the fair sex. It was diffused through centres, popularly called *Asramas* Sri Vijaya was a big centre of learning for Buddhism and Buddhist scholars. Besides the four Vedas, including the *Atharva* and the *Sama*, grammar was studies according to different traditions, Panini's *Astadhyayi* is mentioned in several records, while king Yasovarman had composed a commentary on the *Mahabhasya* of Patanjali. The Puranas were well known. The *Ramayana* and the *Mahabharata* were also studied. People were familiar with the works of Kalidasa especially *Raghuvamsa*. The names of Bharavi, Vasubandhu and Gunadhya also figure in Kambuja records.

Literature

Indian literature was keenly studies in Campa. King Bhadra varman was well versed in the four Veda, while king Indravarman III was proficient in the six systems of Hindu philosophy as well as Buddhist philosophy. King Jaya-Indravarmadeva VII was well versed in grammar, astrology and the Mahayana system of philosophy. According to a Chinese chronicle, after the Chinese General Lieu Fang had sacked the city of Campa, he carried with them 1,350 Buddhist manuscripts. This event took place in A.D.605. Java drank deep at the fountain of Indian literature, and under the patronage of its benign rulers, produced a vast literature, varied in contents. Besides the translations of the two Epics the *Ramayana* and the *Mahabharata*,

Java produced the *Krsnayana* by Triguna dealing with the abduction of Rukmini by Krsna, *Bharata-yuddha* written by Mpu Sedah and *Harivamsa* both based on the *Mahabharata,* during the reign of Jayabhaya—and several works belonging to the Purana class of which special mention may be made of the *Brahmauda Purana.* The Aja-Indumati episode in the *Raghuvamsa* and the *Madana-dahana* episode in the *Kumarasambhava* find their echoes respectively in the *Sumanasantaka* and the *Smaradahana.* There were also works on *Niti* and *Dharma Sastra,* religion and philosophy. Among secular works may be mentioned those on history, linguistics, medicine and erotics. All this was the outcome of an academic discipline, based on the ancient Indian system of education and the patronage extended by the highly gifted and enlightened rulers.

Religion and Art

The greatest impact was in the field of religion and art, the former supplying themes to the artist who tried to conform to the canons of the *Silpasastra.* The religious systems of India-both Hinduism and Buddhism—became deeply rooted in South East Asia. The popular faiths and religious practices in India found an exact replica in those regions. Vedic sacrifices with the setting up of the *yupas* were known in Borneo about the 4th century A.D. the Puranic gods and goddesses and stores connected with them were widely current. Although Saivism was more prominent, Visnu with his incarnations also found numerous patrons and votaries from among the ruling monarchs. Siva with his destructive and renovating powers—and his two *Saktis*, Mahakali and Parvati, along with his *linga* form—is very much in evidence. The images of Ganesa and the war god Kartikeya are also found. Visnu represented with four arms, his *Sakti* Laksmi, as well as his incarnations, especially Matsya, Varaha, Narasimha, Rama and Krsna are all represented. Brahma also figures as the third member of the trinity. Tthe famous Belahan image of Visnu is supposed to be one of the best specimens of sculpture in Java. In Campa, Siva occupied the most important position and an image of him in the form of a *linga* was regarded as the national deity throughout the course of is history. Other deities also were associated with siva, like ganesa, Kartikeya, and even his bull *Nandi.* Visnu was known by various names, and so also his incarnations. Some of the kings after death, were associated with a divinity. There were several other Brahmanical gods, like Surya and Kubera, who also figured in religious life and art in Campa.

In Kambuja the worship of Siva was associated with the cult of Devaraja which comprised the setting up of *linga* on a raised pyramid symbolising the essence of royalty, the deification of royalty and ancestor worship. Tantricism was closely connected with this cult. The Indian Brahmana Hiranyadama particularly taught certain Tantric texts to Sivakaivalya. Pure Saivism is evident from the Siva worship is also noticed both in inscriptions and in art. The composite deities-Hari-Hara and Trimurti are also noticed. As the supreme deity, Siva presides over the famous temple of Bayon. Visnu is also invoked in a number of records under different names and forms. The story of Krsna is depicted in sculptures. There are references to various other Brahmanical divinities suggesting that the Puranic form of worship was very popular. Vedic sacrifices continued to be performed. Sivacarya was the official priest of four successive kings. Suryavarman performed *Laksahoma* and *Kotihoma* sacrifices and gave liberal fees to the Brahmana priests.

Buddhism

Buddhism flourished side by side in South East Asia not as an antagonistic religion but as a supplementary one. Buddha and Siva are associated together, and the former even finds a place in the Brahmanical Trinity consisting of Padmodbhava (Brahma), Ambhojanetra (Visnu) and the Buddha. The assimilation of Buddha in the Brahmanical Trinity is an important feature. Buddhism acquired great favour both in Campa and Java. Dong Duong in Campa appears to have been a stronghold of Buddhists as evidenced by several images of the Buddha, and remnants of a Buddhist temple were found there. In Java the famous *stupa* at Barabudur is a living monument, symbolising the flourishing state of Buddhism in that island. In all these places the religion of the Tathagata was not an antagonistic force set up against Brahmanism but was something friendly or even identical. A Siva-Buddha cult existed in Java, and Siva, Visnu, and the Buddha were all regarded as identical. The international character of Buddhism is apparent from contacts between Suvarnadvipa and India on the one hand, and other Buddhist countries on the other. We have references to Atisa Dipankara of Vikramasila and Dharmapala of Kanci as visitors to Suvarnadvipa.

Temples

Art, as the handmaid of religion, constitutes the greatest living memorial of Indian culture and civilisation in South East Asia. Whether it be the temples of Myson or Po-Nagar in Campa, or those of Angkor Vat and Bayon in Cambodia or the Barabudur and the Candis of Java, they were all inspired by one ideal-the setting up of a fitting monument symbolising the people's religious devotion. The earlier phase in temple construction is completely Indian, either of the North Indian *Sikhara* type or of the South Indian Dravid style, but native genius with a desire for lofty and sky-scraping structures triumphs over the earlier impulse. A colossal character to the whole structure is also given by the grouping of numerous temples in one enclosure. The sculptures and narrative reliefs bear a stamp of their own, whetner they are the *Ramayana* reliefs at Panataran or the Krsna legend at Angkor Vat. In Cambodia one also notices the cruciform plan of the individual towers, like the one in the Kandariya Mahadeva temple at Khajuraho, and also the conception of grouping a number of cellas on a single terrace as in the famous Orissan temples at Bhubanesvar. The artists exhibited mastery of technique with a high aesthetic conception. Withe decay of Indian influence and the final collapse of the Hindu states art received a death below.

North-western Phase

Indian cultural influence extended to West and Central Asia as well. There was no attempt at political expansion in the west, but the assimilation of all the foreigners who came to India Greeks. Parthians, Sakas, Kusanas and Hunas—in the socio religious structure of India was the triumph of Indian culture. This extended even further, Chinese Turkestan, called by Sir Aurel Stein as the innermost heart of Asia, and forming a vast basin was at one time a prosperous country of flourishing cities with their rich sanctuaries and monasteries. The remains in Turkestan and the finds at different sits explored or excavated by archaeologists have established beyond doubt that large number of Indians had migrated from the Punjab and Kashmir and settled in the Tarim basin where they built numerous cities, Indian life and thought were so firmly planted that when Stein was exploring that region he felt as if he was in some Punjab village, although he was nearly 3,220 km, away from the land of the five rivers.

Indian Kingdom in Khotan

There was in an Indian kingdom in Khotan alleged to have been founded by son of emperor Asoka. The names of the early kings all begin with Vijeta. Buddhism was introduced in that kingdom more than a century after its establishment. Vairocana from Kashmir had gone there for that purpose. Later many Buddhist monasteries were set up on the region; two famous one, Gosrnga and Gomati *viharas* were great centres of learning. Many other Indian monks visited Khotan and many Buddhist monasteries flourished there.

Both Prakrt and Sanskrit were studied in Khotan. The whole of Central Asia was a meeting place of different cultures since it contained the famous silk trade route between China and Rome. The northern route touched Kucha (Kuchi), Qara Shaht (ancient Agnidesa) and Turfan, while the southern route passed through Kashgar, Yarkand, Khotan, Niya, Miran and other important centres. The two routes finally converged at Tun-huang on the western border of China, a strong Buddhist centre noted for its famous grottos. Buddhism flourished in all these regions but traces of Brahmanical religion are also found in Khotan and other places.

Besides religion, Indian influence can also be traced in art and architecture. According to Pelliot, some Indian artists from Khotan had migrated to China. Various remnants of frescos leave no doubt that not only the whole iconography but the technique of drawing, conventions and mannerism were derived from the Buddhist paintings in India. The fragments from Dandan-Uliq show Indian influence—the conception, technique and details being all Indian. Even in the last phase, there is nothing which is not a reproduction of Indian models. Stucco figures were modelled on the existing ones at Gandhara. The Indian influence is even more distinctly confirmed by the finds from Khotan, Tumshuq and Schorshuq.

Political and cultural ties between India and Central Asia continued till about the 8th century A.D. The gradual advance of Islam and the suspension of the silk trade on account of insecure conditions resulted in the breaking of political and cultural ties between India and the "innermost heart of Asia".

India and Afghanistan

India's relations with Afghanistan have been closer in the political and cultural spheres. The political boundaries between India and Afghanistan did not exist under the Mauryas, Indo-Greeks, Kusanas and Mughals. The long period of political associations no doubt resulted in closer cultural contacts. Systematic explorations and excavations at Bamiyan, Begram, Hadda Surkh Kotal and other places have brought to light traces of Buddhist settlements. The Gandhara school of art which flourished both in India and Afghanistan is well represented in sculptures, stucco and clay, as well as in mural paintings from the 3rd to the 8th century A.D. The modern village of Hadda (ancient Nagarahara) is the site of 531 *stupas* together with some three thousand statues. It was one of the most important Buddhist establishments in Afghanistan. According to Fa-Hien, one thousand *stupas* were erected to the memory of Arhats and Pratyeka Buddhas. Bamiyan is noted for its colossl Buddha statues and innumerable cave shrines and monasteries. Brahmanism also flourished in Afghanistan as is evident from the find of a unique Surya image in Begram (ancient Kapisa) Indian influence in the field of religion and art continued till the end of the 10th century A.D., when Afghanistan became an Islamic state.

India and Iran

Indian cultural influence in Iran is not as prominent as in other spheres. The relations between the two countries can, however, be traced back to about the 3rd millennium B.C., with close similarity in the field of religion and mythology. After the fall of the Achaemenian empire, the master craftsmen seem to have found shelter in the Mauryan capital. It is quite likely that the Indian and Iranian artists were tackling similar problems under the same circumstances nd with the same material at their disposal. These resembles are therefore, symbolic of link from man to man, mind to mind, giving a proper coherence to the variegated history of civilisation.'

Indian religion and philosophy , however, made a deep impression on the Iranians. The doctrine propounded by Mani, who flourished in Iran in the 3rd century A.D. bears the influence of Buddhism, and a Manichaen treatise refers to him as Tathagata i.e., Buddha. There is also a marked resemblance between their views on asceticism. In the medieval period the Caliphs encouraged the translation into Persian of Indian treaties on medicine and astronomy. The Hindu system of numerals was borrowed from India by the Arabs and they spread it all over the world.

During the long course of history, India's attitude towards political and cultural expansion has never been imperialistic. Armies were never sent to conquer any region. The conquest was mainly intellectual, and incidentally the superior culture triumphed over the native one. Individual men or groups set up kingdoms which in course of time shaped into empires. The contact with the motherland was maintained but India never exploited the colonies for her own benefit. The kingdoms were, however, repositories of Indian culture—replicas of the ones in India. In South East Asia. these kingdoms and Indian culture flourished for nearly fifteen hundred year; in the land beyond the Himalayas their existence was of shorter duration. The spade of the archaeologist has uncovered this phase of Indian history. The degree and extent of colonial enterprise was never uniform, and sooner or later the Indians in their new homes found themselves merged in the local population.

REVIEW QUESTIONS

1. Point out the importance of ancient Indian history.
2. In what ways does ancient Indian history show the basic unity of India?
3. How old is man in India? How did he live in the Old Stone Age?

4. Trace the various phases in the Palaeolithic Age of India.
5. What is meant by 'neoliths'? Give an account of the material life of the neolithic people in India.
6. How did the neolithic culture differ from the palaeolithic culture?
7. How were the Harappan cities planned?
8. Describe the economic life of the Harappan people.
9. Give an account of the crafts and technology of the Harappans. Why is their culture called the Bronze Age culture?
10. Write a note on the religious practices of the Harappans.
11. Give an account of the Harappan pottery and terracottas.
12. Account for the end of the Harappan civilisation
13. Trace the expansion of the Aryans in the later Vedic period.
14. Describe the material life of the later Vedic people. How was it different from the Rigvedic life?
15. What is meant by the Painted Grey Ware culture?
16. Give an account of the political set-up in the later Vedic period.
17. How was society organised in later Vedic times?
18. What kind of religion developed in the later Vedic age?

Select Bibliography

Anderson, P., *The English in Western India,* Bombay, 1854, p. 16.

B. M. Laddell Hart, *Why does not We Learn from History,* p. 2.

Basham. A.L., *The Indian Sub-continent in Historical Perspective,* p. 23.

Burke, Edmund, Speeches in the trial of Warren Hastings, quoted in *Cambridge History of India* (Indian edition), Vol. V, p. 182.

Collingwood, *The Idea of History,* p. 214.

Cunningham, J.D., *A History of the Sikhs* (edited by Garrett and Sethi, 1955), p. 252.

Dobb, Maurice, *Studies in the Development of Capitalism* (London, 1946), p. 121.

Hart, B.M. Laddell, *Why does not We Learn from History,* p. 2.

Heckscher, E.F., 'Mercantilism', in *The Encyclopaedia of the Social Science,* Vol. X, p. 338.

Heckscher, E. F., 'Mercantilism', *op. cit.,* p. 339.

Henderson, S.V.P. *Introduction of Philosophy of Education,* 1947, p. 15.

Hill, S. C., *Bengal in* 1756-57, Vol. I, p. xxxii.

Hunter, W.W., *A History of British India,* Vol. II, p. 273.

Johnson, Henry, *Teaching of History.* New York Macmillan Company, 1940, p. 25.

Lecky, W. E. H., A History of England in the Eighteenth Century, Vol. I, p. 491; Also Phillips, R. H., *Georgian Scrap-book.*

Lipton, E., *The Economic History of England,* Vol. III, p. 155.

Malcolm, J., *Sketch of the Political History of India* (London, 1811), p. 69.

————, *The Life of Robert Lord Cline,* Vol. II, pp. 120-121.

Malleson, *The History of the French in India* (London, 1868), pp. 192-93.

Mill and Wilson, *The History of British India,* (fifth edition, 1858), Vol. I, p. 91, noter

Mill and Wilton, *The History of British India, op. cit.,* Vol. III, p. 60.

Muhibbul Hasan Khan, *History of Tipu Sultan,* pp. 324-29.

Sardesai, G.S., *New History of the Marathas,* Vol. II, p. 430.

Sarkar, Jadunath, *Fall of the Mughal Empire,* Vol. II, p. 128 (Sarkar's use of the term 'grandfatherly' is somewhat inexact, for Abdali was about 35 years of age in 1757).

Sen, S.N., *The Military System of the Marathas* (1958 edition), pp. 78-73.

Seton-Karr, W.S., *Cornwallis* (Rulers of India Scries), pp. 154-155.

Smith, Adam, *The Wealth of Nations,* op. cit., p. 388.

Terry, Edward, *A Voyage to East India* (1777 edition), pp. 5-6.

Thompson, V.M., *Dupleix and his Letters* (New York, 1933), p. 695.

Walsh, *An Introduction to Philosophy of History,* p. 40.

Williamson, J.A., *A Short History of British Expansion,* p 424.

Index

A

Administratibility, 177
Advantages,
  of a Good Text-Book, 155
  of Unit Planning, 129
Affective, 41
Aids, 86
Aims of Teaching History, 35
Ancient Buildings, 53
Ancient History, 19
Ancient Tools, 53
Aptitude and Personality Test, 184
Arthashastra, 255
Aryans, 217
Aspect history, 90
Assignment, 122
Atharvaveda, 217, 236
August, 33

B

Basham A.L., 34
Bhagwad Gita, 257, 258
Bharatasantati, 207
Bharatavarsha, 207
Biological Theory, 91
Black-Board, 194
Bloom's Taxonomy, 39
Blue-print in Constructing Achievement Test, 183
Bollard, 61
Bossing, 127
Brahma, 257, 258
brahmachari, 244
Brophy, 113
Bryce, 163
Buddhism and Jainism, 248
Buddhism, 206
Buddhist Sangha, 253, 260
Bulletin Board, 199
Burckhardt, 3

C

Campa, 268
Carivle, 49
Carlyle, 92
Center for History in the Schools, 114
Chalk Board, 194
Characteristics of a Lesson Plan, 130
Charts, 193
Child Psychology, 160
Chronological Order, 85
Cinema Projectors, 202
Comprehensiveness, 177
Conference Plan, 124
Contents of the History Syllabus, 95

Creative Imagination, 161
Criterion-Referenced Evaluation, 175
Cultivation of Historical Imagination, 142
Cultural Epoch Theory, 90
Curriculum Development, 89

D

Development of History, 3
Diagnosing Weaknesses, 176
Diagnostic and Achievement Tests, 182
Diagnosticity, 178
Different Types of Objective Tests, 185
Discussion Method, 69
Divided-Period Plan, 125
Double-Period Plan, 125
Dr. S. Radhakrishnan, 2
Drama Technique, 121
Dravidian Culture, 218
Dravidians, 217
Drill Technique, 118

E

Early History, 95
Early Kingdoms in Indonesia, 269
Economic History, 21
Effective instructional planning, 174
Egypt, 16
Elements of Time Sense, 138
Essay Type Questions, 180
Evaluation in History, 173
Examination Technique, 119
Excursions to the Sites of Historical Interest, 166

F

Film slides, 195
Fixed Study-Period Plan, 125
Flannel Board, 198
Flash Cards, 197
Flow Charts, 194
Formation of Units, 73
Freeman Butts, R., 115
From Concrete to Abstract, 85
From Known to Unknown, 85
Fu-nan, 267

G

Ganga-Yamuna doab, 236
Genealogical Charts, 194
General School Library, 145
Geographical Boundaries, 14
Germany, 4
Ghosh, K.D., 162
Good, C.V., 59
Green, G.H., 127

H

Harappan Civilisation, 222
Harappan villages, 226
Hasluck, E.S., 17
Henderson, 32
Henry Johnson, 1
Herodotus, 4
Hill, C.P., 102
Hindu Kingdom of Eastern Java, 271
Hinduism, 206, 216, 220

Historical Data, 8
Historical Synthesis, 9
History,
and Art, 27
History and Civics, 26
and Economics, 28
and Geography, 24
and Handwork, 29
and Language, 27
and Literature, 26
and Mathematics, 29
and Physical Sciences, 28
and Sociology, 31
and Theology, 30
as a Science, 6
Department Library, 146
Syllabus, 93
Text-books, 152
Hoppold, F.C., 37
Howell, 170

I

Ideal Materials, 148
Illustration Technique, 121
Imperial Phase, 270
Importance of History Library, 146
India and Afghanistan, 282
India and Iran, 282
India and Sri Lanka, 264
Indian History, 5
Indian Kingdom in Khotan, 280
Indian schools, 5
Indus Valley Civilisation, 214, 217

J

Jainism, 206
Jarvis, 51
Johnson, 1, 24, 26, 96, 152
Jones, 2, 3

K

Kalhana, 34
Kalibangan, 224
Kambuja, 268
Karl Marx, 5, 33
Kilpatrick, 61
Kingdoms in Java and Sumatra, 270
Knowledge,
of Objectives, 40
of World History, 164
Koerner, 24
Kothari Commission, 34, 158

K

Laboratory Method, 58
Late Stone Age, 211
Later Vedic Phase, 235
Layer Charts, 142
Lecture Method, 67
Legends, 51
Leopold Von Ranke, 4
Lesson Planning, 129
Lewis Hasluck, E., 11
Linwood Chase, 38
Literary Materials, 149
Local History, 16, 95
Lord R. Bryce, 158

M

Mahabharata, 208, 257, 259
Majapahit, 272

Majorie Reeves, 100
Majumdar, A.C., 16
Manusmriti, 255
Maps, 141, 192
Measurement of Factual Knowledge, 176
Mediaeval Ages, 19
Metal and Stone Inscriptions, 53
Method of the Study of Local History, 18
Ministry of Education, 103
Miss Drummond, 36
Modern Period, 20
Moffatt, 170
Mohenjodaro, 224
Moral Aim, 38
Morrison, H.C., 74
Motion pictures, 195
Muffut, M.P., 117
Mulavarman of Borneo, 270
Muller, 33
Myths, 51

N

Narration Technique, 117
National,
  History, 15, 95
  Standards for Civics and Government, 114
Need for Separate History Library, 147
New Stone Age, 211
Nietruhr, 4
Non-standardised Tests, 184
Norm-Referenced Evaluation, 175

O

Objectives of Teaching History, 39
Old,
  Coins, 53
  Concept, 4
  Stone Age, 208
  Written Records, 52
Oral Teaching, 87

P

Palaeolithic Age, 209
Patch' Method, 100
Paul Gagnon, 115
Periodic Method, 96
Pictorial Graph, 198
Place Charts, 142
Place of Text-Book, 151
Political History, 20
Preston, 128
Principles of Syllabus Construction, 94
Problem Method, 59
Prof. Ghat are, 94
Prof. Ghose, 2
Project Method, 61
Psychological Theory, 93
Pt. Nehru, 92

Q

Qualities and Qualifications, 159
Question and Answer, 87
Question-answer Technique, 119

R

Rabindranath Tagore, 2
Radhakrishnan, S., 158
Ramayana, 208
Rapson, 2
Reference Materials, 149
Regional History, 16
Regressive Method, 99
Religion and Culture, 244
Religious or Social Bias, 164
Review, 123
Rigveda, 217, 220
Role of Text-books in Teaching of History, 151

S

Sailendra Empire, 271
Samaveda Samhita, 236
Samaveda, 222
Sankhya philosophy, 255
Sardar Patel, 104
Scope of History, 10
Secondary Education Commission, 34
Selection of periods, 90
Self-study Method, 69
Sigmund Freud, 3
Simpson, 59
Sind Valley Civilisation, 215
Smith, V.A., 15
Social, Economical and Cultural History, 95
Source book, 54
Source Materials, 149
Source Method, 52
Special Teacher Plan, 124
Spencer, 8
Sri Ksetra, 266
Stands, L.B., 127
Stevenson, 61
Still pictures, 195
Study Hall Plan, 124
Subject-Matter Organisation, 96
Sumerians, 217
Supervised Study, 123

T

Table Charts, 193
Tamil literature, 218
Taxila, 208
Teaching Aids, 188, 189
Teaching History at the Primary Stage, 41
Teaching of Local History, 18
Terevelyan, 24
Terevelyan, 24
Text-book Method, 56
Text-books, 148, 190
Thailand and Malaya, 267
Thucydides, 4
Time,
  factor, 97
  graph, 139
  line, 139
  sense, 87
Topical Method, 73, 99
Traditional Type of Tests or Examinations, 179
True Stories, 51

U

Unit Method, 71
Unit Planning, 128
Upanishads, 255, 257, 258

Utilising Library Resources, 147
Utility, 178
Utnur, 213

V

Values of Teaching History, 44
VanSledright, 113
Varman Empire in Kambuja, 272
Vedas, 251, 254, 255, 256, 261
Von Ranke, 33

W

Walbesser, 130
Walsh, 9, 99
Wilson, 114
Wineburg, 114
World History, 14, 95

Y

Yajurveda, 217, 236
Yoakam, 59

Z

Ziller, 24

●●●●